A New Nobility of Blood and Soil

A NEW NOBILITY OF BLOOD AND SOIL

–RICHARD WALTHER DARRÉ–

Translated by

AUGUSTO SALAN & JULIUS SYLVESTER

Foreword by
Warren Balogh

English translation copyright © 2021 Antelope Hill Publishing

Second printing 2021.

Originally published in German as *Neuadel aus Blut und Boden* by J. F. Lehmanns Verlag, Munich 1930.
Translated by Augusto Salan (augustosalan@tutanota.com) and Julius Sylvester, 2021.

Cover art by sswifty.
Cover image: *The hunter with his family gathered around the table over supper* by Adolf Eberle (1843-1914)

Edited by Augusto Salan.
Interior formatting by Margaret Bauer.

Antelope Hill Publishing
www.antelopehillpublishing.com

Paperback ISBN-13: 978-1-953730-49-7
Hardcover ISBN-13: 978-1-953730-96-1
EPUB ISBN-13: 978-1-953730-29-9

Dedicated in admiration and friendship to
Paul Schultze-Naumburg

"There will come a time when it will be recognized that man does not live on horsepower and tools alone. There are also goods which he does not want to and cannot do without. And he will learn to economize, and he will not seek to win one thing, only to lose everything else with it. For if man had gained everything that could be gained with his technology, he would have come to the realization that life on the now disfigured earth—which has been made so excessively easy and simple—is actually no longer worth living; that we have indeed snatched everything that our planet had to give away, and in the process we have destroyed it, and thus ourselves, in this extractive work. Each one of us has to take care of his own part, so that the change may come before it is everywhere too late forever!"

Paul Schultze-Naumburg
Heimatschutz I: Die Laufenburger Stromschnellen
(Homeland Conservation I: The Laufenberger Rapids, Kunstwart)

Richard Walther Darré (1895-1953)

Contents

Foreword

By Warren Balogh

This book is the first-ever English translation of the most important written work of Richard Walther Darré, a major leader of the Third Reich and one of the chief ideologists of National Socialism. Darré served as Reich Minister of Food and Agriculture of Germany, Reich Peasant Leader, *Obergruppenführer* in the SS, and as a *Reichsleiter* of the NSDAP, the second-highest political rank of the party.

Born in Argentina to upper-middle class German parents on July 14th, 1895, Darré was sent to school in Germany while still a child. He spent a year as an exchange student at Kings College School at Wimbledon and went on to study colonial agriculture until the outbreak of the First World War. Although still an Argentinian citizen, he volunteered immediately in August 1914 and served in two artillery regiments during the war, both of which suffered heavy casualties. Darré was awarded the Iron Cross, Second Class during the Battle of the Somme, was wounded in 1917 after being promoted to Lieutenant, and went on to serve in the Battles of Verdun, Champagne, and the Spring Offensive of 1918.[1]

After the war, although his life and family fortunes were upset by the instability and upheavals of the Weimar period, Darré married and continued his agricultural studies. Gaining practical farm experience and studying plant and animal breeding, he completed his doctoral studies in 1929. A prolific writer, Darré authored dozens of papers and articles over the course of his career[2] and wrote two books: *Das Bauerntum als Lebensquell der nordischen Rasse* (*The Peasantry as the Source of Life of the*

---

[1] Anna Bramwell, *Blood and Soil: Richard Walther Darré and Hitler's 'Green Party'* (Buckinghamshire: The Kensal Press, 1985), 15-16.

[2] Ibid., 53.

Nordic Race, 1928) and *Neuadel aus Blut und Boden* (*A New Nobility of Blood and Soil*, 1930). That same year, he was recruited by Adolf Hitler into the NSDAP.

"Blood and Soil" was not a phrase coined by Darré,[3] but he did more than anyone else to popularize it, and it is most often associated with his life and work. Its theme is the interconnectedness of a people, race, or nationality and the land which they inhabit. This is a crucial concept in National Socialism, and reiterations of this theme appear throughout Hitler's writings and speeches even before Darré joined the party.

In *Mein Kampf*, Hitler stated that "for myself and all true National Socialists there is only one doctrine: people and country (*Volk und Vaterland*)."[4] In his inaugural speech as Chancellor in 1933, Hitler declared:

> People and Earth (*Volk und Erde*), these are the two roots from which we draw strength and on which we base our resolves.... the conservation of this People and this Soil (*Erhaltung dieses Volkes und dieses Bodens*) can alone represent our purpose in life.[5]

Hitler explicitly invoked *Blut und Boden* in his proclamation at the opening of the Party Congress at Nuremberg on September 6th, 1938, when he described the tasks which the party had to perform:

> It had to break up and destroy the other world of parties; it had to declare unrelenting war on the world of class and social prejudices; it had to ensure that without consideration of birth or of origin the German who was strong-willed and capable might find his way upwards. It had to purge Germany of all those parasites for whom the need of their Fatherland and people served as a source of personal enrichment. It had to recognize the eternal values of blood and soil, and to raise the respect paid to those

---

[3] Troy Southgate, "Blood and Soil: Revolutionary Nationalism as the Vanguard of Ecological Sanity," in *Amerika*, July 28, 1970, http://www.amerika.org/texts/blood-and-soil-revolutionary-nationalism-as-the-vanguard-of-ecological-sanity-troy-southgate/.

[4] Adolf Hitler, *Mein Kampf* (New York: Reynal and Hitchcock, 1939), 288.

[5] Adolf Hitler, "Proclamation to the German Nation," delivered at the Sportspalast in Berlin on February 10 1933, http://www.emersonkent.com/speeches/das_deutsche_volk.htm.

> values until they became the supreme laws of our life. It had to begin the struggle against the greatest enemy who threatened to destroy our people—the international Jewish world enemy![6]

At the time of Darré's recruitment into the NSDAP, his works were already widely read and discussed in racial nationalist circles.[7] His proposals and theories were taken very seriously by Hitler and other leading members of the party, and he was brought in as both an expert on agriculture and on race and breeding. Put in charge of the party's *Agrarpolitischer Apparat* (ApA), Darré was tasked by Hitler with developing agricultural policy and organizing the rural population of Germany into the movement.

Darré set out the new aims and tactics of the agricultural campaign of the party in a series of important directives.[8] Prior to his appointment, the NSDAP tried to organize its own agrarian special interest group to challenge the *Landbund*, the main farmer's association in Germany. Because the *Landbund* had deep ties to the DNVP—the mainstream conservative nationalist party of the Weimar era—external attacks only succeeded in uniting the farmers in the *Landbund* against the NSDAP, which was still too small and lacking in resources to compete.

Instead, Darré's new tactic was to "conquer the existing agricultural organizations from within by form of a factory cell technique."[9] The ApA kept up the pressure by holding meetings and demonstrations to coincide with general meetings of the *Landbund* local committees, and aggressively infiltrated the organization.

> In some cases they were successful in turning the Landbund meeting into a demonstration of support for the NSDAP. By the beginning of 1932, the DNVP regional organization for East Friesland was complaining that "more and more of the committees (of the *Kreislandbünde*) are composed of Nazis." Once a *Kreislandbund* was in the hands of the NSDAP, it could be used

---

[6] Adolf Hitler, *Speeches of Adolf Hitler, April 1922–August 1939, Volume I* (London: New York Oxford University Press, 1941), 121.

[7] Barbara Miller Lane and Leila J. Rupp, *Nazi Ideology before 1933: A Documentation* (Texas: University of Texas Press, 1978), xxi.

[8] Jeremy Noakes, *The Nazi Party in Lower Saxony: 1921–1933* (London: Oxford University Press, 1971), 165.

[9] Ibid., 166.

> as a forum for a much wider audience than would attend a normal party meeting. Above all it could be used to push Nazis into leading positions in the regional organizations.[10]

The ApA organized countless meetings of peasants and published a National Socialist agrarian news magazine that addressed specifically peasant issues.[11] After succeeding in getting NSDAP members elected to the Chamber of Agriculture, Darré was able to increase pressure on the *Landbund* to recognize the party as the leading political advocate of agriculture in Germany. The ApA became "perhaps the most successful of all the party's professional organizations,"[12] instrumental in the conquest of rural communities for National Socialism, which led directly to the seizure of power in 1933.

Germany was still in an extremely precarious position internationally. Encircled by former enemies from the First World War, still recovering from the loss of her eastern territories and colonies, the food situation in Germany was a matter of utmost strategic urgency. The British naval blockade was perhaps the most devastating weapon used against Germany and Austria from 1914–18. From the winter of 1916 onwards, the German people began to suffer from malnutrition and, in some cases, starvation. Pressure to break the blockade led to the German adoption of unrestricted submarine warfare, which brought America into the war.[13] Ultimately, this pressure fomented the seeds of mutiny and revolution, toppling the ancient Hohenzollern dynasty and bringing the German home front to its knees.

When DNVP leader Alfred Hugenberg was forced to resign as Minister of Agriculture in June of 1933, Richard Walther Darré was appointed by Hitler to this vital position. The world was in the grip of the Great Depression, and German agriculture was on the brink of ruin. Around twelve billion Reichsmarks of new debt had been contracted by German farmers between 1924 (when the currency was stabilized) and

---

[10] Ibid., 167.

[11] Franz-Josef Brüggemeier, Mark Cioc, and Thomas Zeller, *How Green Were the Nazis? Nature, Environment and Nation in the Third Reich* (Athens: Ohio University Press, 2005), 133.

[12] Noakes, *The Nazi Party*, 165.

[13] Imperial War Museums, "What You Need to Know about the British Naval Blockade of the First World War," Accessed September 19, 2021, https://www.iwm.org.uk/history/what-you-need-to-know-about-the-british-naval-blockade-of-the-first-world-war.

1932. The total land area of farmsteads foreclosed on and sold at auction was equivalent to a major German state. Proceeds from farm produce were down by about forty percent from 1928–32, not enough to even cover production. Farmers were weighed down by high taxes and intolerable debt payments.[14]

The revolutionary, far-reaching aims of National Socialist agricultural policy were summarized by Darré in an interview with the American journalist Lothrop Stoddard in 1939. According to Darré:

> When we came to power in 1933, one of our chief endeavors was to save German agriculture from impending ruin. However, our agricultural program went far beyond mere economic considerations. It was based on the idea that no nation can truly prosper without a sound rural population. It is not enough that the farmers shall be tolerably well-off; they should also be aware of their place in the national life and be able to fulfill it. Here are the three big factors in the problem: First, to assure an ample food supply; second, to safeguard the future by a healthy population increase; third, to develop a distinctive national culture deeply rooted in the soil. This ideal logically implies an aim which goes far beyond what is usually known as an agrarian policy.[15]

These goals were implemented by three monumental pieces of National Socialist legislation under Darré: the creation of the National Food Estate, the Market Control Statute, and the Heredity Farmlands Law. Stoddard himself, who described Darré as a "big, energetic, good-looking man… one of the most interesting personalities among the Nazi leaders," described the awesome scope of these measures:

> The Food Estate is a gigantic quasi-public corporation embracing in its membership not only all persons immediately on the land but also everyone connected with the production and distribution of foodstuffs. Large landowners, small peasants, agricultural laborers, millers, bakers, canners, middlemen, right down to local butchers and grocers—they are one and all included in this huge

[14] R. Walther Darré, "The National Food Estate," *Germany Speaks: By 21 Leading Members of Party and State* (London: Thornton Butterworth Ltd, 1938), 148.
[15] Lothrop Stoddard, *Into the Darkness* (Los Angeles: Indo-European Publishing, 2011), 81-2.

> vertical trust. The aim is to bring all these group interests, previously working largely at cross-purposes, into a harmonious, co-ordinated whole, concerned especially with problems of production and distribution. The Market Control Statute links all this with the consumer. The aim here is a thoroughgoing, balanced economic structure based on the principle known as the "just price." Everybody is supposed to make a profit, but none are to be out of line with the others. Furthermore, the ultimate consumer is to be protected from profiteering....
>
> The Hereditary Farmlands Law revives the old Teutonic concept that the landowner is intimately linked to the land. It is officially stated that "The idea engendered by Roman law that land was so much merchandise to be bought and sold at will is profoundly repugnant to German feelings. To us, soil is something sacred; the peasant and his land belong inseparably together." Emphasis is thus laid on the "Bauer," imperfectly translated by our word "peasant." The German "Bauer" is an independent landowner, self-respecting and proud of the name. We can best visualize him like the old English yeoman.[16]

Darré already was appointed head of the SS Race and Settlement Main Office in 1932, where he developed marriage guidelines for SS members on similar lines found in *Neuadel*.[17] Now as Reich Minister of Agriculture and Reich Peasant Leader, Darré was in a position to implement his most radical ideas. Readers of this book will immediately recognize the outlines of the Hereditary Farmlands Law in Darré's theoretical plans for the development of the *Hegehöfe*.[18]

Darré's National Socialist policies towards the peasants may be compared to the situation of farmers under American capitalism or Soviet communism during roughly the same period. In the United States, unregulated exploitation of the land led to the Dust Bowl, which displaced millions of American farmers and, along with the mass foreclosures of the Depression, led to historic homelessness and poverty. During the Russian Civil War, the depredations of the Bolsheviks against the peasantry led to the uprising known as the Tambov Rebellion, after

---

[16] Ibid., 82.
[17] See Chapter VII.
[18] See Chapter V.

which tens of thousands of Russian peasants were starved, tortured and murdered by the dreaded Cheka.[19]

The success of Darré's programs is conceded even by mainstream historians virulently hostile to National Socialism such as Adam Tooze. In an exhaustive study of the economic history of the Third Reich, he is forced to admit:

> What the RNS [National Food Estate] was able to achieve was not only a substantial increase in domestic food production, but also a substantial improvement in the resilience of German agriculture in the face of shocks.... When we bear in mind the disastrous situation of world agriculture in the 1930s it is clear that German farmers, in fact, enjoyed a historically unprecedented level of protection and it is hardly surprising that this came at a price. In return for the exclusion of foreign competition from home markets, peasant smallholders had to accept comprehensive regulation and control. Farming in Germany, as in Europe generally, from the 1930s onwards resembled less and less a market-driven industry and more and more a strange hybrid of private ownership and state planning. The true story is told by the level of prices paid to German farmers compared to those that German farmers would have received if they had been exposed to the full force of foreign competition. On this basis the record is completely unambiguous. Though it is true that grain producers clearly enjoyed a larger margin of protection than dairy farmers, for all major types of farm produce the prices paid to German farmers under National Socialism were at least twice those prevailing on world markets....
>
> The promise Hitler made on the night of 30 January 1933 was to restore the economic fortunes of the German peasantry within four years and the RNS certainly made good on that pledge. According to figures calculated by Germany's most authoritative economic research agency, total farm income, of which animal products accounted for more than 60%, rose by almost 14% in 1933-4 and by another 11.5% in 1934-5. At the same time the burden of taxes and interest payments fell significantly. When we

[19] "Tambov Rebellion," Wikipedia, last modified September 15, 2021, https://en.wikipedia.org/wiki/Tambov_Rebellion.

> allow for the general deflation in prices, increases in money incomes on this scale more than made up for the Depression.[20]

As Reich Peasant Leader, Darré presided over the Third Reich's massive annual harvest celebration at Goslar, called the Reich Harvest Thanksgiving Festival.[21] In the gently rolling hills around this ancient medieval town, which was once the capitol of the Holy Roman Empire,[22] the National Socialists paid tribute to the accomplishments of the peasantry in speeches and events that dwarfed even the huge Nuremberg rallies held for the annual Party Congress. The festival was attended by about 1.2 million people in 1937, and it was here that Hitler announced the passage of the Hereditary Farm Law in 1933.[23]

Over 700,000 farms were established along the *Hegehof* model under this law, a great achievement.[24] Lothrop Stoddard visited a number of the farms established by this law, and he left behind an extremely interesting (and very positive) anecdotal description of them from an American perspective.[25] The long-term success of the Heredity Farm Law is difficult to assess, because the war later put enormous stresses on agricultural labor and production, and because the law itself was repealed by the Allied occupation.[26] Because the law concerned the long-term racial and demographic regeneration of the German people, one cannot appreciate its full effects without the benefit of observation over decades or even centuries. However, one aspect of the law that might interest modern readers is highlighted by Hitler biographer Brendan Simms:

> Unlike the previous late nineteenth- and early twentieth-century Prussian agrarian legislation, which had been designed to protect Germans against Slavic subversion, mainly by Poles, the criteria of

---

[20] Adam Tooze, *The Wages of Destruction: The Making and Breaking of the Nazi Economy* (New York: Viking Penguin, 2007), 195.
[21] A summary of the Fourth Reich Farmers' Rally, held in Goslar in 1936: https://research.calvin.edu/german-propaganda-archive/bauerntag36.htm.
[22] Bramwell, *Blood and Soil*, 104-5.
[23] "Reich Harvest Thanksgiving Festival," Wikipedia, last modified July 7, 2021, https://en.wikipedia.org/wiki/Reich_Harvest_Thanksgiving_Festival.
[24] Darré, *Germany Speaks*, 148-9.
[25] See "Chapter IX: The Battle of the Land," *Into the Darkness*, 84-95.
[26] "Law No. 45 of Feb. 20, 1947 on 'Repeal of Legislation on Hereditary Farms and Enactment of Other Provisions Regulating Agricultural Forest Lands,' OG/CC, No.14 at 256 (May 31, 1947)," available at http://starweb.hessen.de/cache/ANL/1947/00003.pdf#page=6.

> the *Reichserbhofgesetz* were racial, rather than national. Those specifically excluded from "the capacity to become farmers" were Jews and Africans. By contrast, the law placed peoples of "tribally related blood" on the same level as non-Jewish "Germans." The Ministry of the Interior defined these as peoples who "had lived in coherent national settlements in Europe some time back in historical time." Gypsies were explicitly excluded, even if they were sedentary, but the list of acceptable farmers included not only all supposed "Aryans," but also many other "races" such as the Hungarians, Estonians, Finns, Slavs, Danes and Lithuanians. If they had German citizenship, they could become or remain farmers. In other words, the potential racial pool comprised virtually the entire European continent.[27]

This interpretation of the law, which could be described as "White Nationalist," was also commented on by Darré's biographer Anna Bramwell:

> Since his 1933 legislation attempted to put his major ideas into practice, it is worth looking at Darré's actual method of racial selection, once he was given the opportunity. It does seem to demonstrate that a coercive racial selection was not envisaged, and lends emphasis to the distinction, drawn earlier, between a defensive intra-racial eugenics, which aimed to prevent the disappearance of a group, and the expansionist super-stud mentality popularly associated with Nazis. Under the Hereditary Farm Law, only farmers of German and "similar" stock, who could prove descent back to 1800, could inherit the protected farm...this definition included Polish farmers.... Racial education was part of the curriculum of the peasant university at Burg Nauhaus and the SS Racial Office (part of the SS Race and Settlement Main Office). Examples of this work include a circular sent to the SS education department, suggesting that a textbook be produced showing photographs of good racial stock. Darré offered a textbook on horses as an example. SS leaders were shown films on Blood and Soil, harvesting, ploughing, to persuade them of the desirable nature of the life.

---

[27] Brendan Simms, *Hitler: A Global Biography* (New York: Basic Books, 2019), 226-7.

> The key point, though, is the voluntary nature of these activities. Darré did not try to enforce compulsory breeding laws. He did not incite riots against Poles and Jews and demand the compulsory sterilization of the unfit.... He looked to racial education to create what he called a "positive racial consciousness," rather in the way in which today, especially in the USA but to some extent in England, television and other media make special efforts to present the black minority in a favorable light in drama series, children's programmes, and so on. Darré wanted farmers and their families to be educated into racial consciousness—White is Beautiful—as part of a process of instilling a sense of identity. It was seen as a rescue operation for a vanishing breed.[28]

During the Second World War, Darré's political career went into decline. As a man best suited to the realization of visionary long-term goals in peace time, and due to the difficult demands of the wartime economy, he was eventually replaced as Minister of Agriculture by his technocratic deputy Herbert Backe in 1944. After the war, Darré was convicted at the Nuremberg trials and spent five and a half years in prison at Landsburg (in the same prison where Hitler wrote *Mein Kampf*), before his release due to declining health. Of his interrogation by Allied forces, Bramwell remarks:

> What does emerge clearly from all his interrogations is the ignorance of the American interrogators of the structure and functioning of the Third Reich. The whole process seems to be motivated by a vengeful incompetence, in part fueled by the salacious hate-propaganda of the American Press. Even as late as 1946, the mass suicide of Russians who had fought for Germany and were to be repatriated back to Russia, was headlined by the USA Army paper *Stars and Stripes* as "Red Traitors Dachau Suicide Described as Inhuman Orgy." Darré found his hereditary farms described as "Teutonic Breeding Centers."[29]

---

[28] Bramwell, *Blood and Soil*, 71-2.
[29] Ibid., 183.

A typical example of this "hate-propaganda" may be seen in a supposed "secret speech" of Darré printed in *Life* magazine in December, 1940 under the heading: "Secret Nazi Speech: Reich Minister Darré Discusses the World's Future Under Nazi Rule." At the time of this writing, an excerpt from this article is the only "quote" by Darré included on his Wikipedia page:

> [A] new aristocracy of German masters will be created [with] slaves assigned to it, these slaves to be their property and to consist of landless, non-German nationals... we actually have in mind a modern form of medieval slavery which we must and will introduce because we urgently need it in order to fulfill our great tasks. These slaves will by no means be denied the blessings of illiteracy; higher education will, in future, be reserved only for the German population of Europe...[30]

The original *Life* article, sandwiched between garish advertisements for Coca-Cola and other consumer products, is accompanied by an editor's note in very tiny print:

> How *Life* came into possession of this amazing speech delivered in early May 1940 by Richard-Walther Darré, Germany's Minister of Agriculture, to a group of high Nazi officials, cannot be divulged. Nevertheless, after thorough investigation, *Life* has satisfactory reasons for believing this speech is authentic as briefed on these pages. An even better reason for printing this secret address exists in the fact that, even if it was not delivered exactly as recorded here, it might have been. Readers should therefore regard it not as a mere journalistic scoop but as something far more important—a fair sample of the kind of doctrine that is currently being voiced by highly placed members of the Nazi government.[31]

---

[30] "Richard Walther Darré," Wikipedia, last modified August 3, 2021, https://en.wikipedia.org/wiki/Richard_Walther_Darré.

[31] "Secret Nazi Speech: Reich Minister Darré Discusses the World's Future Under German Rule," *Life*, December 9, 1940 (Ginger Rogers cover), 43–44, https://books.google.com/books?id=QUoEAAAAMBAJ&printsec=frontcover#v=onepage&q&f=false.

With the first-ever publication of *Neuadel* in English by Antelope Hill, American readers can now, for the first time in ninety-one years, decide for themselves whether the words above accurately reflect the views and sentiments of the real Richard Walther Darré!

One aspect of Darré's life and legacy that has attracted significant controversy in recent decades is the assessment that he was one of a number of "Green Nazis," or members of the Third Reich who represented early ecological interests and concerns. In this context he is labeled as a major influence on what is pejoratively labeled "ecofascism."[32] This view was first put forth by his biographer Anna Bramwell in her book *Blood and Soil: Richard Walther Darré and Hitler's 'Green Party'* and expanded further in *Ecology in the 20th Century*. Leftist academics have since viciously attacked her views,[33] while others have validated her claims. According to Bramwell, writing in the 1980s:

> Today it would be difficult to ignore fears about erosion, the destruction of animal species, anxieties about factory farming, the social effects of technology and the loss of farmland.... When Rachel Carson wrote *Silent Spring*, she focused the world's attention on the ecological destruction caused by pesticides and other chemicals in the lakes and earth of North America.... It is not widely known that similar ecological ideas were being put forward by Darré in National Socialist Germany, often using the same phrases and arguments as are used today. He began to campaign for these ideas, especially organic farming, from 1934 onwards, and during the Second World War stepped up the effort to introduce organic farming methods into Germany. After the war, as a broken, discredited politician, he continued to write about soil erosion, the dangers of artificial fertilizers and the need to maintain the "biomass," until his death in 1953. Two decades later, these ideas about man's relationship with nature and the

---

[32] See Janet Biehl and Peter Staudenmaier, *Ecofascism: Lessons from the German Experience*, (1996), https://ecologyviewedfromtheright.files.wordpress.com/2019/03/janet-biehl-and-peter-staudenmaier-ecofascism-lessons-from-the-german-experience.pdf.

[33] Frank Uekoetter, *The Green and the Brown: A History of Conservation in Nazi Germany*, (New York: Cambridge University Press, 2006), 202-3.

> organic cycle of animal-soil-food-man known as organic farming, had gained wider attention.[34]

Bramwell also cites examples of Darré's post-war activities as evidence of his early environmentalism:

> Another move to form a German "Soil Association" was made in December 1952, when Darré met the Town Clerk (*Oberstadtdirektor*) in Goslar at the Hotel Niedersachsischer Hof, and made notes about a society to be called "*Mensch und Heimat.*" Its function would be to further "organic ideas, a healthy soil and care for the homeland" (*Heimatpflege*).... During the years after his release, he wrote steadily, articles with titles like "The Living Soil," "Peasant and Technology," and "Mother Earth." The articles on organic farming were usually inspired by English works, such as those by Sir Albert Howard, Sir George Stapledon, and Lady Eve Balfour, although he also referred to the USA's "Friends of the Soil," and American efforts to combat erosion. In 1953, he enthusiastically reviewed Lady Eve Balfour's *The Living Soil*. As in the 1930s, he wrote about the American dust bowl, this time under the pseudonym of Carl Carlsson, and called for Germany to adopt soil protection measures of a similar kind to America's 1947 anti-erosion law....[35]

There is no doubt Darré was a nature-lover and a conservationist,[36] as were many of the leaders of the Third Reich,[37] but what is perhaps more troubling to the modern Left is the fact that the racial views of National Socialism exist very comfortably along the same moral-ideological continuum as concern for nature and the land. The word "ecology" itself,

---

[34] Bramwell, *Blood and Soil*, 171-2.

[35] Ibid., 196-7.

[36] See Dedication; Chapter IV; Chapter V.

[37] Biehl, *Ecofascism*, p. 17. Besides Darré, the other leading National Socialists described as belonging to Hitler's "Green Wing" typically include Deputy *Führer* Rudolf Hess, Inspector General for German Roadways (builder of the *Autobahn*) Fritz Todt, and the horticultural architect Alwin Seifert. But this could also easily include *Reichsmarschall* Hermann Göring (as *Reichsminister* of Forestry, author of the national conservation law, also author of a total ban on vivisection as Minister President of Prussia; see *The Green and the Brown*), and even Hitler himself, who was a lifelong nature-lover and vegetarian.

coined by nineteenth-century Romantic, nationalist, racialist, and zoologist Ernst Haeckel,[38] implies the relationship between species and their environment. So in that way, the concepts *Volk und Vaterland, Volk und Erde,* and *Blut und Boden* are inherently ecological, insofar as *Volk* and *Blut* are conceptualized in racial-national terms.

Care for the health of the land and wild spaces was not something separate from Darré's racial views, but wholly integrated with them. What mainstream scholars and critics of "ecofascism" never seem to reconcile is the idea that there is a real ideological and moral continuity between care for the race and care for the land. Both positions challenge the view, common to both liberal capitalism and Marxism, that man is somehow separate and above nature, that the laws of nature do not apply to man, or that "the environment" can be compartmentalized as an issue unconnected with the long-term development of racially healthy peoples and their connection with the land. One could go so far as to say so-called "ecofascism" is not a synthesis of two separate strands of political thought, but rather that National Socialism—as an ideology rooted in the unity of People/Race/Blood and Land/Earth/Soil—is inherently ecological. The question modern environmentalists must wrestle with is: can any ideology grounded in an objectively false and unscientific egalitarianism, such as liberalism or Marxism, ever truly solve world ecological problems?[39]

Richard Walther Darré received hundreds of letters of support after his release from prison, affectionately addressed to "Herr Minister."[40] He continued to write articles attacking large corporations and opposing exploitative attitudes to the land[41] until he was too ill to continue. He died in 1953 at the age of fifty-eight and was buried in Goslar, the site of his former greatest triumphs. His funeral was attended by hundreds of local residents, but his grave is covered by an unmarked stone, and all traces

---

[38] Ibid., p. 7.

[39] This controversy blew up in 2019 with the release of the film *Planet of the Humans.* Writer/director/producer Jeff Gibbs and executive producer Michael Moore were attacked as "ecofascist" because they dared to dispute that a growth-driven consumerist economy could innovate its way out of major ecological problems through the mechanism of private "green energy" industry chasing the profit motive, rather than through responsible population planning and reduction of wasteful consumption. The film was even temporarily deplatformed off YouTube shortly after its release.

[40] Bramwell, *Blood and Soil,* 195.

[41] Ibid., 197.

of his life and accomplishments have been carefully scrubbed from occupied Germany.[42]

Darré's face and voice are forever immortalized in Leni Riefenstahl's film *Triumph des Willens*, where he briefly appears as one of a number of NSDAP leaders to address the 1934 Nuremberg rally on his favorite subject: peasants and the land.

A New Nobility of Blood and Soil is an essential work of National Socialist thought. In keeping with Darré's tendency to support visionary goals and ideals with grounded, pragmatic reasoning, the book not only outlines several detailed proposals for the coming Third Reich but also explains the principles behind them. A careful reading of the text reveals both the subtle and nuanced considerations by which Darré reached his conclusions, and the brilliant and sensitive mind behind them. At times—and especially compared with the obscene vulgarity of what passes for "political thinking" in the early twenty-first century—one feels one is not reading the thoughts of a man from the past, but of the meditations of some moral and intellectual superman of the future.

On October 16th, 2017, upon accepting the Liberty Medal by the National Constitution Center in Philadelphia, the American Senator John McCain exasperatedly exclaimed, "We live in a land of ideals, not of blood and soil!" He decried "any dogma consigned to the ash heap of history" and reaffirmed the values of liberal-capitalist globalism.[43] The Senator—who has himself since passed onto the ash heap of history—was reacting to the fact that, two months earlier, young White men marching in Charlottesville, Virginia had chanted the old slogan of Richard Walther Darré.

That the public invocation of this phrase is still capable of shaking the elites of the present world order to their core is proof its powerful resonance will only grow louder in the future.

Warren Balogh

Hillsboro, West Virginia
September 19th, 2021

---

[42] Ibid., 198.
[43] Sam Kestenbaum, "John McCain Uses Nazi 'Blood And Soil' Slogan In Stark Warning About Trump," *Forward*, October 17, 2017, https://forward.com/fast-forward/385410/john-mccain-warns-of-blood-and-soil-nationalism-in-trump-era/.

Preface

The present work is the logical continuation of the basic ideas of my book *Das Bauerntum als Lebensquell der Nordischen Rasse (The Peasantry as the Source of Life of the Nordic Race)*, which discussed tangible proposals for a German Reich of the German people—a Third Reich—to which we all aspire to. It may seem astonishing that I begin these proposals not with the peasantry but with the nobility. I must counter that in the correctly understood Germanic sense of the word, there is probably a degree of difference between the nobility and the peasantry (in the sense that both were incorporated into the Germanic rural estates with different tasks), but there is not a fundamental difference. It therefore is the essential task of this book to explain such relations in more detail, and also to show that the caste-like stratification of nobility and peasantry—which has developed in German society since the Middle Ages—is both thoroughly un-Germanic and un-German, two terms which today basically mean the same thing.

In the following poem, Baron Börries von Münchhausen out of an unshakeable German feeling captures the essence of the nobility, at least as it should be, and presents it:

This is us!
Born to helmet and shield,
Chosen to protect the land,
To the king his officer,
Faithful to our old customs,
In the midst of our peasants,
This is us!
We sow our fields,
We cherish our forests,

For child and grandchild.
You mock the ancestors?! The guardians
They are of the only goods,
Which are not for sale to you.
We stand with a stiff neck
In the market's haggling and toiling
In strict knighthood.
In silence we want
To preserve the country's best:
German peasant strength!

If we view the nobility in such a way that the nobility is not the lordship superior to the peasantry, but a leadership cadre that is of the same nature as the peasantry and endowed with special responsibilities, then the following becomes understandable. If I wanted to help our German peasantry, I had to first and foremost turn to the question of identifying a leadership appropriate to its nature, namely, a leadership that would secure for the peasantry its place in the German nation, which it may claim on account of its double task of being the source of both the people's renewal by blood and its nourishment.

Until now, the task of creating a new nobility has been, so to speak, merely a task of class creation in the field of agricultural activity. But as the peasantry is the true and original source of blood renewal of the nation, so is it the source of the nobility incorporated into it. In its capacity as a result of peasant select breeding, the nobility is the natural-born giver of leadership for the whole people—provided that the terms peasant, people, and nobility are understood in the Germanic sense.

This book is an attempt at a theoretical blueprint, i.e. it attempts to transform this trinity of peasant, people, and nobility into a unity; I have endeavored to form and round out this draft into a completed whole. In this, I was guided by today's special circumstances—the call for a new nobility is today more widespread than we would initially assume given the present conditions in Germany. Such sentiments are encouraged by the newly gained knowledge of heredity and the surprisingly flourishing racial studies. Plans and drafts for the formation of a new nobility appear everywhere—no less than a renewal of the existing nobility is striven for and demanded. But what is missing from all such proposals, as far as I have seen, is a clear and well-rounded understanding of all aspects and activities of nobility; an extremely narrow point of view is usually taken, and then only from there is the question discussed. In this way, however, it is not possible to create something palpably useful, no matter how witty and creative some of the suggested ideas may be. This circumstance convinced me to bring together into one framework all those sub-areas which must be taken into consideration in the creation of a new nobility, in order to establish a preliminary overview from which the basic plan for the solution of the question can be derived. I have endeavored to comprehensively describe both an overview of the responsibilities of the German nobility and a plan for its reorganization, so that a perspective can be obtained which permits a more or less clear judgment and which removes the whole matter from the realm of misty wishful thinking and castles in the air and places it on the ground of realizable possibilities.

I am aware that any possibility of realizing the ideas presented here presupposes the restoration of our national liberty and independence. This goes without saying for a thinking man, but I mention it nonetheless as it is useless to argue about this precondition. What matters first of all is exclusively whether our people desires to realize the thoughts laid down in this text, which, however, should by no means be considered any kind of recipe. Only when the *Whether* is decided will it be possible to find the ways and means for the *How*.

The impetus for this work came from a quote from the late *artaman*[44] leader Hans Holfelder: "We need a new nobility!"

I have to thank lecturer R. Eichenauer, who had the kindness to proofread this typescript. But I have to thank especially the generous hospitality of the Schultze-Naumburg family, who made it possible for me to conceptualize and complete this book.

R. Walther Darré
Certified agriculturist and certified colonial manager
Saaleck, spring 1930

[44] Editor's note: The *artaman* concept was developed by Dr. Willibald Hentschel, founder of both the *Mittgardbund* (Brotherhood of Midgard) and the *Artamanen Gesellschaft* (Artaman League). The word was a combination of the Middle High German words *art* and *manen*, meaning "agricultural man." The organization advocated for physical fitness, environmentalism, vegetarianism, and rural living as important means for the regeneration of the Nordic race. Deeply anti-Slavic and anti-Semitic, a main focus of the League prior to the rise of the National Socialist German Workers' Party (NSDAP) was the prevention of Polish settlement in eastern Germany.

I

Introduction

"The destruction of the law and the shaking of the social order are only the result of the weakness and insecurity of those in power."

Napoleon I

1

It is an indisputable fact of history that the growth and prosperity of a people is directly related to the health of its nobility, both physically and morally. A healthy nobility is capable of leading a people to the highest flowering of civilization and government; but if it fails or perishes, the fate of the people will be sealed if the people does not pull itself together in time to create a new class of leaders. Treitschke writes:

> If a ruling or privileged nobility diminishes in wealth, education, and political devotion—or if the other estates reach it in all of these respects—the nobility loses its innate right to rule, the state falls ill, and a transformation of society is inevitable.

Therefore, there is a close relationship between the fate of a people as a whole and of its leading class.

But history also provides us with this fact: where a people had the will and the strength to replace its degenerate or otherwise weakened nobility, it was spared the fate of degeneration and was able to assert itself in the struggle of the peoples for existence. Perhaps the most famous example of this is prehistoric Rome—after internal struggles between the patricians (the peasant families who formed the nobility) and the plebeians (the other families living in the country, predominantly of a non-peasant class), the old Roman *nobilitas* emerged in the fifth century B.C. from the best of both the plebeian and patrician families. This Roman nobility, which from the fourth to the first century B.C. knew how to lead the Roman state unerringly and powerfully, was also the creator as well as the guardian of the old Roman republican political system until a completely different political system developed with its demise and the rise of Gaius Julius Caesar. The old Roman concept of freedom for the people was transformed into the late Roman despotism introduced by Caesar, a system of government that was clearly influenced by the Orient and Asia, i.e. an arbitrary and coercive rule over the people from above. At the time of Caesar, Rome no longer had the power to form a true nobility from within itself. Although a new upper class emerged and was based on noble principles, it was nevertheless different from the *nobilitas* that had previously existed.

This is why E. Mayer once said quite correctly, "It cannot be about whether an upper class is there at all, but only about how it can be there with beneficial effects." An upper class is always there, the only question is whether the people has a sanguinary connection with its upper class (as was the case with the old Roman *nobilitas* with regard to the plebeians), or whether the people merely tolerates its upper class, which became customary in Rome from the advent of the Caesarean concept. This brings us to the question: what actually is nobility?

This query will be answered in the following sections, since—as you will see—we as Germans can only judge this question from a German, and in this case, Germanic, point of view. But this much may be said here—an upper class only becomes a nobility in the German interpretation of the word when it consists not of individuals but of families, whereby it is initially irrelevant whether these families represent the best of the people—i.e. are, in a sense, the expression of a leadership—or whether they rule over the people as oppressors without any connection to them. In the Germanic sense, however, nobility represents a selection of valuable families which are legally indistinguishable from the other families of the national community, except that an attempt is made through a system of breeding laws to maintain the hereditary high quality of these families. Furthermore, through an educational tradition that correctly guides the noble youth, virtues are cultivated which teach everything that is absolutely necessary for the leadership of a people or a state.

It must be emphasized that, although an upper class composed only of the best of a people is a leader class, it is far from being a nobility in the German-Germanic[45] sense of the word, because one of the characteristics of German or Germanic nobility is necessarily that measures are put into place that ensure the hereditary transmission of its proven leadership talents. We could even say that the essence of the genuinely German concept of nobility in the Germanic sense is a consciously cultivated leadership on the basis of selected hereditary material.

If the leading class of a people is composed exclusively of its best elements, without any provision being made for the inheritance of its talents in any form, the people will, under all circumstances, deplete its abilities and talents. There is no doubt that such a form of exploiting talents may cause a temporary flourishing of the people, but this state of affairs is not permanent. Almost all historical democracies of the modern era offer examples of this, because the establishment of a democracy in a state that was previously noble-led creates a general power vacuum in which gifted individuals can, with some luck, work their way up to the upper echelons of the people. But it is precisely this peculiar democratic tendency of denying any hereditary bond and even refusing to recognize the hereditary inequality of individuals which makes it difficult or even impossible for recognized valuable talents to be hereditarily anchored in the nation. This is the key to the riddle of why democracies, after a short historical period of flourishing, always very quickly show a decline in their ancestral talents and therefore die culturally.

If, on the basis of the above findings, we consider the question of whether our people still has a nobility, and if so, whether it can still be described as healthy, then unfortunately we must answer with an unsparing "no." Neither do we possess nor do we have any means of retaining our precious leaders' hereditable traits (a situation which, incidentally, the German democracy of 1918 is causally responsible for), nor can we claim that our nobility still represents the leadership of our people, let alone that it is healthy. If we take Treitschke's famous words as a basis, "Either there is a political nobility or there is none at all," it

[45] Editor's note: "German" is a translation of the word *deutsche*, which is typically used to describe the peoples of Germany from the eighth century forward. "Germanic" is a translation of the word *germanen*, which is used to describe the people of Germany before then. Therefore, something that is German-Germanic is reflective of both ancient and modern Germans.

must be said that there is apparently nothing left of our nobility—otherwise, it would have already reappeared, albeit in a very different way, in the fateful years for our people since 1918. It cannot be argued that the war losses of 1914–18 played a role in this—we only have to browse Theodor Häbich's compilation of the still-landowning nobility in *Deutsche Latifundien* (*German Latifundia*, second edition; Königsberg 1930). It is clear to see that the ratio of the nobility—which is barely noticeable in the state life of our people—to the whole of the people is a surprisingly small one, while the ratio of the land area still at the disposal of the nobility to the land area of the Reich's territory is quite obviously much larger. The ratio of the nobility's land ownership to its political influence is therefore unhealthy. If this fact alone exposes the inner weakness of the nobility, then the impression of a failed nobility becomes even clearer if we take the trouble to investigate when and where the nobility has played any significant role in the enormous struggle of our German youth (since about the turn of the century, but especially after 1918) for a race-appropriate German state structure.

No, the failure of our German nobility has deeper causes than the losses of the World War. The roots of this phenomenon go back to the Middle Ages. Strictly speaking, we have had no nobility in Germany since the Germanic nobility of its inception—bred on the basis of leader performance—was transformed into a ruling class based on outward appearances and closed off to the outside world. Incidentally, Treitschke's well-known essay in Karl Walcker's *Staatswissenschaftliche Aufsätze* (*Essays in Political Science*, 1877) contains this insight, "The Prussian nobility as a class has done nothing but mischief for three centuries." As an additional example, Freiherr vom Stein demanded the renewal of the nobility more than one hundred years ago, proposing that the most competent members of the people should be able to supplement the nobility, as is customary with the English nobility (from his November 24th, 1808 open letter to von Schön, known as Stein's Political Testament).

Today, at the time of writing this book, our nobility is in dire straits. With few exceptions, the post-war German nobility has done relatively little to rebuild our Reich or our people, so much so that only in isolated cases can it claim to be respected or be regarded as the favored leadership of a future new German Reich. Apart from the *Adelsgenossenschaft* (noble cooperative), which at least makes an attempt to save what is valuable in the nobility and to pave the way for its renewal, the remnants of our nobility (isolated honorable exceptions cannot change the picture as a whole) are sitting on their estates or on their bank accounts, in order to—as G. Ferrero once said with biting derision about the Roman nobility in the first century B.C.—at least save themselves and their possessions in the general confusion of the decline of the state, and to cloak this endeavor in the word "conservatism." Elsewhere, the nobility of today prefers to use its name recognition in the cities, especially in Berlin, to attend the societies and receptions of the nouveau riche, who had risen through war and upheaval, as well as of the new rulers, to create a glittering social framework.

No, we no longer have a nobility in the German-Germanic sense of the word. Some members of the nobility may not only be innocent of this state of affairs, but may even be fighting through ideology and action for a renewal of the nobility, thus consciously or unconsciously proving the reality of their own existence.

But as a people, we cannot do without a nobility. We all aspire to a Third Reich! Its existence and validity will depend largely on whether we still have the will and the strength to create a new nobility. It would be a mistake to assume that the Third Reich could be maintained exclusively by a ruling class built on individual achievement, but there is no doubt that only such a ruling class can one day create it. Nobility is the selection of gifted generations, bred through special measures, from which only the high performing individual nobles are promoted into an achievement-based leadership stratum, whereby promotion or non-promotion becomes a kind of continuous performance test and proof of achievement for future noble generations. Once again, the purpose of nobility as an institution in the German-Germanic sense of the term is to preserve the heritable biological traits relevant to leadership talents in order to create a kind of pool, so to speak, from which the leadership class of the people can source a never-ending influx of genuine leadership. This is why the following demand arises from us—we must revive a genuine nobility for our people.

2

Since the founding of the German Empire in 1871, Paul de Lagarde has repeatedly pointed out in his political writings[46] that we need a new nobility, indeed, he has already come forward with several proposals in his works. After him, individual champions of this idea appeared more and more frequently, the strongest corresponding proposals are to be found in the years after 1918. From the literature presented in recent years, only the following will be mentioned here: Boesch, *Vom Adel (Of the Nobility)*; Johannes, *Adel Verpflichtet (Nobility Obliges)*; Hentschel, *Mittgardbund (Brotherhood of Midgard)*; Harpf, *Völkischer Adel (Völkisch Nobility)*; Mayer, *Vom Adel und der Oberschicht (Of the Nobility and the Upper Class)*; von Hedemann-Heespen, *Die Entstehung des Adels (The Emergence of the Nobility)*; Goetz, *Neuer Adel (New Nobility)*. To these must be added the various essays in periodicals which deal with the question of the nobility and call for its renewal, especially the essays in the *Adelsblatt (Noble Journal)*, the journal of the *Deutsche Adelsgenossenschaft (German Noble Cooperative)*. But all these proposals and attempts at solutions are not quite satisfactory, because they either overlook quite essential points of the question, or they only pick out sub-areas with which they are familiar, or they do not take historical experience into account. Some of these proposals want to rely too much on regulations and laws and do not take into account the blood or genetic value that the nobility should possess. Another one simply wants to "command" the remnants of the Nordic race (Germanic peoples) in Germany into a kind of nobility, without taking into account that a master class of the Nordic race over a non-Nordic population is not nobility, as nobility and Nordic race are by no means be the same thing. Or be it finally the one, by W. Hentschel of the *Mittgardbund*, which correctly understands the breeding and selection processes for the formation of a new nobility and makes corresponding proposals, but through institutions such as his *Mittgardbund* rejects a basic tenet of any reasonable nobility—namely a family tradition based on the idea of paternal law. Such proposals are also reappearing today,[47] which deny the hereditary nature of blood and

[46] See *Schriften für das Deutsche Volk (Writings for the German People)* (Munich: J. F. Lehmanns, 1924).
[47] Such as Bruno Goetz's *Neuer Adel (New Nobility)* (Darmstadt, 1930).

speak of a "nobility of the spirit." Nietzsche has already given a clear answer to such demands in *Der Wille zur Macht* (*The Will to Power*, page 942):

> There is only nobility of birth, only nobility of blood. I'm not talking about the little word "von"[48] and the *Gothaische Kalender*[49] – a preoccupation for fools. Those who speak of an "aristocracy of the spirit" are generally trying to conceal something; as is well known, it is a favorite phrase used by ambitious Jews. The spirit alone does not ennoble – there must first be something that ennobles the spirit. And what is that? Blood.

This much is certain: Whoever wants to take a stand of any type on the question of nobility in our people and comes forward with proposals for its renewal or with drafts for recreating it completely must first of all clarify what the history of our nobility actually is. Hardly in any other field do principles of historical experience apply so much, something Treitschke once expressed as follows, "The persistence of the past in the present proves itself inexorably even in the histories of those peoples who do not want to believe in this historical law."

But if German history is really to be the teacher, it must also take into account a law which Vollgraff of Marburg paraphrased as follows, "All phenomena of civic and political life, from marriage to the forms of governance, will remain unexplained and obscure if we do not take into account the racial make-up of the people being studied."

Unfortunately, both of the above-mentioned laws lead us into a very peculiar dichotomy with regard to the historical German nobility. We have to realize that although it was the Germanic race or, as we say today, the Nordic race, which breathed blood and life into this German nobility and helped to determine the laws of expression of its civilization's creations, all that we are accustomed to speaking of as the "historical German nobility" has hardly anything to do with Germanic ideas about nobility. All of our historical German noble privileges and conceptions

---

[48] Editor's note: The word "von" served in Germany and Austria as a noble predicate (*prädikat*, from the Latin *praedicatum*, meaning rank designation) and is a name suffix or form of address for a nobleman.

[49] Editor's note: The *Gothaische Kalender* was (and is) the reference work for aristocratic genealogy commonly used in noble families.

are completely un-Germanic, and are, for the most part, even un-German, and owe their origin to foreign ideas about rule and the leadership of a people. It must be said that during the millennium of the so-called Holy Roman Empire of the German Nation, the Germanic nature of our people, along with its nobility, was put into a kind of straightjacket to an ever more pronounced degree. We do not have to examine here whether this was always and in all things something undesirable or useless; however, it must be emphasized that without a clear understanding of this fact, German history cannot be understood,[50] especially not state upheavals such as the Peasants' Wars[51] or the infiltration of the so-called Ideas of 1789[52] among our people.

Thus we cannot avoid first ascertaining the nature of the Germanic people's conceptions of their nobility. For if it is true what we said above in Vollgraff's words—namely that race determines the essence of a people, then we must also try to approach the solution of our task from the racial essence of our people. This racial essence of our people is *Germanentum* (Germanism)—it is the foundation of our being.

---

[50] After completing this work, Darré became aware of a work that clearly elaborates this idea: H. Wolf, *Weltgeschichte der Revolutionen und das Recht des Widerstandes (World History of Revolutions and the Right of Resistance)* (Leipzig, 1930).

[51] Editor's note: The German Peasants' War (or Revolution of the Common Man) is the term used to describe the series of uprisings of peasants, townspeople, and miners that broke out in 1524 for economic and religious reasons in large parts of southern Germany, Austria, and Switzerland, during the course of which the peasants, with the Twelve Articles of Memmingen, made demands for the first time that are regarded as an early formulation of human rights. The uprisings were put down by landlords and sovereigns between 1525 and 1526, resulting in the deaths of an estimated 70,000 to 75,000 people.

[52] Editor's note: A term popularized by German sociologist Johann Plenge, the "Ideas of 1789" represented the ideas of the French Revolution—namely the rights of man, democracy, individualism, and liberalism—which stood in direct opposition to the "Ideas of 1914," represented by National Socialism.

II

On the History and Evolution of the German Nobility

"A nation that does not retain a living connection to its origins is close to withering away, as surely as a tree that has been severed from its roots. We are today what we were yesterday."

Heinrich von Sybel

1

The reasons why the historical German nobility cannot claim to have ever been the pinnacle of the hierarchy of blood or the perfection of the German-Germanic man (and thus to have become nobility in the Germanic sense) lie in the following.

In general, the view prevails that the Christian German nobility evolved gradually from the pagan Germanic nobility, eventually forming the so-called German "high" nobility after the emergence of the so-called *ministeriales*[53] in the High Middle Ages, whose remnants were then buried in 1918. However, this view overlooks a fundamental circumstance.

The nobilities of the pagan Germanic peoples and of the Germanic peoples who converted to Christianity no longer had the same conceptions of nobility and were, in essence, complete opposites. This is not altered by the fact that large parts of the old pagan Germanic nobility

[53] Editor's note: The *ministeriales* were a class of serf-born individuals elevated to positions of authority in the Holy Roman Empire. They possessed social rank despite not being free men and held a variety of positions ranging from military service to imperial management.

were undoubtedly absorbed into the Christian Germanic nobility, so that, for example, the German nobility of the Middle Ages, even if perhaps not equivalent in public law, were in fact regarded and respected in some regions in much the same way that the pagan Germanic nobility had originally been. V. Dungern[54] is therefore undoubtedly right when he describes the medieval German nobility as the ideal of combined, highly-bred *völkish* power; we shall see that this praise is only valid with reservations.

The nobility of the Germanic peoples—like that of the Indo-European peoples—was based on a knowledge of the hereditary inequality of human beings. According to the conception of the time, the cause of this hereditary inequality was divine ancestors. It was believed that "blood" was the bearer of a person's qualities, that the physical and psychological qualities of a person were passed on from ancestor to offspring, and that noble blood also transmitted noble qualities; accordingly, it was also believed that an ancestor could be "reborn" in the offspring. Breeding laws of almost uncanny consistency ensured the purity of the blood. Von Amira states in *Grundriss des Germanischen Rechts (Outline of Germanic Law)*, "The Germanic noble families could be diminished, but not supplemented or increased." This explains the strikingly rapid extinction of the pagan nobility of some Germanic tribes during the Migration Period.[55] We do not know the reasons behind this sharp distinction of blood between the Germanic nobility and the Germanic freemen, but we do have the option of explaining it on the basis of more recent discoveries in the field of heredity by assuming the employment of breeding laws, about which I provided more detailed information in my book *Das Bauerntum als Lebensquell der Nordischen Rasse (The Peasantry as the Source of Life of the Nordic Race)*.

The pagan Germanic nobility was therefore exclusively a nobility of dynasties which only included families distinguished by clarity of descent. They were the noblest and the best of the Germanic peoples—people of noble blood. They drew the moral justification for their existence and their breeding laws from sacred ideologies. Even if the

[54] See his *Adelsherrschaft im Mittelalter (Noble Rule in the Middle Ages)* (Munich: J. F. Lehmanns, 1927).

[55] Editor's note: The so-called Migration Period, in its most narrowly defined sense, is the migration of mainly Germanic groups into western and southern Europe during the period starting from the Hunnic invasion of Europe circa 375 until the Lombard invasion of Italy in 568.

ancient Germanic nobility did not possess any privileges of a public-legal nature over the other freemen of their tribe, but merely had social and material advantages, their influence was nevertheless reliant to a significant degree on the respect which the people had for these noble dynasties. We have absolutely no example from the whole of later German history which could even approximate to this relationship between the Germanic nobility and the Germanic freemen, which was built on moral ideas and hereditary facts. "With all their sense of freedom, the people were proud of their lordly dynasties. Not with jealousy and envy, but with joy and love, with veneration and gratitude—the people looked up to them," wrote W. Arnold in *Deutsche Urzeit* (*German Prehistory*).[56]

An external marking of nobility was unknown to Germanism, as were external rank decorations such as crowns and scepters, thrones and princely dress; the well-known Iron Crown of Lombardy is only a work of the fifteenth century, using an iron bracelet from around 900. As Otto Lauffer wrote in *Germanische Wiedererstehung* (*Germanic Resurgence*; Heidelberg, 1926):

> Courtly ceremonies and corresponding insignia increasingly penetrated the Germanic princely courts only after the migration of peoples from Byzantium. The emperors at Constantinople, for example, granted friendly Germanic princes a kind of nobility charter, by which they conferred on them the title of consul or *patricius*, granting special privileges with regard to honorary dress and forms of address. The Germanic princes adopted these distinctions primarily in consideration of their formerly Roman provincial subjects.

---

[56] Actually only in England do we have something that approximates this relationship between the nobility and the people found among the Germanics. See Dibleius, *England* (England, Leipzig and Berlin: 1929) vol. I, 146: "Above all, however, the idea of natural leadership by old families is so deeply rooting in English popular beliefs that all modern egalitarianism is thrown out the window. For every ministerial post, for every honorary position in the state and municipality, the noble candidate is the first to be considered." Incidentally, we shall see in the following sections of this book that the position of the English nobility in the English people is by no means a coincidence—in addition to the still strong Germanic influence among the English, it can be traced back to the fact that the English nobility were able to avoid certain development that the German nobility fell into.

A reminder of this Germanic conception of nobility has been preserved in Sweden—a country in which some ancient Germanic customs have survived to the present day—in the fact that the oldest noble families of the country, e.g. the (translated here) Ochsenstern (not -stirn as in Schiller), the Schweinskopf, the Silberschild, the Lorbeerzweig, the Adlerflug, the Ehrenwurzel, and others exist in the unpretentious garb of a name that seems bourgeois (i.e. non-noble) to us Germans.

The free and noble Germanic peoples knew only *Du* as a form of address among themselves, without regard to differences of class. It was only later, following the Roman and Byzantine example, that kings were addressed as *ihr*,[57] over time this becoming generally accepted; it was not until the Carolingian period that the thoroughly un-Germanic and un-German[58] courtly and noble ceremonies began, which developed more and more in the Middle Ages and reached their climax in the time of absolutism, reaching in 1918 their (hopefully!) final grave.

The conversion of the Germanic peoples to Christianity, i.e. to the doctrine of the Anointed One, deprived the Germanic nobility of its moral foundations.

We cannot imagine the magnitude of upheaval of moral concepts brought about by the German peoples' conversion to Christianity to sufficiently understand the dissolution with regard to customs and law. In sharp contrast to the idea of the hereditary inequality of human beings, Christianity proclaimed "the accident of birth" and promoted the idea of the equality of all, imparting human traits to the throne of moral concepts. The Germanic nobleman had hitherto regarded himself as a guardian of divine order, placed in this world via the continuing power of procreation and originating from a divine ancestor. Consequently, he could not receive justification from the "self"; rather, he received it exclusively from what he was worth to the community or nation he led. With his conversion to Christianity, he was completely and thoroughly

[57] Editor's note: Addressing in the second person singular of the personal and possessive pronoun (*du, dich, dein,* etc.), colloquially called *duzen*, is the grammatically direct and simplest form of address that underlies all Indo-European languages. The *ihr* for individuals (*ihrzen*) of high rank is an outdated form of address in standard German.

[58] As early as the eighth century, the collective name *deutsch* (German)—*thiodisk*, from *thiod*, meaning "people," became commonplace among the Germanic tribes, particularly the West Germanic tribes of the mainland, while the name *germane* (Germanic) was used by Celts and Romans, but was not common among Germanic tribes.

deprived of the moral ground of his own sense of self as well as his social—and not least his ideological—position in the nation. Regarding the nature of things, it was no longer a question of fulfilling a task in this world on the basis of special innate predispositions, but things were turned upside down, in that the assessment of every moral task fulfillment was, so to speak, turned from the eternal into the temporal, and from the temporal towards a beyond. The Germanic had hitherto, on the basis of his pagan faith, carried within himself a kind of divine moral law, to which he subordinated the worldly things of his earthly existence. Suddenly all this was worth nothing, and he had to make an effort to first attain the hereafter by living a life pleasing to God on this earth. The individual was no longer evaluated by the people on the basis of a moral order that was known and sacred to everyone and in the fulfillment of which he first had to prove himself, but he was now evaluated exclusively according to how he solved the task of securing a privileged place in the hereafter through an individually purposeful life, for only this was—thought through to the last—pleasing to God. Thus the value of the noble birth was actually destroyed in thought, for everyone was now equal to every nobleman in the competition for the salvation of the soul in the hereafter—which was now the actual moral task of life. The supremacy of this concept over all worldly things cleared the way for the noble and free Germanic peoples to be ruled by non-noble officials, and later, in the case of the Franks, even by non-free officials, for this, which was monstrous to the heathen Germanic, was self-evident the moment it was done in the service of Christian thought. Therefore, the conversion of the Germanic peoples north of the Alps to Christianity, from the Franks onwards, was not primarily a matter of divinity, but a political measure conducive to the purpose of the kings, who thereby consolidated their rule.

If the feeling of the Germanic peoples had not been so thoroughly noble, if an actual trait of Germanism had not been the desire for the order of all things—a desire that hates every "disorder" in the depths of the soul, then the effects of the conversion to Christianity could have easily taken on the proportions that today's Bolshevism has managed to reach. For just as Bolshevism in Russia turned the whole previous conception of authority and morality completely upside down, so did Christianity at first among the Germanic peoples. And it must unfortunately be said that Christianity does not differ so much from Bolshevism in the crudeness of the means employed in realizing its plans.

In this question, however, a sharp distinction must be made between what Christianity professed as a message of salvation and what was useful for certain kings who used it as a means to pursue selfish goals under a moral idea.[59]

Experience has shown that today's Germans generally find it difficult to comprehend the full impact of the conversion of the Germanic tribes. It has been so hammered into our heads that the conversion of the Germanic tribes to Christianity was a step forward on the path towards the general development of mankind (and that it was done for the good of the Germanic tribes) that we are hardly able to grasp the idea that the conversion of the Germanic tribes to Christianity was primarily a measure of political expediency on the part of ambitious kings and not a matter of inner conversion to a higher knowledge of God.

At the heart of this matter is the attitude of Germanism towards the concept of the state. This is in no way to suggest that the Germanic people already had clear ideas about a state and its nature in the sense in which we have understood a state since the existence of the ancient Roman Empire. However, the Germanic peoples had very clear ideas about the way in which communities, peoples, and associations of peoples could be united in a unified order that overlapped them. Such orders simply grew out of the needs of everyday life. They had the individual community as their foundation and were dependent on the feelings of kinship between the peoples and tribes, especially with regard to matters of faith; furthermore, they depended on the natural conditions of their land, and finally—but not least, on the ruling power of individual people's kings or chiefs. The essential point, however, is that the system, as well as the representation of the entire order to the outside world, was of quite incidental importance and only came to the fore on special occasions where it was the main matter. The system grew from the bottom upwards, and had the father of the family (not every freeman, since only landowners were full members of the Thing[60])—and thus the family—as the actual bearer of influence; it then branched out from the family to community representation and from there on to the national assembly and so on, but in each case structured itself logically from the

---

[59] In more recent colonial history, too, Christian missionaries have often been used and deployed without their knowledge to advance political goals that could never have been dared to be said publicly.

[60] Editor's note: People's assemblies (*volksthing*) and Germanic court assemblies were called *Thing* or *Ding*.

bottom upwards, rather than from the top downwards. It was a system whose foundational laws were determined by the Germanic peasants' ideas of self-government, and whose composition depended on the more or less randomly assembled set of the lowest and smallest units, i.e. the landowners of each individual community. In this structure built on pure self-governance, any leader, no matter where he came from, was a commissioned leader—his status as a leader was not vested in any legal power or concept aside from free self-governance. In other words, the leader was never a source of law in himself or through the position he held, like the late Roman Caesar. Accordingly, and in essence also logically, every leader could be called to account by their legal peers in the self-governing body, and the Germanic peasants, if necessary, did not hesitate to lay their heads before the feet of their kings. The position of the Germanic kings and chieftains was thus far more what we would call today a "commissioned manager hired on notice," than a king in the sense of our more recent German history. This explains why the Germanic king was not a distinguished ruler, but always remained an equal among equals, who was only endowed with special powers on a case-by-case basis and for the fulfillment of special tasks. He was then, however, allowed to wield these powers with all ruthlessness because of the responsibility he had assumed.

The strength of this Germanic political system (the basic tenets of which, by the way, passed over into the medieval German political system and are something which we have been consciously struggling to revive since Freiherr von Stein) lay in the fact that the law was upheld and the inner and outer freedom of the Germanic freeman remained untouched. Its weakness, on the other hand, lay in the fact that this system, built on a perfect foundation of natural law, lacked a firm structure, precisely what we today call the state and state borders. Thus, it also lacked a united external representation, as well as any outwardly directed purposefulness in general. This is the explanation for the fact that the foundations of early Germanic states, while astonishing in their perfect internal justice and their both artful and functional internal structures, are at the same time so conspicuously vacillating and aimless in their foreign affairs, with their cohesion against foreign enemies often entirely dependent on the personality of the individual leader.

When the Germanic peoples clashed with the Roman Empire, the late Roman political system and relationship of the individual to the state stood in stark contrast to this Germanic concept of the parts of the people united under one leader. Admittedly, the ancient Roman Empire had originally grown out of patrician institutions, which were more or less the same as those possessed by the Germanic peoples in their early days. But after the defeat of Carthage, the internal laws of the Roman Empire changed. The civil servants no longer felt themselves to be the agents of self-governance, but slowly and imperceptibly transformed under the influence of the moneyed people who were gaining more and more power in the state; they became the actual masters and developed into an independent leadership. The civil service, although still supplemented from the old Roman families, turned into the tool of the bankers. This state of affairs only became apparent in the time of Caesar, especially after his assassination, when the people began to deify his person in the oriental sense. Such a process would have been unheard of earlier in the Roman Republic, and it proves the Roman people's complete turning away from the old Roman way of thinking and their accustoming to an unconditional leadership. With this, the path was clearly marked out and Augustus consequently followed; he designed the Roman state as an institution of expediency structured from top to bottom, which was fundamentally superior to the rights of the individual and served to carry out the subjugation of the peoples according to expedient points of view, irrespective of their uniqueness or peculiarities. Through this system the Roman state was able to weld together the Mediterranean basin into a kind of economic unit. At the same time, of course, the power of economic interests, which, through the influence of the bankers, was becoming more and more equal to that of the state, had priority over the interest of the personal freedom of individual citizens. Its success was ultimately an outwardly more or less clearly delimited empire with astonishingly developed institutions of expediency with regard to its domination and to the economy. There is no doubt that the Roman Empire of the Caesars realized, in a certain sense, the supranational world economy that we are striving for again today, for the Mediterranean basin was initially its own little world for the peoples living along the Mediterranean. But this Roman Empire, as far as man is concerned, was built over the peoples!

This is a fine example—Rome's battles over Gaul prove it most clearly. Rome needed Gaul's wealth and later needed Gaul as part of its economic zone from the Atlantic Ocean to the Orient. It was in the time of Augustus that this process was both initiated and completed, and we can clearly observe it historically. In carrying out his plan, Augustus resisted the tribal idiosyncrasies of the Gauls as well as other ethnic concerns. It is revealing to note that Augustus then deliberately set about suppressing ethnic issues in Gaul through measures that would take us far too long to discuss in detail here. His attempts to bring the Germanic tribes into the same economic dependence as the Gauls in order to protect the eastern border of Gaul failed. When the Roman governor Varus, who had been trained in the Orient and had been transferred from there to Germania, also tried to impose a tribute plan on the Germanic tribes—as was common practice in the rest of the Roman Empire—the well-known uprising in 9 A.D. arose, which, with the battle in the Teutoburg Forest,[61] put an end to such Roman efforts for centuries to come.

The late Roman empire was thus a fully constructed system, the external boundaries of which were, as far as possible, oriented towards the material laws of the economy and whose inner workings were also oriented towards this goal. The human being played a secondary role. The laws of blood were either not taken into account at all or only to the extent that they did not disturb the state as such nor its activities.

Nevertheless, despite its disregard for human freedom and the human dignity of each individual, this Roman Empire was built on the recognized inequality of the human race. The inequality was no longer driven by noble patrician dynasties that could be confident of their people's admiration because of their divine descent, but by property and economic wealth; the idea of the hereditary inequality of human beings was thus transferred from blood to the ownership of property. But this empire of the Roman Caesars, despite its immoral political system, remained insurmountable as long as this idea of the hereditary inequality of humanity was maintained. That is why this empire collapsed only with Christianity. The time of the actual collapse can be placed quite precisely in the years between 235 and 285 A.D. G. Ferrero has recently demonstrated this in his very readable study, *Der Untergang der Zivilisation des Altertums* (*The Decline of the Civilization of Antiquity*; Stuttgart 1923, second edition). He says, for example:

---

[61] In the Battle of Varus (also known as the Battle of the Teutoburg Forest or the Battle of Hermann, and referred to by Roman writers as the *clades variana*, or "Varian disaster"), which took place in the second half of 9 A.D., three Roman legions, together with their auxiliary troops and support forces, suffered a crushing defeat in Germania under Publius Quinctilius Varus against a Germanic army led by Arminius ("Hermann"), a prince of the Cherusci.

> The Greek and Latin civilizations both rested on the basic noble principles of a twofold, unavoidably necessary, and divinely willed inequality—the differences of race and class.... Almost everywhere in the Greek and Latin cultures, governments were aristocratically based on the hereditary prerogative of a small oligarchy capable of governing alone.... Rome was never governed democratically, not even in the stormiest times of the Republic; even the ruling class of the Roman Empire until Caracalla, that is, until the beginning of the third century (only a century before Diocletian), can still be described as having an aristocratic selection of a nobility. The senatorial and knightly classes, which enjoyed the privilege of occupying all high imperial positions, were a selection from the totality of Roman citizens, who in turn were formed from the noble and lowly, rich and poor, educated and uneducated, together forming a second class within the imperial population, itself endowed with important privileges and subject to its own laws. The Greco-Latin selection was on the basis of the principle that individuals and peoples are not equal in their moral dispositions, but rather unequal.... Christianity, through its doctrine that all men were equal as the children of the same God, had shaken the aristocratic fabric of ancient civilization to its foundations.

Until the third century after Christ, there was no difference between the Germanic and Roman peoples in the fact that both were convinced of the hereditary and divinely ordained inequality of human peoples. However, the Germanic and late Roman peoples are sharply opposed to each other in the way they perceive the relationship of the individual to the people as a whole, or of the citizen to the empire.

In the third century A.D., the Roman Empire began to collapse for entirely internal reasons. Under pressure from Asiatic nomadic hordes, the Germanic peasant tribes flooded the territory of the Roman Empire at a moment when it was no longer able to defend its borders. That the Germanic tribes "conquered" the Roman Empire is historically inaccurate. For "conquest" as it is understood in this context presupposes the will to attack a country in order to rule over it. Such a will is nowhere to be found among the Germanic peoples (apart from the Lombards, who did not break into upper Italy until the sixth century)—they merely sought land in order to settle. The Germanic peoples were, in fact, quite willing to serve the Roman Empire if they were allowed to live according to their customs on lands assigned to them. However, late Roman law and Germanic law are two things that contrast like fire and water, and were so opposed that they could not coexist. Thus we see this time of general confusion, which is somewhat inaccurately called the "Migration Period," filled with a push by Germanism to establish itself within the territory of the Roman Empire. This could not last and either perished, like the Vandals in Africa, or was pushed out, like the Visigoths from Italy. The latter finally found a place to stay in Spain, i.e. in a very remote corner of the Empire. Only in Gaul were the Franks able to gain a definitive and unrestricted foothold. Accordingly, it was in Gaul that the conflict between late Roman and Germanic law, and between the late Roman and Germanic political systems, came to a head and initiated a struggle that lasted through the millennia until it was conclusively decided by Napoleon I, who finally and conclusively imposed the late Roman administrative system.

We must keep in mind, however, that the Franks brought personal freedom to Gaul with their law and accustomed its people, which had completely degenerated and been enslaved in the mire of late Roman civilization, to freedom and human dignity again.[62]

But the Franks were also adaptable. In the south of their empire, where no rural Frankish settlement had taken place and the Franks only

---

[62] Strictly speaking, the French Revolution of 1789 can be called a joke of world history in its justifications. Louis XIV had imposed absolute monarchy in France. H. von Moltke writes in *Die Westliche Grenzfrage (The Western Border Question)*, "This transformation of France under Louis XIV may justly be regarded as a Gallo-Roman reaction against the Germanic element which had hitherto still prevailed in France, as an annihilation of both the old Frankish popular liberties and the representation of the estates, and as a return to the former Roman despotism, such as what had been indigenous to Gaul for five hundred years from Caesar down to Clovis." The French people rose up against this despotism and simply demanded back the safeguards of the old Frankish, old Burgundian, and so on constitutions, i.e. the old Germanic institutions of the original assemblies, the army, and the imperial assembly. But it is a great irony of world history that these demands of the French, certainly no longer a very Germanic people, had to be forced upon their still predominantly Germanic, i.e. blond and blue-eyed, nobility. Meanwhile the French revolutionary, who boasted of wanting to chase Germanism back into the forests of eastern France and who was not afraid to send a blond and blue-eyed man to the scaffold—even if he was not a nobleman, and who presented himself as the guardian and heir of Roman liberties, simultaneously demanded Germanic institutions from his Romanized nobility of Germanic blood. With which things were indeed turned upside down in every respect!

ruled their territory as landlords, the Roman administrative institutions had remained more or less intact, so that the Franks had the opportunity in their own empire to learn about the expediency of these institutions. They learned that Germanic law, while perfectly capable of preserving the human dignity of the law-abiding individual, was less useful for administering and managing an empire according to the interests of a centrally directed state. While in one part of Gaul the Frankish self-governance prevailed, the Roman administration prevailed in another part—an empire came into being whose Germanic leader was given the opportunity, in a thoroughly peaceful way, to train himself in Roman administrative and ruling customs and to learn to appreciate the Roman state institutions as excellent aids in creating a kingdom independent of the people—in this case, independent of the entirety of the Franks. The situation arose in which the Frankish king, who had been "commissioned" as king by his fellow Franks on the basis of Frankish law, believed that he could best satisfy his desire to expand his personal power by justifying his ambitions on the legal basis of his Gallo-Roman subjects. The advantages of the Frankish kings were best preserved by adopting Gallo-Roman legal views, and it is understandable that Frankish kingship began to lean in that direction. In those times, however, Christianity, as the previous Roman imperial religion, was synonymous with the Roman conception of state and law. It therefore makes sense that the Frankish king Clovis I, who converted to Christianity together with other Frankish leaders, in this way consolidated the foundations of his royal power and proceeded to rule in a decidedly un-Germanic manner. His Franks at first did not think at all of following him down this path, and it took centuries for all of the Franks to accept Christianity. But since the Frankish system of self-governance, with its commissioned kingship, could only be transformed into an autocratic kingship (complete with a civil service responsible only to the king) if this transformation was based on moral reasoning, it is logical then that the Frankish kings turned their attention to evangelizing Christianity among the Franks and promoted conversions to the best of their ability. Once all Franks were Christians, their king and his officials could rule over them—regardless of whether these officials were of free Frankish or non-free origin. At the end of this development, and representing it most fully, was a Frankish king who was not even descended from a noble Frankish family, but who nevertheless firmly and securely ruled the Frankish Empire through his retinue of officials of diverse origins who were devoted only to him—Charlemagne! With Charlemagne, the late Roman conception of the empire and the state had for the first time gained a firm foothold on purely Germanic soil and was able to assert itself.

From the Catholic side, we learn much from Dr. Eugen Mack's *Kirche, Adel und Volk* (*Church, Nobility and People*; Wolfegg 1921, page 3), which describes how closely political and religious aspects interacted during the development of the Frankish royalty, and how it favored the emergence of a Frankish Christian nobility which no longer had much to do with the old pagan Frankish concept of nobility, but which nevertheless was to become of the most lasting significance for Germanism. Eugen Mack explains:

> Exactly one hundred years before the Treaty of Verdun, in 743, we have a great turning point with regards to the Church and the Franks. The organizer of the Church in Germany, Saint Boniface, was at work. Pippin, the majordomo of the Merovingian house, who politically favored the work of Boniface, installed, after an interregnum beginning in 737, what would be the last Merovingian king—Childerich III (743). The state alone was not suitable for establishing a Frankish Christian nobility, and so it had to involve the Church as an authority superior to the state and work harmoniously with it. The Church itself came to this decision—at a synod in Eistinä (Estinnes) in Hainaut, where the spiritual and secular nobility met, it was decided that part of the church property secularized by Charles Martell (Majordomo 714–741) should be returned. If this was not possible for the time being, they would remain in the hands of their owners as precarious property. This meant that the owners would pay an annual tax and that their property would revert to the church in the event of their death, if the heir was not in need. This is the beginning of the feudal system, and in a certain sense also of the *Leibfall und Gnadengüter* (mortuary).[63] The Church began the system of fiefs on a grand scale. It bound land and soil and created for itself a tribal estate, and in later development a *fideicommissum*,[64] subsequently

[63] Editor's note: The mortuary was a payment in kind due to the feudal lord on the death of one of his bondmen.

[64] This sentence could be misunderstood: The Church did not bind land for the first time, since land had already been bound among the Germanic peoples, as the

serving as a model for the empire. As large landowners, the Church and the nobility formed a close alliance that lasted until secularization in 1803.

2

The actual Christian German nobility begins with the year 496, when the Frankish king Clovis I—along with some of the great men of his empire—converted to Christianity for thoroughly political reasons. The conversion of the Franks was not carried out directly by their king, but by non-Franks, mainly Romans from beyond the Alps or Anglo-Saxons such as Willibrod and Winfried Boniface, who had particularly close relations with Rome. These missionaries were essentially evangelizers of un-Germanic legal concepts and convinced the Frankish kings to use the dominance of their kingship—which was opposed at the time to Roman ideas—to expand their own power. Thus Roman and Christian ideas worked hand in hand to make an independent king out of a king originally dependent on a free people and to endow him with rights of his own legal source. In this way, the king's former fellow citizens became subjects. Germanic democracy was replaced by Germanic monarchy. The path was cleared for only those whom the king appointed to serve as the king's officials, rather than those who had emerged from the self-governance of the Germanic national community on the basis of their intrinsic values. In this way, a civil service was established above the people ("people" is always understood here to mean the free or noble

---

following sections will explain. However, the Church began to provide the families it liked with tied property—the system of benefices, in order to anchor its influence in the country and to keep the families in question dependent. At that time, land ownership was synonymous with economic power and, as a result, also with political power. Accordingly, Mack says quite correctly in another place, "The papacy would not have been able to project its power so effectively if it had not also had external political and economic influence through the significant land and properties which had been acquired by the Papal States, especially since Pippin, the father of Emperor Charlemagne. In 756, two years after the death of Saint Boniface, then the archbishop of Mainz—Germany's largest archbishopric, Pippin donated the conquered Ravenna and the surrounding pentapolis to the Roman See by laying the keys of the conquered cities on the tomb of Saint Peter. From that time, this development had a very great significance on the history of the power of the Church over the peoples of the world, lasting at least until the end of the Papal States."

Germanic) which no longer needed to be in harmony with the people in terms of blood value. From this Frankish civil service developed a very substantial part of the new German nobility. It is very difficult to say how we should judge this German nobility of the Early Middle Ages in terms of race. Certain indications seem to suggest that some very un-Nordic (un-Germanic) blood flowed into the medieval nobility through both the Frankish Carolingians and their officials. For example, von Giesebrecht in *Geschichte der Deutschen Kaiserzeit (History of the German Imperial Era)* describes Giselbert, Duke of Lorraine, who lived around 921, as follows:

> The Lorrainian was considered ambitious and greedy and at the same time fickle and scheming, he liked to change masters and allegiances according to his advantages. He is described as a man of short, stocky build with enormous strength; his eyes rolled restlessly in his head, so that no one could distinguish the color of them, his speech was broken, his questions tempting, his answers unclear and ambiguous.

The characteristics described here are anything but Germanic!

Frankish rule was so thorough that no other Germanic tribe could claim to have completely converted its pagan nobility into the early medieval Christian nobility. It is proven that the old pagan nobility have survived longest among the Frisians, where—according to von Amira—pagan nobles could still be found as late as the sixteenth century in some old established chieftain families. The Saxons, who would have been the most likely candidates to convert their old pagan nobility into early medieval German nobility, probably lost the main part of their nobility at the well-known slaughter of Saxon nobles in Verden an der Aller,[65] as well as through the subsequent dispersion of these families by Charlemagne. However, it is necessary to counter the opinion, which can often be heard today, that Charlemagne had carried out the slaughter of thousands of Saxon nobles only out of a base hatred of the noble. Charlemagne was far too soberly calculating a statesman to have allowed himself to be carried away by such an unrestrained course of action. The situation was different—if Charlemagne wanted to extend his empire

[65] Editor's note: The execution of 4,500 Saxons near Verden an der Aller on the orders of Charlemagne in 782 is known as the Blood Court of Verden, Verden Blood Court, or the Blood Bath of Verden.

over the Saxons, he had to substitute paganism for Christianity, because otherwise he would have had no moral justification for bringing his non-Saxon Frankish officials—the Carolingians—to Saxony. For the Saxons, however, their paganism was inseparable from their nobility. In other words, as long as the Saxon nobility existed, the Saxon commoner would not become Christian, because the concepts of his nobility and Christianity were mutually exclusive. Consequently, the position of the Frankish Carolingians also hung in the air as long as the Saxon nobility existed. The energetic Saxon people could not be repressed in the long run by force of arms alone. The situation arose that either Charlemagne abandoned Saxony or the Saxon nobility did. Importantly, old Germanic paganism was thriving in undiminished strength in the northern reaches of Saxon territory. A simple expulsion of the Saxon nobility would have only driven them to the north, from where their influence on the remaining Saxons would have been all the stronger—this scenario did indeed occur several times. Charlemagne's attempts to gain control of the pagan Baltic region failed, as the Swede E. Almquist-Westervit has convincingly demonstrated in *Archiv für Rassen und Gesellschaftsbiologie* (*Archive for Racial and Social Biology*; volume 19, page 418). This Baltic failure must have led Charlemagne to decide to wipe out the Saxon nobility, much like Alexander the Great untying a Gordian knot with one blow. As Wilhelm Teudt-Detmold has demonstrated in his very readable article "Karl, Westfrankenkönig, Römischer Kaiser" ("Charles, King of the West Franks, Roman Emperor") article in the newspaper *Die Sonne* (*The Sun*; volume VI, pages 7-8), the slaughter of the 4,500 Saxon nobles in Verden happened in a very methodical way, which, considering the current state of affairs and the possibility that the Saxon nobility could escape to the pagan north at any time, it may have been a political necessity—particularly if Charlemagne had already reconciled with the underhanded idea of slaughter. The reason for the murders was therefore hardly the hatred of the high-bred by the low-bred, but may have been the result of very sober reasoning and political considerations. This, however, by no means should be regarded as a moral justification, at least not from a German point of view. But the fact that Charlemagne did not represent the Germanic side in this struggle between Roman and Germanic forms of government and political systems—wanting to impose Roman thinking on Germania and succeeding in doing so—proves that Charlemagne could no longer have been a pure Germanic, or at least that he no longer had any understanding for the significance of the Germanic nobility, precisely because of his deficient Germanic blood heritage. This fact has already been pointed out by Meckel in *Altgermanische Kultur* (*Ancient Germanic Civilization*; 1925), who states that Charlemagne was an exemplary student of his Roman teachers.

Verden is of decisive importance in the history of the development of the German concept of nobility. On that day in 782, the change that began in 496 with Clovis I's conversion to Christianity, came to its conclusion. From the year 782 onwards, Germany was ruled by a Christian nobility that had been developed from the official Frankish nobility of probably dubious Germanic blood value, which was only replaced and supplemented by better blood over the course of time—probably achieving significant improvement only since the reign of King Henry I the Fowler (876–936). The development of the German Christian nobility from the Frankish civil service nobility is essentially the reason why, in contrast to the pagan Germanic nobility, it no longer served as a leadership incorporated into the people, but as a self-contained layer above the German people, which was not to be redrawn until the time of the Crusades.

This replacement of the Germanic nobility by the new German nobility of the Early Middle Ages was directly dependent on the development of Christian kingship in western and north-western Europe. This is the reason why the degree that the old Germanic nobility (and its reputation) was preserved among the people is in inverse proportion to the success of Christianization among the Germanic tribes. We could almost draw a gradient which, starting from the Frankish Empire, its preservation increases towards the north. This is why Swedish royal founders such as Erich Emundson in the tenth century had so little influence that when they established their Christian kingship they were unable to turn their people into subjects, which also explains why in Sweden the old ideas of nobility have been able to survive in certain respects to the present day.

In German lands, the freedom of the common free person received its most significant blow at the beginning of the tenth century. It was a time of decline for the East Frankish Empire under Louis the Child, before Henry I's clear view and firm hand was able to put things back in order. At that time, very few were strong enough to defend their patrimony against both external and internal enemies—those who were unable to do so had no alternative but to enter the service of a powerful ecclesiastical or secular lord. Poor crop yields and Hungarian invasions devastated the commoners' fields, while at the same time they were being repeatedly called to arms to protect the land. Thus, many a commoner was forced by circumstance to buy protection and security from powerful men in exchange for interest payments. Even if the common freemen initially retained their freedom, it no longer had the same value for them, since they lost the means to assert themselves against their patrons. It was easy enough for them to be reduced from an interest-paying debtor—which in those days was a kind of bondage anyway—to the status of actual bondage. This in turn resulted in exclusion from the legal system (the Thing of the Free) and subordination to the court law of their lord.

It was only then that the free Germanic peoples of Germany began to divide into two large, separate masses—the peasantry proper, soon consisting predominantly of interest-paying servile people, and the commanding warrior class, which was able to monopolize power. Wherever one looked, new service and dependency relationships were developing to diminish the old freedom of the people. Throughout history, individual tribes of small and medium-sized free landowners and peasants have survived in remote regions, such as in the high Alps, in the Frisian marshes, here and there in Westphalia, and in Scandinavia. But in general, the number of free people who built and protected their own farms has visibly diminished. A peasant was no longer endowed with his fief by the divine—by "God in heaven and the sunlight"—but by the feudal lord, who determined whether he would be saddled for the master's service (military service) or harnessed to the plough (peasant labor). Even though the feudal system had only been known in German areas for a century, it was from here that the real shaking of the old communal way of life was to start. If we consider the words of Mack in *Kirche, Adel und Volk (Church, Nobility and People)*, quoted above, it quickly becomes clear to us why the feudal system had to result in the destruction of the old communal traditions and was very probably originally brought to Germania explicitly for this purpose.

In addition, those vassals who were able to preserve their honor—and their personal freedom—through arms in the service of their patron were mainly reserved for court and military duties and were soon no longer employed in actual peasant work. Moreover, vassal service did not offer meager wages—it helped to achieve wealth and honor; extensive fiefs and shares in the spoils of war were rewards for the brave. Even if the fiefs were not hereditary at that time, they nevertheless granted the enfeoffed person honorable prosperity. This was to become more and more important as the endless wars of the coming centuries elevated the man who was skilled in arms above all others. So it is understandable that many good people were drawn to vassalage, widening the gap between them and the fully free peasantry.

The social standing of the peasantry was further damaged by the development of unfree servants in arms. As it became customary and necessary for great lords to surround themselves with unfree men-at-arms, a permanently mobilized "retinue" developed from them. And these unfree servants—the *ministeriales*—quickly equated their unfree servitude with the vassalage of free servants, elevating their position and, of course, only deepening the gulf between vassals and peasants.

In the eleventh century, this development was driven towards its completion. With Emperor Otto III (the son of a Greek princess), the foundation stone was laid for an occidental world empire that at least equaled that of Byzantium in its claims. This empire was a repetition of Charlemagne's empire, for it placed the emperor at the center of all power. Thus a rule was established that had little in common with the limited princely power that had been customary in Germania from time immemorial and was reminiscent of the despotism of the old Roman emperorship and that of Byzantium, even if it never reached it in its true form. However, it should be noted—see Chapter II, Section 1 above—that our word *Kaiser* (Emperor) is merely the German name for the founder of Roman despotism, G. J. Caesar. The early medieval empire was both a warrior state and a clerical state, which can be understood if we consider the above-mentioned ideas about the three concepts of church, nobility and rule. Its power was based on the sword-tested arm of the vassals as well as on the clergy, a circumstance that initiated the close interweaving of emperorship with the pilgrimage to Rome, and which, even with the best intentions in the world, cannot exactly be described as a stroke of luck for our people. Even if it were wrong to assume that this empire should be equated with the autocracy of later centuries—the time of so-called absolutism, the principle of ancient Germanism that every fully free person, provided he was a landowning householder, cooperated in building up the state leadership, was broken in favor of a power that set out to assert its independence downwards, even if it never managed to fully achieve its goal. It should be noted in passing that this emperorship, built on vassalage and the Church, bears a striking resemblance to certain warlike nomadic rulers of history, who, as is well known, basically ruled from above with swords and faith, and whose administrative and ruling institutions were not conceived for the uplift and promotion of the people's forces, but for their merciless exploitation.

In the times of the eleventh century, Germany was in the midst of tremendous turmoil. The German way of life was taken in a different direction by the unstoppable advance of the ideas of feudalism, as favored by the emperor and the Church. With the traditional regional states dissolved, ecclesiastical and secular powers divided up the old dominions. The formerly free states were largely replaced by the bishops, abbots, and counts, with only a minority managing to remain free of the empire. More and more commonly, military honors, knightly service, and position in the imperial army determined status and no longer, as before, an individual's degree of freedom. As early as 1024, at the coronation of Conrad II in Mainz, feudal service so determined a man's honor that in the order of oaths taken for the king, individual men of free status without a fief came last, even behind the vassals, i.e. the common knighthood.

In those times, bishops, abbots, counts, and lords began to build stone castles in order to manage the peasants' labor from the safety of a fortification and to be able to defend themselves against the neighboring lords. In my book *Das Bauerntum als Lebensquell der Nordischen Rasse (The Peasantry as the Source of Life of the Nordic Race),* I attempted to describe in more detail the un-Germanic and thoroughly nomadic character trait that came to Germany with this system of fortresses.

Finally, it should also be mentioned that at around this time, the independent development of urban life began. Soon, the city dweller increasingly separated himself from the peasant and looked down on him.

Thus was introduced in those centuries a mentality common amongst Germans today that farm labor was an occupation unworthy of a freeman. Necessarily, this resulted in nobility and peasantry standing against each other like two irreconcilable opposites. Virtually nothing remained of the old unity of nobility and peasantry, of sword and plough—the basis of all Germanism.

3

In Germany, it was not until the tenth century that the concept of noble status was introduced.

The reason for this was the constant expulsions and devastation in the Danube lowlands caused by the nomadic Hungarians, who from time to time raided Germany on a massive scale. The slow-moving armies of the free Germanic tribes were no match for such sudden attacks by cavalry-based forces, primarily because at that time the Saxons considered only service on foot to be worthy of a freeman. King Henry I, following the example of the Frankish armies of knights (whose emergence was also due to attacks from nomadic peoples, namely the Arab raids on the south-west of the Frankish Empire), created a cavalry force from the infantry ranks of his Saxons, as well as of other Germanic tribes, which later proved to be a capable match for the Hungarians. In this way, however, Henry I had initiated a development in German warfare which was bound to weaken the old freedoms of the people, and indeed did weaken it. Whereas until then every freeman had been able to raise arms and weapons for military service without difficulty, this was no longer the case. The many civil wars under the successors of Henry I soon made military service on horseback such a burden that the less affluent freemen could no longer afford the necessary expenses. Over time, the knights gradually replaced the traditional military service, finally turning the people's army into a vassal army. The vassal army, permanently mobilized, increased in popularity because these knights were not only excellent at serving in arms, but were also available at any time, a factor that played no insignificant role in the perpetual competition of the great men of that time for sinecures, among other things. To the same extent that the armies of knights gained honor, the infantry service lost it. More and more, the words *warrior* and *knight* became synonymous. The army of the people became an army of knights. Whereas the Germanic freeman had known the plough and the sword as a unit and as the insignia worthy of a freeman, the two were now separated. It became customary to speak of a military rank and an agricultural rank. This marked the beginning of a development which, given the nature of the Germanic people, would inevitably lead to the upheavals of the peasant wars in later centuries and, after their failure, to absolutism. But such a German nobility not only had nothing in common with the Germanic ideas about nobility, it was the exact opposite.[66] Whereas the Germanic free peasants had admired their nobility because the noble families actually represented the most morally, mentally, and physically well-bred individuals, now, after the failures of the peasant wars, the descendants of formerly free Germanic peasants had to be held down by rod and force of arms so that the German nobility, which was built on outward appearances and not on performance, could keep itself alive and in control.[67]

Nevertheless, the development in Germany described here also had its good side. For without this emperorship, which in its innermost essence is actually un-Germanic, the Germanic would never have arrived at a clear conception of a German state, or, at a minimum, the Germanics would never have been able to resist the predatory incursions of the Asiatic nomadic hordes. Due to his inner nature, the Germanic would perhaps not have been able to create his state without external pressures, because it is precisely his abilities in just self-governance and his capacity for developing internal state structures that prevented him from grasping the external aspects of everyday state life with the clarity and emotional certainty that these questions require. This is probably connected with the fact that throughout history the Germanic peoples have been proven to be far less effective (or completely ineffective) in shaping the states of their core countries, while finding more success in peripheral regions. The reasons can perhaps be found in the fact that where the Germanic peoples were able to stratify themselves over a population of a different race and employ their gifts of self-governance only amongst themselves in smaller circles (which, however, had a significant effect on the subjugated population in the sense of just leadership), their attention was directed more readily and more clearly to foreign affairs, which offered incentives if it could be mastered. In any case, it is a striking but undeniable fact that the most powerful state formations of the Germanic peoples in modern times arose on colonial soil, e.g. Austria, Prussia, England, and a few more. On the other hand, Germanic core countries

[66] This should be clear to all racial researchers who want to evaluate the medieval German nobility for insights into the soul of the Nordic race.

[67] The Swedes were more fortunate in this respect. In the heroic Wasas dynasty, the peasants still found old, genuine, Gothic nobility (the Wasas, especially the famous Gustav Adolf, prided himself on being of Gothic descent), which provided them with leaders in their fight against a foreign nobility, mostly of German origin. In this way, the Wasas prevented the Swedish peasant from coming under the pressure of a noble class. Hence the bundle of ears of corn in the coat of arms of the Wasas and their motto, "All through God and the Swedish peasantry."

such as northwest Germany, which is still predominantly populated by Germanic peoples, did not produce any Germanic states of significance, but, importantly, their blood was decisive in determining the statesmen of other countries. Treitschke occasionally points out that every reasonably important German statesman usually has a parent, or at least a grandparent, of Lower Saxon—generally peasant—blood.

The Germanic state of the Germanic peoples, correctly structured in terms of space, economy, and blood—from the bottom up and from the top down—as well as clearly delimited and purposefully managed, is still waiting to be created today. The Prussian state of the Hohenzollerns may have come very close to this goal,[68] at least in its basic ideas, but it was still not perfect. The renewal begun by Freiherr vom Stein attempted to incorporate the Germanic concept of self-governance into the Prussian state, but this attempt was ultimately unsuccessful. The task of creating the Germanic state of the Germanic peoples or, which is the same thing, the Germanic state of the Germans, is still before us and is still to be mastered by us and our successors. This is the Third Reich we confidently hope and strive for. For the time being, however, we have not even fulfilled the demand that E. C. Jahn was able to outline with the brief words, "The state is the basic structure of the people, the people's external structure and appearance."

To sum up, we can say that over the course of the first millennium of our era, a clear conception of the state asserted itself amongst the Germans, replacing their old conception of nobility with a completely new one. Outwardly, the reason for this was their circumstances, while inwardly the reason lay in moral terms, with Christianity, which no longer wanted to and could not tolerate the concept of a nobility originating from divine ancestors. Therefore, the second millennium of German history, dominated by the idea of emperorship, began with a completely new conception of nobility in the core of German thought. Our historical nobility goes back to the Christian German nobility established at the beginning of the second millennium, not to the pagan nobility of the Germanic tribes, even if the blood of the pagan Germanic nobility may have largely been passed down to the Christian nobility. It is now well understood why I said in Chapter I, Section 2 that the considerations of race and the considerations of German history lead us

---

[68] The Swedish state created by the first Wasas kings, including Gustavus Adolphus II, could also be mentioned here in some respects.

into a dichotomy with regard to the history of the development of the German nobility, which can only be overcome when we realize that the contrast exists in the philosophical differences (though perhaps not so much in blood) between the pagan and the Christian nobilities of the Germanic peoples.

III

Means and Possibilities for the Formation of a New Nobility

"Those who want success must also want the means."

1

What we Germans need is a genuine nobility in the old Germanic sense. In some way, we must return to the Germanic concept of nobility.

Since we have a scientifically established theory of heredity, the moral justification for any demarcation of rank based on outward appearances and not on hereditary blood value, together with the associated prejudices of rank, has collapsed. To the people of our time who have advanced our understanding of heredity, it seems ridiculous when the bearer of a noble name is at the same time the bearer of hereditary physical or mental inferiorities. It is precisely the modern and progressive branch of our science, natural science, which has opened up for us paths that lead back to the morality of our Germanic ancestors in a very interesting way. For their morality was based on the recognized hereditary inequality of humanity, and today's natural science is returning to this realization. In any case, it is of no importance whether or not the Germanic peoples were on the right path regarding the details of heredity and in the knowledge of its causes.

If we want to build up the actual core of a new German nobility based on the Germanic concepts of nobility, then we must first and foremost lead the thoroughly un-Germanic form of noble stratification, which began with the German Early Middle Ages, back to its original form based on the integration of the nobility into the people and built on the basis of innate values. Our new German nobility must again become a living source of highly-bred leadership talents. It must have institutions that retain blood of proven value in the hereditary line, repel inferior blood, and guarantee the possibility of absorbing newly emerging talents from the people at any time.

Nevertheless, it is important to note that among the Germanic peoples, nobility was not only a matter of blood, but as a concept also depended on other circumstances that will play a role for us here. The documents for the following can be derived directly from the remains of ancient Germanic legal literature. Where these have gaps or are ambiguous can be filled-in directly in two ways. Firstly, there is ancient Indo-European legal literature whose often peculiar synchronicity with Germanic legal literature astonishes us and allows us to assume that the Germanic legal sources we are missing were the same or at least very similar to the Indo-European ones; and secondly, the known land laws of the Germanic tribes from the Middle Ages can help us. There is undoubtedly a connection between Germanic and Indo-European rights in the history of legal development, making it possible through comparative jurisprudence to use old Indo-European legal literature and the Germanic land laws of the Middle Ages to carefully supplement or make comprehensible what is missing or unclear in the Germanic legal literature in question.

The Germanic nobleman—it was the same with the Indo-Europeans—derived his origin from a divine ancestor whose blood (in other words: genetic material!) had to be passed on by the descendants to the offspring in the purest possible form. Such a passing on of the blood was symbolically linked to the eternally burning hearth fire. This hearth fire, which had to be continuously maintained, represented, so to speak, the visible soul (central tenet) of the idea. The roof belonged to the hearth fire as its protection and thus also the house. To the house belonged the family that kept the whole system alive—in our German language the term *haus* (house) for "family" has survived. For example, we say "House Habsburg" and mean "the Habsburgs," or we say "*ich und mein ganzes haus*" and mean "everything that belongs to the family." House, hearth, and family were definitely synonymous concepts for the Germanic people.

If the family unit was to be kept viable, its nutritional basis had to be ensured. Therefore, a defined landholding was the legal basis of this institution. How closely land ownership was perceived to be included in this term is evident from the fact that far into German history – in custom even into the nineteenth century – a land purchase only became legally binding when the buyer extinguished the old hearth fire and rekindled it.

In the essence of this institution, which links land ownership directly with religious ideas and the family, the Germanic nobleman does not differ from the Germanic common freeman. Common to both – as well as to the Indo-Europeans – is also the view that such a structure, which is born of religious and legal concepts of life, can only tolerate monogamous marriage; where we see evidence of polygamous marriages, however, it is always obviously also a matter of several hearths, i.e. households; I am not aware of any instance of several equal and legally married wives living together under one roof. This is not, however, the case with unfree women, whose position as a wife did not affect the wife's position as a mistress.

In contrast, there seems to have been quite a difference between the Germanic noble and the Germanic common freeman in the way land ownership was inherited. This fact is important!

The common freeman was called *bauer* (peasant) among the Germanic peoples because of a direct connection with the dwelling, the "house," of which he was the head of the household. Particularly, the term traces its roots to the Old High German *bûr*, meaning "dwelling" or "house," a word that according to Heyne and Weigand has survived with us in *vogelbauer* (birdcage). Since only the land-owning head of the household was a full citizen and thus a fully valid individual in the eyes of the law and in the Thing, it is important to note that the word "peasant" represented a title of honor and an expression of personal freedom. This is important to emphasize because it shows most clearly how much things were turned upside down in the second millennium of German history, when the very concept of peasantry was associated with the concept of subjugation. From a Germanic point of view, the word "unfree peasant" is a contradiction in terms. Certain people would like to deny this fact by saying that only the Germanic nobleman was free, while the Germanic peasant was basically in bondage. For the supporters of this view, who are mainly to be found in the field of economics, we should refer to the history of the development of Holstein, where old Germanic customs have survived for a relatively long time. At the Diet in Oldesloe in 1392, free peasants appeared for the last time on an equal footing with the nobility and prelates at the regional assemblies, where occasional blood feuds would be negotiated. This is the last national assembly where peasants were seen to appear! Later nothing more is heard of them; they disappear into the gloom of serfdom. The old *volkstage* (assemblies of the people) are replaced by the state assemblies of the estates.

Since the house and the family associated with it, as well as full legal freedom, are the hallmarks of the Germanic peasantry, the land area of such a Germanic peasant was only as large as was needed to feed the family. However, a "family" at that time also included unmarried relatives and the servants, so it was usually significantly larger than a family today.[69, 70] Therefore, Germanic peasants were allotted land of a size that ensured the family's nourishment, but had nothing to do with any kind of template land distribution or allotment. Von Amira writes in *Grundriss des Germanischen Rechts (Outline of Germanic Law):*

> The unit of measure of possession is the *hufe* or the *lot* or the residential land or the plough land. Everywhere this unit was understood to be the land which was necessary on average for the maintenance of a family, and which, for this very reason could not be the same size of area everywhere, i.e. could only become a fixed area of measure at the regional level. The shares in the use of common land not subject to cultivation were usually based on this measurement.

Where Germanic peoples did not settle in individual farms but rather in village cooperatives, the peasantry of a village would form a margraviate. On a case by case basis, this cooperative had the authority to redistribute available agricultural land whenever circumstances made this measure appear advisable. We do not know the reasons which could lead to a redistribution of the plough-land, but we may assume that such a thing happened only rarely and on special occasions; the minimum extent of a

---

[69] This form of Germanic peasantry has been preserved in its old form among the so-called Couronian royal peasants in Courland (Latvia) and in an even more ancient form among the twenty-eight farms on the island of Runö (Estonia) in the Gulf of Riga, where customs and traditions can still be found that we otherwise only know from ancient Germanic legal literature. See W. Ziercke, *Mecklenburgische Monatshefte (Mecklenburgian Monthly Bulletins)*, February and August 1927.

[70] Editor's note: the ancient Germanic farming practices described here in both Courland and Runö Island were exterminated following the end of the Second World War and the voluntary or forced removals of the Germans living there.

plough-land could never be less than that required for the nourishment of the family to which the plough-land was allotted. In this respect, the margraviate differs quite fundamentally from the Russian *mir*, which we will get to know in more detail in the next section. The Russian *mir* disregards the livelihood of households and only takes into account an individual's hunger for land, regardless of whether or not the land allotted to the person concerned will be used to feed him and his family. In contrast, the Germanic margraviate was a cooperative of household heads—their decisions on a redistribution of plough-land therefore always took into account the livelihood of cooperative's households. Since the head of the household was always at the same time the head of the family living in the house, it is understandable that every land reallocation or redistribution was always carried out by clan. In this respect, the Germanic traditions are unambiguous and in this area also agree with ancient Indo-European traditions, including the fact that, if possible, only one third of a conquered land was ever taken from the subjugated population for their own settlement purposes. The land distribution of the Ostrogoth king Odoacer in Italy, for example, is very clear. Since the sources expressly tell us that the Goths lived on these lands according to their customary rights, and history tells us the same thing about Ariovist and the Suebi, there is no need to doubt about whether this is indeed an ancient Germanic institution. Anyone who is even somewhat familiar with these connections knows that all interpretations which would like to compare Germanism to "soil communism" are grossly missing the facts. Certainly, the Germanic people did not enjoy any freedom with regards to an individual's usage of land—but this land-boundness did not arise from communist thinking, rather it arose from the simple fact that land was included in the concept of godhood and the family idea derived from it, belonging to the family like a roof to the house. To the Germanic, land was only a necessary link in the unity of the clan, which was built up according to their way of life and religious beliefs, and it would have seemed inconceivable to him to value agriculturally-usable land independently of the idea of family.

The Germanic nobility seems to have been independent of the constraints of a cooperative decision, i.e. they did not have to make their land available in the event of a redistribution. Not that the nobility was in a position to appropriate land at will and bequeath it as they saw fit, but it seems as if the Germanic nobility had an inherited estate which they bequeathed to others independently of the margraviate. In any case, our word for nobility is derived from such a hereditary seat. According to Heyne, our word for nobility originally meant nothing more than the cooperative of landowners (it would probably be better to say: cooperative of those owning hereditary property)—Middle High German *adel* and Old High German *adal,* in the diminutive of Old High German *uodal,* meaning "hereditary seat." Weygand has the following derivation: Old High German *uodil/uodal,* Old Saxon *odil,* and Old Norse *odal,* all meaning "hereditary property" or "home." With von Amira we find: the word for hereditary or ancestral estates was derived from the Old Norse *odal* (elsewhere in the north meaning "real property" in general), Old German *edel* (until about 900), Old Saxon *odhil,* Old High German *uodil,* and probably the Frisian *ethel* in its early medieval form. In some of these, not only was the owner's power of disposition limited, but the male line was also granted the right of first refusal over the property, as in the Norwegian *odal* and the Old Saxon *edel.* The indivisibility and inheritance of the ancestral property to the oldest male heir was also characteristic of those forms of hereditary property which appeared during the Early Middle Ages in Upper Germany as *hantgemahele* (contracted as *hantgemâhl*) in the possession of fully free and, as a rule, knight-born people. In the Early Middle Ages, Norwegian law, specifically West Norwegian law, distinguished between those who inherited a manor (*odal*) or had a claim to it, and the ordinary old or common freeman (also called *bonde*). Among the Anglo-Danes of the tenth century, too, there was a difference in value between *hold* and *bonde,* which was based on ownership.

This shows, first of all, that our word for nobility is derived from a Germanic institution that granted an inalienable and indivisible inheritance to a family, the enjoyment of which was reserved for either the eldest or the most important son (*holdr* signifies hero!). Inheritance was linked to the obligation to marry, and the concepts of inheritance, nobility, and monogamy seem to have been so intertwined that, for example, the term *adhalkona* for the wife has survived in Icelandic up to the present day. In other words, nobility among the Germanic peoples was an institution that concerned property for the preservation and multiplication of proven blood value. We shall see that this Germanic conception of nobility lasted the longest in England.[71]

---

[71] The connection between land ownership and nobility in the sense of a head of household on a hereditary estate is particularly evident in England from the local

Let us bear the following in mind: in a region or a country there is a fixed number of hereditary seats. The succession to each hereditary seat is only ever possible for a son, who at the same time must show himself worthy of this distinction through proven performance. Linked to the acceptance of the hereditary seat is the obligation to marry, in accordance with the idea developed above that the sacred fire of the hearth must be maintained by the same blood that lit the fire in ancient times. Connected with the idea of marriage is monogamy and the idea that the blood of the ancestor must be passed on to the offspring in the purest possible form, i.e. the evaluation of a spouse with regard to the offspring, i.e. breeding. In other words—only the best of the young people inherited the hereditary seat and married, thus placing themselves in the best possible position to bear the largest number of offspring. These leading people were then the actual nobility, while their brothers and sisters, as far as they did not also marry on a hereditary seat, were presumably no longer counted as part of the nobility, although they were of course descended from the nobility by blood. In general, the non-inheriting sons did not marry or had to obtain an opportunity to marry outside the country. The Norman Empire in Sicily, for example, owes its origin to such non-inheriting sons. Its founder and the Norman nobility invited into the country by him were this very same sort of non-inheriting sons of the Norman nobles of northern France; the phenomenon is quite similar to the *reislauf*[72] (going for a journey) of the non-inheriting Swiss peasant sons. The custom relating to the bachelorhood of the non-inheriting sons continued in places into the nineteenth century. These sons are called *junkers* among the nobility, and uncles[73] among the peasants.

---

nobility designation "lord." Lord, from the Anglo-Saxon *hlaford*, meaning "brother"/"bread keeper," which in turn comes from *half*, meaning "loaf" or "bread," and *weard*, meaning "keeper" or "guardian." Correspondingly, Lady is from the Anglo-Saxon *hlafdige*, meaning "brother"/"bread issuer," in turn from *hlaf* and *dige*; probably related to the Old Swedish *degja* or *deja*, meaning "issuer" or "caretaker."

[72] Editor's note: The *reisläufer* were Swiss nationals who left Switzerland in huge numbers to seek status, adventure, or wealth as mercenaries in European militaries from the fourteenth century until the 1874 amendment to the Swiss constitution that banned participation in foreign conflicts. World-renown for their fighting abilities, they played a role in virtually every European conflict of the era. The Vatican's Swiss Guard is today the world's last remaining Swiss *reisläufer* force.

[73] In a healthy modern state, these non-inheriting sons of landowners must be the real and never-ending source of renewal for the non-agricultural professions.

While the number of marriages on the Germanic hereditary seats was limited, the best of the young were given every opportunity to reproduce and did not have to worry about the number of their children—indeed a large number of offspring seems to have been obligatory. Thus the hereditary seats acted like filters, purifying the blood of the individual generations to ever higher perfection. This probably explains why the Germanic nobility of some tribes achieved pure thoroughbred breeding, which in principle did not allow any foreign blood to flow into the noble families.[74]

We hear nothing of any other privileges for the nobility in any other area. The view often found in economics that the Germanic peasant was obliged to the Germanic nobleman in the same way that a bondholder is to the lord of the manor is nowhere to be found in Germanic law. Even if we assume only a very loose relationship between landlord and bondsman, the unique—and we could even say socially ideal—Thing law of the Germanic peasant would still not be explainable. Von Amira, for example, says:

> The original Germanic system of governance left no room for the power of individual rulers. The head of state was the *Landsgemeinde* (People's Assembly). Apart from the *Landsgemeinde* and the *Hundertschaftsversammlung* (Assembly of Hundreds), there were no other state organs or officials—indeed, apparently the only officials were those who were elected by the *Landsgemeinde*. Certain basic features recur uniformly in the character of Germanic kingship, for example, the king's personal responsibility for his functions. Additionally, the ancient Germanic king lacked any and all independent legislative power—he had no greater right to vote in the *Landsgemeinde* than the next best free peasant.

To the Germanic sensibility, privilege was always only a personal reward for duties performed or to be performed, in proportion and in accordance with the actual scope of the duties, but not, for example, in accordance with actions that were not needed. The Germanic was imbued with the thought—power is only justified insofar as it means service.[75]

---

[74] For more information, see Darré, *Das Bauerntum als Lebensquell der Nordischen Rasse* (*The Peasantry as the Source of Life of the Nordic Race*), sections IX and X (1928).
[75] An excellent introduction to the basic ideas of Germanic law is offered by Merk, *Vom Werden und Wesen des Deutschen Rechts* (*On the Development and Essence of*

If, therefore, economists want to maintain the view that the Germanic was a landlord, then it can only maintain its assertion if it stamps both the Germanic peasants and the Germanic nobles as landlords. But that makes no sense, because the landlord theory in economics is concerned with drawing a line between the Germanic nobles and the Germanic peasants by making the nobleman the landlord and the peasant the landholder. This is an attempt to explain why the spreading feudal system destroyed the old common freedoms of the Germanic peasants and transferred them to the landed Christian lordship. In the preceding section, however, we see that things are quite simple in this regard. Moreover, the landlord theory of economics is contradicted by the history of law, the history of settlement, and also by the word "peasant" itself, as was pointed out in Chapter II, Section 2. Far more probable would be the assumption that E. Meyer, for example, expressed in his research on the ancient Germanic nobility, namely that the Germanic peasants arose from the younger sons of Germanic noble families who were able to establish a household, but who through their descendants remained subordinate, so to speak, to the lineage of the eldest son.

Let us summarize: by providing hereditary seats, to which the heir was only entitled to after proven performance and on which marriage and breeding laws applied, the Germanic peoples not only held on to proven leadership blood, but multiplied it and thus deliberately bred it. Incidentally, there is no evidence of any privileges enjoyed exclusively by the nobility, so that there can be no doubt that a separate noble class did not exist. The Germanic nobility seems to have been nothing more than the division of the nation according to different bloodlines, based on the ideological affirmation of the hereditary inequality of mankind, for the purpose of providing well-tested hereditary material for the selection of suitable leaders. The Germanic nation was thus, within the framework of its tasks at that time, a thoroughly structured whole, i.e. a life structure, with living content and purposeful division. Although the law applied equal rights for all,[76] not everyone was expected to bear the same level of responsibilities, but rather everyone was expected to do what could be expected of them on the basis of their hereditary status.

German Law) (Langensalza, 1926).

[76] "Equal rights for all" applied first and foremost to the Germanic freemen in their various ranks within the legal cooperative.

We must fall back on this basic idea of Germanism if we want to create a new nobility for our people.

2

The idea of creating a new nobility on the basis of recognized hereditary seats has already been brought to fruition in one European state—Hungary. It was the imperial administrator Horthy who achieved this. For us, it is essential that Horthy's successes in this field free us from any doubts as to whether it makes sense to revive old Germanic ideas of nobility in a modern guise. Horthy has proven that the path can be followed. We will first describe here what Horthy has created.

Horthy wanted first and foremost to counter the destructive ideas of Bolshevism, which threatened Hungary. Bolshevism is, in its deepest sense, nothing more than Tartarized Marxism, i.e. modern nomadism. Bolshevism is actually, albeit through different means, exactly the same as the nomadic attacks on Germanic Europe by the Huns, Hungarians, Tartars, Turks, and so on. Horthy knew of no better way to counter the predatory and destructive ideas of Bolshevism than with the ideas of the homeland, soil, and blood. It was the rootedness of the Hungarians that was of primary importance to him, through which the old Hungarian nomadic idea was replaced by a Germanic one. Furthermore, Horthy's great care in providing the Hungarian people with a sufficient number of leaders was driven by a sense of responsibility for the future. Perhaps he was also aware that in the future, the old Hungarian nobility would no longer be in a position—purely in terms of numbers—to provide the independent state of Hungary with a sufficient number of leaders.

Treitschke once stated that in the fate of a people, it is not so much the knowledge of a leader that is ultimately important, but his character, that is, the firmness of his human soul. Probably from a similar train of thought and on the basis of the experiences of the past World War (1914–18), Horthy concluded that the frontline soldiery that had proven itself in the four difficult years of the war undoubtedly represented a selection of the people with genuine strength of character and useful leadership abilities; at least he did not think he was making a mistake when he tried to preserve the humanity of the frontline soldier in as many descendants as possible for the Hungarian state.

Horthy's idea was first and foremost to provide proven frontline soldiers with amenities that would reinforce their roots in Hungary, and secondly would preserve them for the Hungarian people through their descendants. He gathered proven frontline soldiers of the World War, namely officers, non-commissioned officers, and enlisted men, into a heroes' cooperative. A member of a heroes' cooperative was rewarded with a small estate, a so-called heroes' or noble domain. The counter-obligation of the feoffed, both towards the heroes' cooperative and towards the state in its capacity as the patron of the heroes' cooperative, consisted of not monetary or other economic recompense, but exclusively in moral value. First and foremost, the feoffed had to exemplify real leadership to the Hungarian people through impeccable conduct of life, continue to be devotedly loyal to the fatherland, cultivate this spirit of loyalty in his house, and finally by marrying a healthy woman to ensure that numerous healthy and valuable offspring was born to him.

With this institution, Horthy hoped "to bring into being a new class from the stratum of the nation which was undoubtedly the most valuable and the healthiest, which could serve as a model for everyone, and which would continue to cultivate the traditional virtues of the Hungarian race." A title of nobility is attached to the noble domain, which is only granted to the feoffed—in this Horthy evidently followed English custom. The noble domain belongs to a nobility chapter, to which the feoffed is also subordinate. The nobility chapter regulates, among other things, the inheritance of the noble domains; the heir is generally the eldest son if there are no physical, mental, or moral reservations against him. In accordance with the feudal nature of the entire system, an heir's siblings are naturally not compensated, but the brothers, provided they are suitable, are given preference in the civil service or in the allocation of new noble domains.

The land for the noble domains owes its origin to voluntary donations; these donations either took the form of voluntary cessions of land or of periodic financial subscriptions which enabled the noble chapter to acquire land on the property market. It was also stipulated that not just anyone could donate something to the noble chapter, but only those Hungarians whose personal and professional impeccability could be proven. The names of the donors were published.

If we think through what Horthy created in terms of its fundamental ideas, we realize that Horthy, whether consciously or unconsciously, revived the old Germanic concept of nobility and integrated it into a modern state. If Horthy had only endowed proven frontline soldiers with landed estates in gratitude for their services and in order to bind them to himself, as it were, but without requiring them to incorporate breeding responsibilities, then he would have merely repeated the medieval feudal system built on sinecures. But it is precisely the feoffing for the purpose of rooting a family and its mission of producing valuable offspring that proves that this is only outwardly a repetition of the medieval concept of fealty, while in reality it is beyond that—it is a connection to the oldest Germanic ideas of nobility. Like the Germanic peoples, Horthy is also carried by the idea that every moral upward development of a people is causally and thus inevitably dependent on the promotion of valuable hereditary tribes within the people, but not primarily dependent on the promotion of the individual members of the people.

The talent of a people, which rests in the hereditary stock of its generations, is basically the only real source of value because all other value can only come to life through that talent. Nothing comes from nothing![77] The hereditary talent of a people is therefore its only real good, out of which it produces all values. This is a truth that many of our contemporaries find very unpleasant to hear, but it nevertheless forms the cornerstone of all cultural realities. Thoughtlessly or maliciously squandered endowments cannot be replaced—they are irrevocably gone. The causes of the decline of states and civilizations in history can be traced back to this fact to a large extent—this is no longer a mystery to natural science today, but is clearly and openly revealed. Here, divine nature, disgraced by our obsession with progress, smilingly confronts us with iron laws, the fundamentals of which, however, no subhuman or inferior will ever want to recognize, for these laws speak his judgment.

The thinking of many of today's German contemporaries is infested with the ideas of Marxism, and so they resist the scientific findings of the fundamental hereditary inequality of human beings. But Marxism, by its very nature, is not concerned with how values come into being. With the blind narrowness of nomadic grazing instinct, it stares only at the task of how the goods and values of this world are to be utilized, without wasting a single thought on the laws that condition the creation of those values; the questions of the laws of value creation is as far from Marxism

---

[77] Even an *idea* is inherently incapable of imposing itself against the inadequate echo of a talentless people. In these cases, i.e. among less gifted peoples, ideas are only realized when they become flesh and blood in a man and this man, in a very sober and calculating way, more or less forcibly converts the people to this idea with the strength of his personality and energy.

as, say, the cow is from the question of how the hay it has just eaten came into being. At its core, Liberalism is not so far removed from Marxism; although it has grasped and affirmed the economic laws of the creation of value and the production of goods, it nevertheless tends to persist in purely material thinking and wants to know nothing of the people's way of life, or, in the truest sense, of the decisive forces which condition and constrain the human being who produces value—a reality that Liberalism believes it is entitled to disregard. Liberalism and Marxism are directly responsible for today's state of affairs, where our way of life is disregarded and ridiculed in our national bodies. Only in this way can it be explained that the Germans, a people of such high-quality endowment and disposition, have the madness to make the healthy support the inferior and, by means of extensive—allegedly social—legislation, also see to it that the inferior are given the widest possible opportunities to live, while the valuable who are in need of help are denied help.[78] Or is it not perhaps madness that healthy German married couples today cannot find a place to live, while huge sums are spent on making prisons and asylums as comfortable as possible?

Horthy is absolutely right: establish institutions that favor the advancement and multiplication of the valuable, while at the same time inhibiting the possibility of multiplication of the inferior. This, and only this, purifies a people over time by removing the worthless components from its genetic material, ultimately developing it into an ever more unified whole. It was right that Horthy began with the creation of a new nobility, because for the implementation of a state idea based on value-creating traits, a tested and trained leadership class is as important to it as the officer corps is for an army.

For the tasks we are to solve here, the essentials are clear—both from the old Germanic nobility tradition and from what Horthy has created, to the effect that hereditary seats, i.e. hereditary estates, are necessary for a new nobility to be created. In any other attempt at a solution, the

---

[78] It should be emphasized here that Darré is not speaking out against unemployment welfare. The unemployed as such are first and foremost only proof of an economic disorder within the national body, but not necessarily proof of his own inferiority; this can be the cause of his unemployment, or better, of his lack of will to work, but it does not have to be. The present army of the unemployed is the most visible symptom of the incompetence of German economic management since 1918, but it is not the consequence of a professional or character inferiority of the unemployed per se.

continuity of the system and of the idea would suffer and the founding of families would become too easily dependent on unpredictable circumstances, as history teaches us. Moreover, unfavorable external conditions could also lead to fewer births, thus endangering the basic idea of the whole system. Finally, and this is almost the most essential point, the rearing of children under unfavorable conditions is detrimental to their soul and health. In any case, it is a fact that the Germanic family has never been able to live or maintain itself for a long period of time in an urban area or in circumstances otherwise detached from rural life without the necessary counterbalance of land ownership. Other races and peoples seem to have been better prepared for an urban existence detached from the land and rural life—perhaps because their ancestors, as nomads, were once accustomed to an unpredictable way of life[79] and to rocky landscapes or treeless steppes without green and fresh forests. For the Germanic peoples, such developmentally favorable requirements for urban life are not present, and for all of known history the Germanic has hated the city with all the fibers of his heart, probably out of healthy sentiments. Where the Germanic did become a city-dweller, this obviously always happened by force and never did him any good without the counterweight of a country home. It is very significant that all the Germanic tribes of the Migration Period almost fearfully avoided settling in Roman cities. As late as the eleventh century, for example, the small landowners of Lombardy, the *vavasours*,[80] were the population in whom the Lombard blood had been preserved in the most unmixed form. The aversion to urban areas can be traced back to the Lower Saxons of King Henry I—who resorted to choosing by lot those who were to live in the cities and castles that he founded, since the Saxon did not want to separate himself from the countryside—through to the Anglo-Saxons of today's England, who seek their dwellings outside urban areas if at all

[79] In any case, animal breeding knows similar examples of this. For example, it is easy to get a tamed Norwegian rat to reproduce, even under the simplest and most meager conditions, whereas the house rat, although just as easily tamed, can only be made to reproduce if the keeper has special skills. The situation is similar with the house sparrow, which, despite its habituation to humans, reproduces only very rarely in captivity. This is obviously a matter of certain basic physiological laws that we have not yet fully explored—we might conclude that species and breeds adapted to a migratory life are less sensitive to changing environmental influences than sedentary ones.

[80] Editor's note: *vavasours* were vassals or leaseholders of a baron that also had vassals or leaseholders under themselves.

possible.[81] Since German civilization is based on Germanism, we must also take its living conditions into account if we want to ensure a continuous upward development of German civilization.

The way in which hereditary property can be created will be shown in detail in the next section. However, one point should be mentioned here—the designation for such a hereditary property. Horthy speaks of a "noble domain." A domain is a crown estate, so for the still royal Hungary, the word noble domain is justified. However, we cannot use this term, firstly because it is doubtful whether a monarchy will ever again arise in Germany, and secondly because even in the case of a returning monarchy, under the current circumstances, the old Germanic people's kingship would still be conceivable, that, by its very nature, could not effectively distribute "domains." The word "noble estate" would perhaps be the closest term in accordance with the old Germanic meaning of the word "nobility." However, there are concerns with this; for example, that the word nobility is no longer understood by our people in the Germanic sense of the word, and misunderstandings would be likely to arise. More seriously, however, is the fact that today in East Elbia, various estates still bear the designation *Adlig Gut* (Noble Estate) and are registered accordingly in the land register. I would therefore like to avoid the word nobility in the terminology of the hereditary estate.

The word *hegehof* is hereby proposed.[82, 83] This word unmistakably expresses what is to be cherished in blood and soil.

---

[81] This is significant—when the French moved into Wiesbaden in 1918, they preferred the good flats close to the city center for their officers and officials. When the English occupying force of Cologne came to Wiesbaden a few years later and replaced the French, the English avoided the flats in the city center as much as possible and looked for flats in the urban outskirts or in the good villa areas of Wiesbaden.

[82] This word was found in Johannes, *Adel Verpflichtet* (*Nobility Obliges*), 2nd ed. (Leipzig, 1930); a quite excellent novel in which, with poetic vision, things and people are foreseen as existing which could perhaps one day become reality on the basis of the proposals for the creation of a new nobility proposed here.

[83] Editor's note: the etymology of *hegehof* appears to come from the words *hegen*, meaning "to preserve" or "nurture," and *hof*, meaning "manor" or "farm." The plural is *hegehöfe*.

3

Horthy, as already reported, endowed the noble domains with a title of nobility which was only borne by the feoffed. The title question is of fundamental importance. In order to be able to answer it, however, we must briefly clarify the meaning of a title of nobility.

In the previous chapter we already saw that the Germanic peoples did not know any title-like address of their nobility and that the whole title system only penetrated into Germanism from Byzantium, i.e. from oriental influence, compare Chapter I, Section 2. It would also have been absurd if the Germanic noble had wanted to be addressed with a title by the Germanic peasant, for he was noble by virtue of his being and confirmed by proven achievement—not by any outward appearance, especially since titles first takes appearance into account, whether the title as such has been acquired justifiably or unjustifiably.

From the Early Middle Ages the use of titles emerges: *Freie und edle Herren* (Free and Noble Lords). This was a title that indicated ownership and descent, and later evolved into the title of baron. Conversely, all other titles that would go on to become titles of nobility, including the titles of nobility that we are familiar with in German history, were not originally titles of nobility but titles of office—this applies to titles up to the rank of duke and margrave.

The counts were at first nothing more than Carolingian tax officials, presumably not of noble or even commoner Germanic blood to any large extent. If our present-day district council offices were hereditary to a family and after a certain period of time marked their holders as members of the nobility, i.e. if the title of district councilor became a title of nobility, we would have a similar development.

If we took into account the contrast between the late Roman and Germanic conceptions of administration described in Chapter II, Section 1, we would have to admit that there could undoubtedly have been nobles among Charlemagne's counts. But the very nature of the Frankish office of count makes it improbable that the noblest Franks would have pressed themselves into this service. We can assume, however, that the Carolingians, especially Charlemagne, would have avoided appointing both noble and common Franks to the position of count as much as possible, as it could become inconvenient to them.

How the title *Freie und edle Herren* came into being in Germany is still unclear. Presumably, the Germans simply modified the un-Germanic title customs that had penetrated Germanic culture into something that better suited their own nature, bringing this title—which characterized the true nobleman of the Middle Ages—into being. All the other German titles of nobility only came into being later, over the course of German history.

One circumstance in particular was to become significant for our national development. Originally in Germany, the Germanic principle that nobility only applied to the owners of land was adhered to. This view has persisted in England to the present day, where—with the exception of hereditary baronets—only landowners are holders of a hereditary title of nobility. For our German nation, we have received a very nasty cuckoo's egg in our nest; during the age of knighthood, the noble name and partly also the noble title passed to all sons of a nobleman without distinction, regardless of whether the son had landed property or not. This circumstance has become of more incisive importance for our German nationhood than we might at first assume; more details about this can be found in the final section of this book. Here it should be said only briefly that the unfortunate policy of the German chivalric period just mentioned is one of the main reasons why it was so difficult for a unified upper class to form in Germany and why tensions arose so easily between the nobility and the other sections of the people. If only the holders of a country seat were allowed to bear the title of nobility and a noble name, while their brothers and sons remained bourgeois, as is the case in England, a sharp demarcation of the nobility from the bourgeoisie never arises.

The Constitution of the German Republic of 1918 made a very unfortunate decision in this matter. Instead of resolutely and ruthlessly putting an end to the development of the noble titles and noble names established since the age of chivalry by abolishing both, it decreed: Article 109: 1. Privileges shall be abolished. 2. Titles of nobility shall be considered only as part of the name.

Thus the previous noble name becomes an extended civil name. So it is no longer Prince William, but "Mr. William Prince of Prussia," because "Prince of Prussia" has become the civil surname and "William" the first name. This often leads to lengthening. The civil surname Count von Posadowski-Wehner Baron von Postelwitz (without comma) might be a bit lengthy.[84]

From a German point of view, things really are completely upside down. If the pagan Germanic nobility was purely based on merit, then the medieval Christian German nobility, even if it had a different foundation, was at least eventually evaluated according to the same laws and German sentiments as the pagan nobility. Today, the possibility is such that even the most incompetent can walk around with a noble name without having to show even the slightest merit. Moreover, the case will generally be that in polite society even the most stupid fool with a noble name will often take precedence over most able commoner, because in these matters respect for traditional protocols ultimately plays the decisive role. The rift that has run through the upper classes of our people since the age of chivalry has not been closed by the constitution of the German Republic of 1918. There may no longer be a legal difference between the nobility and the bourgeoisie, but it in fact still exists. Thus, not only is the emergence of a unified German upper class formed from the blood of proven leaders and supplemented by proven performance made impossible, but—this is actually the worst thing—through the incompetent and often unworthy bearers of noble names, the idea of hereditary leadership is undermined in our people and thoroughly wrong ideas of nobility emerge both in noble circles themselves and within our bourgeoisie. If Article 109 of our Reich Constitution does not owe its origin to a well-intentioned thoughtlessness, we would almost be inclined to assume that it was created with the deliberate intention of eradicating the idea of hereditary selection of leaders in our people.

For the idea of the *hegehöfe* developed here, according to what has been said and considering the current circumstances, we can only conclude that we must revert to the Germanic and German idea that only a person entrusted with a *hegehof* may be permitted to bear a noble name or title or any other corresponding identification.

First of all, Article 109 of our Reich Constitution would have to be expanded to the effect that the formerly noble characteristics of current bourgeois names would also be dropped, including the little word "von." Furthermore, the families that were granted a *hegehof* would have to be granted the right to consider themselves a true nobility again, in the same

---

[84] See Haafe-Faulenorth, *Das Heutige Adelsnamenrecht (Today's Law on Noble Names)*, August 31, 1929.

sense and sentiment as the pre-Christian Germanic nobility.[85] Then, these new noble families would have to be identified somehow.

In order to find an appropriate designation, we actually have no choice but to fall back on the oldest of German noble titles, *Freie und Edle Herren*, because all other German noble titles are completely out of the question in this context. However, even this title is not readily usable, not even in its variation as *freiherr* (baron) or *edler herr* (noble lord), because these two titles would not properly express the meaning of the *hegehof* idea and because they are both still present today in names that have now been naturalized, for example Jakob Graf und Edler Herr von und Zu Eltz gennant Faust von Stromberg.

In contrast, I propose the good old German word *edelmann* (nobleman) in addition to "of *hegehof* so and so" at the end of their name, not as a form of address, but rather to fully serve the purpose of establishing a thoroughly clear marking.

One advantage of this proposal is that it would make it independent of whether the old nobility wanted to discard their bourgeois noble names or not. After all, the addition of the name "*edelmann* of *hegehof* so and so" can just as easily be added to a bourgeois name as to a noble name of the present day. For example, "Adolf Wenck, *edelmann* of *hegehof* Eifelberg" is just as unambiguous in this respect as "Anton Ernst Graf Wuthenau, *edelmann* of *hegehof* Schwaigern."[86]

With this form of nobility identification, no misunderstandings about the new nobility can arise, nor would the valuable part of the old nobility feel moved to be hostile to the *hegehof* idea in defense of their previous names. On the contrary, we could imagine that the path shown here would makes it appear to the valuable portions of our old nobility that cooperating with the *hegehof* idea would be a chance to prove their own

---

[85] To be clear, we emphasize here that we do not mean that the new German nobility must be non-Christian.

[86] Originally, it was believed that the addition of the name "of *hegehof* so and so" would suffice. However, such an addition to the name can easily lead to difficulties and confusion of a different kind, because life on a *hegehof* is not only limited to noblemen. Where, for example, the *hegehöfe* also serve as a postal station—this would probably be the case quite often in remote areas—confusion related to the names of all the people living on a *hegehof* and the *hegehof* in question would arise for purely postal reasons, which would be quite undesirable. Not only would this open the door to abuse, even without bad intentions, but the distinction of nobility could not be protected with the care that is absolutely necessary for the way of life and moral effect of the whole *hegehof* idea.

noble worthiness before the German people, as well as have an educational effect within the totality of the *hegehof* nobles by consciously cultivating good noble traditions.

The designation *edelmann* would only be granted to the person entrusted with a *hegehof*, not to his children. The *hegehof* heir remains a bourgeois until he actually accepts the inheritance, i.e. until he is a nobleman on a *hegehof*. Nevertheless, the nobleman who passes his *hegehof* to an heir must be granted the right to add the distinction "*alt-edelmann* (retired nobleman) of *hegehof* so and so" to his name; more will be said about this in the coming sections.

We may wonder as to whether or not the wife of a nobleman should be granted the appropriate designation "*edelfrau* at *hegehof* so and so." For women, the label is not necessary, because the wife of a nobleman is a noblewoman by virtue of her marriage. The English nobility, for example, have this point of view. However, it is perhaps expedient to grant the wife of a nobleman the designation "*edelfrau* or *alt-edelfrau* of *hegehof* so and so" in the interest of providing emotional support.

4

The question of who is to be promoted into the new nobility on the *hegehöfe* cannot and need not be decided here, but it will at least be briefly discussed.

A good sign of true nobility is undoubtedly when an individual does not allow his actions to be driven by egocentric goals, but rather by goals that are superior to his ego; in this regard we must consider the German people as a community superior in this sense. If by "people" we do not mean the purely numerical grouping of all the individual persons whom chance has brought together within the present borders of the Reich, instead referring to those who profess their German blood and a commitment to Germanism, then we create a concept of "people" which is closer in essence to the Germanic sense. This is an even more perfect prerequisite for nobility "since our past has certainly been based in blood and there is no reason to assume that this will change in the future" (Ernst Hasse). With this commitment to German blood, we will also have a German man whose judgment and German sentiments will probably not be subject to any doubt. Treitschke once said:

> If we assume that human beings are descended from a pair, and if we are also convinced of the equality of all human beings before God, then the differentiation of species lies an infinite time behind us. But once nature has accomplished the differentiation, it is well known that it does not want a regression to take place. She takes her revenge by punishing the mixing of different species, so that the higher is depressed by the lower. But for those among today's Germans who still find it difficult to understand this new emphasis on the value of blood in the future German national community, and who are still caught up in the colorless idea of "humanity," we serve them with well-known words of Immanuel Kant, "This much can probably be judged as likely: that the mixture of tribes, which gradually extinguishes their characters, is not beneficial to the human race—all so-called philanthropy notwithstanding."

In a nutshell: a German comrade in the above sense who meets the blood conditions and regulates his actions according to the words, "As a German, always act in such a way that your fellow Germans can choose you as their example!" will undoubtedly have grown from the very wood from which a new German nobility will be carved.

Such Germans are not just found in one class today, but in fairly equal numbers in every strata of our people. The proof that this is really the case was provided by our experiences at the front in the 1914–18 World War—probably the most impactful revelation experienced by frontline soldiers; Ernst Jünger elaborated this insight brilliantly in his war books.

Thus we can say that every real German who dedicated his life to the service of the German people in order to ensure its continued existence during the difficult years of deprivation from 1914 onwards, or who has tried to lead it out of the mire into which it has been dropped by certain people who, in the words of Oswald Spengler, see in politics only the continuation of private business by other means, is useful raw material for the creation of a new nobility. For we will not find a better proof of performance than the conduct of a German during Germany's greatest time of need. If we preserve this blood, then we will under all circumstances preserve a useful stock of bloodlines which, even in future times of need, are likely to provide the German people with leaders who will be equal to their task. After all, the German language says quite cleverly: "*Einer sache gewachsen sein*" (To be equal to a task), i.e. to be able to master it by virtue of certain innate qualities that have grown with the human being.

IV

Basic Questions of German Agriculture

"Better to have the most oppressive taxes on luxuries, better, like Pitt did, to tax all the elements of the Earth, than to burden the sweat of the farmer."

Motz

1

Today's urbanites have lost their understanding of the laws of agricultural life to such an extent that, unfortunately, even the most self-evident necessities of a healthy agricultural life can no longer be taken for granted. But even agriculture itself—having gone mad—is already beginning to adopt the rootless ways of thinking of the urbanite. Under the whisperings of "modern" trends, people have begun to open the gates to the doctrine of a financial system independent of land and soil. We could look on calmly if this apparent progress were not in reality accompanied by one of the most terrible imaginable degenerations in the field of nationalism. This forces us to discuss some basic questions of German agriculture, because otherwise I must fear that this *hegehof* proposal will not be understood by the reader or that it will lead to errors due to unclear preconditions.

Our people today have become ill in their economic thinking and seriously imagine that everything promoted by the financial system is synonymous with cultural progress. If such shifts in economic thinking had not occurred in our people, then certain false ideas about agriculture would not have been able to take root in the minds of many Germans in the way that is unfortunately the case now. Our grandfathers had a stronger relationship; they had not yet lost their connection with the land.

The essential question here is that land has been deprived of its moral and vital functions and has merely become part of the means of production which are left to the exploitative will of the owner.

The root of this evil is our people's abandonment of the old Germanic concept of property. We may argue whether this departure was wrong for our trade and industry, but for any thinking person there can be no doubt that it has been disastrous for agriculture and therefore for our people.

The Germanic concept of property cannot be separated from the basic Germanic idea of the family as a sequence of dynasties. This was causally connected with Germanic religious concepts, as well as with the worldview of the Germanic peoples in general. We have already explained the essentials of this in Chapter III, Section 1, but we should also refer to the excellent work by Kummer in *Midgards Untergang (Midgard's Downfall).*

Just as there has been a struggle between the Germanic and late Roman political systems and concepts of state administration since the Germanic peoples met the Roman empire of the Caesars, there is also a struggle in the field of the concept of property. This is natural because the political system and conceptions of property more or less always interact with each other.

The patrician families of ancient Rome were Indo-European. If no fundamental dividing line can be drawn between ancient Indo-European and Germanic legal concepts, since both obviously go back to the same racial background and were originally formed in the same environment of a primordial homeland, then in the case of the Roman patricians it must be said that ancient Roman and Germanic legal concepts are still very similar. In particular, there is no difference between the ancient Roman and Germanic conceptions of the relationship between family and land. The land of a family is not a matter of the head of the household's ego, but part of the idea of the family itself, in the sense of a succession of dynasties. Thus the ego, including the ego of the head of the household, is always only one part of the family, as the family itself is the superior whole, and the head of the household is obligated to serve the land with regard to the family and its preservation. The selfish possessiveness of land is fundamentally alien to both the ancient Roman and the Germanic sense of justice, because every ego-related claim to land ownership necessarily presupposes the detachment of the ego from the idea of family.[87] However, this deferral of the ego, which serves the family, has nothing at all to do with soil communism, nor is it connected with the Russian *mir*, that peculiar Russian concept of the right of the entirety to land ownership. *Mir* is the Russian word for a peasant village community in Russia, and also for the concept of common ownership of land by the peasant community. This form of land ownership can be traced back with certainty only to the beginning of the seventeenth century. Apparently, the *mir* is the result of general serfdom and a tax levied on each soul in the community, for which the community (not the individual soul) was liable to pay. Since each member of the *mir* had to bear the same tax burden, they were also allocated an equal share of the communal land: the necessary balance between rights and burdens was established by regular redistribution every fifteen years. This Russian *mir*, which already comes very close to communist ideas (even if it never reaches them) is essentially the reason why the Russian peasantry did not show the same fierce opposition to communist tyranny as our peasants have to communism in the years after 1918.

The Russian *mir* and the Indo-European/Germanic soil-boundness differ fundamentally in that the former only takes into account the whole of a community and subordinates the family as such to it, thus also recognizing, for example, marriages on an insufficient nutritional basis. The latter, however, fundamentally subordinates the individual and the people as a whole to the idea of family. It may seem to be only a subtle difference that separates these two forms of rootedness. But this difference is of a very fundamental nature, because history teaches us that the subordination of the family to the whole, as with the Russian *mir*, must always lead to grief for the family when agricultural space becomes scarce and—since all civilization grows from the family—necessarily also to the degeneration of civilization. Conversely, the Indo-European conception places the family or the dynasty above the tribe, for the tribe is the sum of the families (not, as in the case of *mir*, the sum of all souls),

---

[87] This linking of the Indo-European/Germanic concept of the family to the concept of property, especially with regard to the ownership of land by a family, is so pervasive that we can say: If we dissolve this conceptualization of property and make property an independent, freely disposable commodity—a selfish thing in itself—then we necessarily destroy the Indo-European/Germanic idea of family; which is why Hardenberg's economic measures a hundred years ago initiated Germany's economic prosperity in the nineteenth century, but at great expense to German customs and civilization, which was based on the old German idea of family.

and places the viability of the family above everything else. Under this conception, it may have to limit the number of family foundations if the area under cultivation remains the same and the number of people grows; but through this very measure it also maintains the physical health of the families and thus also a vibrant civilization.

Again, the communist concept of land ownership can be distinguished from both of these conceptions, and can actually only be explained by assuming that it has developed gradually from the grazing customs of nomadism. Strictly speaking, soil communism regards the individual only as part of a horde, to which it grants the benefit of the horde's property. Although the family is not necessarily eliminated, it is not given any special consideration. The only difference between soil communism and the Russian *mir* is that the former proclaims the right of the individual to benefit from the yields of the soil, without making any considerations for families in particular or for how these yields come about, whereas the Russian *mir* at least still speaks to the right of an individual family to cultivate a part of the communal property, without raising itself to the heights of the Indo-European conception, which further subordinates the right to cultivate the soil to the idea of family.

It is unfortunate to say that our economists in general do not bother to distinguish these fundamental differences between soil communism, the Russian *mir*, and Indo-European/Germanic soil-boundness, or even care to establish clear definitions for these terms. This explains why there is such a confusion of opinions today about the concept of soil-boundness.

The reason why the old patrician conception of land law,[88] which was quite similar to the Germanic conception, was able to change in such a dramatic way that it appeared in late Roman law as the unconditional antithesis to the Germanic conception, lies with internal developments in Rome. When Rome gained control of the economic nodes of Mediterranean trade following the defeat of Carthage, financial thinking began to prevail and the old patrician conception of life and the state was pushed aside. This development began after the First Punic War and was basically completed by the end of the last one, although it was not until the time of Caesar that the final dividing line was drawn between the old

---

[88] The term "land law" is actually wrong here, because the land, as part of the family idea, could only be a part of family law with regard to dynastic succession; it initially had no law of its own.

Roman and the new Roman political systems. Thus a Roman law came into being which no longer had very much in common with the old patrician law and which seemed to be the unconditional antithesis to Germanic law. We are still familiar with these things today, as the slogan of the antithesis of Roman and German law attests.

As far as the family is concerned, the old patrician concept in ancient Rome was that the family was a sequence of dynasties (a more or less vertical attitude to the idea of family). This concept later evolves into one that regards a family as merely a group of individuals, with the father of the family (*pater familias*) at the center (thus essentially a horizontal way of looking at things). In the old patrician view of dynastic succession, a dynasty was, so to speak, a tree rooted in the ground. It is therefore more than natural that the land belonging to one dynasty was awarded undivided to the heir; the ever-burning hearth fire, the monogamy, and the indivisible land ownership formed and remained a thoroughly living unity. With the transformation of the idea of the succession of dynasties into the idea that the family represents a group of individuals with the father of the family at the head and as the center, the uprooting of the family was sealed, because it now remained indifferent as to where this group of family members resided.[89] From then on, it was not much of a leap to the view that the head of the household could dispose of property independently of the family, and, hand in hand with the increasingly dissolving concept of the family, a private law centered on the individual had to come into being. This individualist legal form was developed to perfection in late Roman law.

Such a development of Roman law from the original idea of family protection in the broadest sense to the unconditional affirmation of the individual led not only to a political system that regarded the people merely as a sum of individuals, but also completely shattered every idea of family. This development had a particular effect in two directions which concern us: first, marriage was no longer necessarily a matter concerning the family or the production of children, but became a purely I-and-thou affair, in which the production of children was left to the discretion of the individual; and secondly, land was now managed

[89] It should be noted in passing that this form of grouping family members under one family father corresponds to the custom of patriarchy found among nomadic peoples, a practice which in its essence has nothing whatsoever to do with the Indo-European concept of dynastic succession, although there may be developmental connections in prehistoric times.

according to a purely individual-centric concept of property, and it did not even occur to anyone to consider it in terms of the nutritional or economic basis of a family. In other words, the moral connection between marriage and land ownership had been thoroughly torn apart.[90]

The Germanic tribes brought with them a concept of marriage that corresponded exactly to that of the patricians. Thus, just as ancient Roman and late Roman marriage law contradicted each other, so did late Roman and Germanic marriage law. The Germanic peoples' ascendancy in and mastery over Western Europe following the Migration Period allowed Germanic law to initially become authoritative or, where it did not directly replace Roman law, indirectly influence it. Naturally, Germanic law was also influenced by late Roman law in return.

The Germanic states established in Italy fell in line with late Roman legal ideas relatively quickly. This is particularly true of the Lombard Empire. Even if Christianity certainly influenced this development, another circumstance also played a decisive role and is important for us to learn about—late Roman law particularly benefited trade. Trade, however, thrives best in urban centers. The Germanic peoples, however, settled outside the cities, living in the countryside according to their own law. Thus, the very un-Germanic institution of the city was relatively untouched by Germanic influence, meaning that late Roman legal ideas were able to survive well in Roman cities. Under these circumstances and due to the nature of the times, the cities gradually gained economic predominance over the countryside. Through this urban economic supremacy, the victory of late Roman legal ideas over Lombard ones was decided.

In the Frankish Empire, the development took a somewhat different path, in that the much stronger influence of Germanism made it possible to establish a Germanic political system before late Roman law was able

---

[90] This is also the reason why all Roman attempts from Caesar onwards to mitigate the sudden decline in births among the valuable Roman families (with exceptional laws, bachelor taxes, child premiums, tax relief, and so on and so forth) failed completely. This is also connected with the fact that the Germanic tribes, which in this time were increasingly settling in the Roman Empire, did not bring about any significant change in the situation, despite their natural fertility. When a state, through the law, gives precedence to the individual over the idea of family—all family-related things, both in terms of civilization as well as the production of children, inevitably decline. To try to counteract this inevitable development with temporary laws is like drawing water with a sieve or nurturing a tree while at the same time removing the earth from its roots.

to establish itself. Therefore, the penetration of law was directly a matter of the political system. We have already shown how French absolutism under Louis XIV the "Sun King" brought about the victory of late Roman law and its political system.

The penetration of the late Roman conception of law into Germany has mainly taken place in recent history and in two primary ways: firstly, absolutism in its various forms, which helped the late Roman legal ideas break through, and secondly, the economic development of Germany in the nineteenth century. It is strange that Prussia, which since the time of the Great Elector[91] had increasingly transformed absolutism into a more highly developed form of German state (finally freeing Germanism from the concept of absolutism), would be the state that would emphatically hand over Germanism to non-German legal concepts in the field of economics. In view of the close interweaving of economic concepts with the civilization and customs of a people, this means that the same state that was both directly and indirectly the bearer of German development from the Peace of Westphalia onwards—and was paramount in granting Germanism its place in the sun—had also indirectly become the destroyer of Germanism by opening the way for the penetration of un-German economic concepts within the German nation and for helping them to victory.[92]

It was the responsibility of Hardenberg, the Chancellor of Prussia, to decide on the German economic direction and it was he who opened the door to an un-German, purely individualist financial attitude. Hardenberg had a great opponent in this matter, Freiherr vom Stein. Few people today in Germany know of Freiherr vom Stein's struggle against Hardenberg, and even fewer have grasped the significance of this struggle. Our people have generally paid little attention to this clash, even though Hardenberg marks the beginning of an economic chapter of our people that quite logically ends with Gustav Stresemann and would have gotten to that point much earlier had Bismarck had not delayed this development for decades.

---

[91] Editor's note: "The Great Elector" refers to Frederick William of the Hohenzollern dynasty. The Elector of Brandenburg and Duke of Prussia from 1640 until his death in 1688, he greatly developed the duchy through his political, economic, and military achievements.

[92] The reader can learn more about this question in Treitschke's well-known *Einleitung zur Deutschen Geschichte im 19. Jahrhunderts Nachlesen (Introduction to Nineteenth Century German History).*

It was the greatness of Germanism that it derived its laws from its concept of God and from this belief placed life-promoting laws above the laws of the economy and the individual. In other words, blood and—as part of the idea of blood—soil stood above all individualist economic considerations. This basic attitude of the Germanic people towards the economy remained unbroken into the nineteenth century, and despite all the shocks to which it was subjected to over the course of history—often pushing it to the brink of ruin—the old conception triumphed again and again. It was only in the nineteenth century that this pattern came to an end, and we could almost say that the much-praised BGB[93] of 1900 was the key reason.

The following is essential for us here—the related Germanic ideas of the succession of dynasties, with marriage being bound to the land, and the inheritance of landed property, were preserved in German law despite the replacement of their ideological Germanic foundations by Christian ones and despite of their subsequent replacement by feudal and landlord customs. This is evident by the fact that the Germanic custom of inheriting landed property (i.e. only one son inherited the landed property at a time) remained in force. In some cases where landed property was or had to be divided among several sons, this division never went so far as to shake a family's basis for subsistence. This family protection was of decisive importance in medieval town law. Certainly, it is true that in some parts of our fatherland the peasant custom of inheritance, i.e. inheritance to a son, goes back to a landlord's decree. But there is also no doubt that the basic ideas of this are clearly marked out in the very essence of Germanism and not in late Roman law, which is why we must link the Germanic custom of inheritance to Germanism in historical terms and not describe it exclusively as a medieval economic development of the landlord system, as is done by some economists today.

It is often said today that the origin of this custom of passing on the estate or the farm to an heir is indeed a Germanic custom, but that it essentially arose from economic necessity, because in a time of purely self-sufficient economies, the distribution of land ownership must remain limited. While this explanation may be plausible from today's economic

---

[93] Editor's note: *Bürgerliches Gesetzbuch* (BGB) or the German Civil Code is the central codification of German private law. The BGB regulates the legal relationships between private individuals and is thus distinct from public law.

perspective, the Russian *mir* and the non-Germanic economic systems of the Irish, Welsh, and Scots in England prove that this explanation is not compelling. Furthermore, the erroneous nature of this view is clear to anyone who is only somewhat familiar with the Germanic concept of property, which is rooted in the idea of family.

We might now think that these past things are a very unimportant matter for the present day and are basically a dispute about the emperor's beard. But that is not the case! We will soon see that these things are of drastic importance for our time.

According to the Germanic and ancient German-Christian sense of justice, the privilege of the inheritor was generally linked to the obligation to marry, so the idea of dynastic succession was always in the foreground of the custom. The acceptance of an inheritance was therefore linked to the fulfillment of a task. Accordingly and strictly speaking, there was also no "disinheritance" of the non-inheriting sons, because such a thing presupposes an individualist concept of ownership, which is not inherent in Germanic man. Legal entitlements of the non-inheriting heirs in the sense of compensation do not exist in ancient Germanic law, and this is quite logical, because such claims would be absurd in view of the Germanic concept of property which was linked to the succession of the dynasties.

If, however, we examine this question in terms of today's economics, i.e. if we simply imagine today's self-centered thinking about property existing in those times, then the Germanic form of inheritance of land ownership suddenly takes on a fundamentally different face. We might then believe that the custom of inheritance was an economic necessity for certain periods of time. But as soon as the old German obligation to marry and to continue the family is suppressed and the inheritance is thus regarded as purely an increase in net worth for the heir, the impression of a great injustice arises. Consequently, compensation must be demanded for the departing heirs when a more highly developed economic system replaces the old purely self-sufficient economy, i.e. either when business management technology has progressed so far that a division into smaller estates or farms becomes possible, or when the economic system permits compensation on a monetary basis. The justification of this line of thought is certainly debatable as long as the idea of lineal succession is not disregarded and compensation for the relinquishing heirs is therefore only demanded to the extent that it does not shake the idea of lineal succession. But this point, namely that of the succession of dynasties, is obviously not at all important in certain political circles, which is why it is never mentioned, while the rest of the issue is used to make completely different demands.

In a footnote (87) above in this section, it has already been pointed out that the Germanic idea of family, with its lasting effect on customs and civilization, cannot be better undermined than by making property a movable and freely disposable commodity. It now very much looks like this is also the purpose of the doctrines promoted by certain circles of economists. In particular, this refers to the theory of an English banker known as Ricardo's basic rent theory, to which a large number of economists subscribe to today.[94]

Ricardo's basic rent theory presupposes firstly the un-Germanic concept of individual ownership of land. It further presupposes that when land is settled, the distribution of the land is initially based on economic criteria, i.e. that the best land is taken first and then subsequent increases in population forces the cultivation of worse quality land. All of this is undoubtedly not wrong and has happened more than once in modern colonial history, whereby colonial development even seems like a special proof of this theory because it already takes place within the framework of an individualist modern concept of property. But Ricardo's presuppositions are wrong for the history of Germanic settlement.

Ricardo concluded that the economic costs that regulate the market price of agricultural products is determined by goods grown on inferior soils because their owners want to cover their costs and make a profit. The owners of the better soils also obtain the same price for their products on the market, however, they earn more because the costs of production are lower for them. Thus, Ricardo devised a sliding scale of profit and the price of rent based on soil quality. According to his law of rent, everything that exceeds the yield of the least productive land is now rent. Here we already come across a serious calculation error in the rent theory, because it ignores the influence of the owner's aptitude on the management of his farm. It also forgets some other imponderables that play into the agricultural business. With this basic rent theory, an excellent means had been found to detach the concept of land ownership from that of the family, and this seems to have been Ricardo's ultimate aim.

---

[94] Editor's note: Ricardian rent is distinct from and should not be confused with contract rent, which is the payment tenants make to a property's owner for its use.

Because they fell back on the fact that the disinheritance of the non-inheriting sons was an injustice, a further conclusion was that all the people who no longer lived on the land were in a certain sense disinherited and that it was therefore only an act of economic justice if these people were somehow compensated. A direct compensation of the disinherited through the allocation of land—i.e. an expropriation of land from those who possess it and its distribution to their fellow citizens—is neither economically feasible nor necessarily desirable for a nation with a highly developed national economy. But with the concept of Ricardian rent, we now had a means of compensating for this injustice. We only had to tax away this basic rent and the balance was already created. It was one of Ricardo's successors in particular, Henry George,[95] who stated this clearly:

> I do not propose either to purchase or to confiscate private property in land. The first would be unjust; the second, needless. If they wish, let individuals retain possession of what they are pleased to call their land. Let them continue to call it their land. Let them buy and sell, and bequeath and devise it. We may safely leave them the shell, if we take the kernel. It is not necessary to confiscate land; it is only necessary to confiscate rent.

With that, we are already in the realm of Marxism and its conception of the relationship between an owner and his land.[96] But we have seen that the basis of the Marxist conception of land ownership, namely rent theory, is a kind of sleight of hand. By means of this false presupposition, Marxism then builds up its doctrines of land ownership into more and more audacious lines of thought. On the basis of such presuppositions, of course, everything can be proved logically.

Leaving aside the economic nonsense that is inherent in rent theory (especially as it is theorized by H. George, where the productive capacity of a piece of land is regarded as a perpetual motion machine and the

---

[95] Henry George, *Fortschritt und Armut (Progress and Poverty,* German translation by D. Reclam Haeck*)*, 350.

[96] It is to be noted, unfortunately, that the work of Rudolf Böhmer in *Das Erbe der Enterbten (The Inheritance of the Disinherited),* written with such a warm heart and enthusiastic will to act, has taken these Marxist views as the basis of its arguments. The effect of which is that Böhmer, who wants to defeat Marxism, does not in fact get free from Marxism in his arguments.

"owner" of this beautiful thing as a second perpetual motion machine, which repeatedly does work for no cost whatsoever), compare this Marxist view of the relationship of the owner to his land with that of the Germanic peoples, with their incorporation of the concept of property into the idea of the succession of dynasties, and we do not need much thought to realize that a world of contrasts opens up here. Marxism builds on George and Ricardo as both conceive the relationship of land to man as a purely economic association. Our German peasantry, however, derives their relationship from the Germanic conception of family. Therefore, Marxism and a German peasantry based on Germanic fundamental ideas are, by their very nature, irreconcilable mortal enemies. It is quite logical that the Marxist rulers of Germany today see their real enemies not in the German bourgeoisie nor in the landowner or the small settler, but in the peasant, for it is in the peasant that most of the basic Germanic concepts, ideas of life, and family structure are still alive today. This is also connected with the supposedly contradictory facts, which in essence are quite logical, that Marxism expels hundreds of German peasants out of their homes and farms and into foreign lands, but at the same time eagerly favors the small settlements of internal colonization; the consideration must be added that internal colonization cannot hurt Marxism in the long run. There is no doubt in my mind that if Marxism is ever overcome once more in Germany, the standard-bearers of this struggle will be the German peasants.

Only from these facts can the anti-peasant rhetoric of Marxist leaders be understood, for example, this statements by:

> Karl Marx: "The peasant economy is the most habitually lazy and irrational business. No better is the peasant himself."
>
> Or August Bebel: "It proves true here once again that there is no class more selfish, ruthless, and brutal—but also no class more narrow-minded—than our peasant. Those, therefore, who love backwardness, as they find satisfaction in it, may find satisfaction in the continued existence of this class. Human progress requires that it disappear."
>
> Or Friedrich Engels: "We shall everywhere and always strive to hasten the downfall of the small-holding peasant, even in agriculture."

> Or Geck-Karlsruhe: "Social democracy must take away the peasant's monkey-love of landed property."

Liberalism goes hand in hand with Marxism. Regarding the land question, Liberalism is Marxism in reverse, i.e. it does not proclaim the right of the general public to the land's rent, but the right of the owner to his land's rent. Liberalism, however, does not recognize the idea of blood, i.e. that the owner of land has—in addition to the enjoyment of his property—a blood duty either in the old sense to his race or in the modern sense to his people. The ideological foundations of Liberalism in this question are essentially the same as those of Marxism. We could almost be tempted to say that Liberalism and Marxism are two worldviews that have been devised in order to, in one way or another, deal a death blow to the German idea of blood and soil. Thus, after Hardenberg opened the way for liberal economics in Germany, Liberalism, in cooperation with its twin brother Marxism, unleashed a fury against everything that—on the basis of the old German sense of justice—did not allow individuals unconditional freedom in the use of property. Thus, late Roman economic law and late Roman idolatry of the individual, which even the age of absolutism could not fully impose on Germany, finally made their unconditional and unrestrained entry into Germany. It is no exaggeration to say that what Varus failed to impose on the Germanics almost two millennia ago was ushered into Germany during the nineteenth century and has been made a reality in the years after 1918.

It is natural that the old German conception of the economic order has lasted longest in German agriculture. But it was a fatal mistake on the part of the German agricultural leadership that it was unable to effectively enlighten the German people about the moral tasks which landowners must fulfill in addition to their economic tasks. If the German people as such are to remain alive, such a campaign was and is vital in the defensive struggle which German agriculture has been waging against Liberalism and Marxism for about a century now. From a German point of view, it must be said that the moral tasks of the idea of blood must actually precede the economic tasks of the peasant, or should at least be placed on equal footing with them.

Liberalism and Marxism attacked German agriculture on the basis of purely economic questions. It was fatal for German agriculture that its leaders took up the fight on these terms without emphasizing from the outset that these economic questions were only a fraction of the matter and that the final decision had to be made with regard to questions of blood. In this way, the agricultural leaders became, to a certain extent, the proverbial knight with a wooden sword taking on opponents armed with steel weapons. For nowhere in history has agriculture, or at least not peasantry, been able to sustain itself on the basis of a purely individualist financial attitude with regard to land ownership. If some German princes had not held on to their traditional duty of preserving agriculture, what we are experiencing today would have happened decades ago.

2

A purely *geldwirtschaftliche* (monetary) approach to the relationship of the owner to his land always has a devastating effect on peasants for two reasons: firstly, due to the incorrect organization of the inheritance of agricultural property, and secondly, due to the free economic competition on the commodity market. We need to get to know both of these aspects in order to understand them.

The inheritance of agricultural property can take place in two ways: by real division and by right of inheritance.

Real division means that the property is divided equally among the heirs. In this way, one farm or estate becomes several, and each of these new foundations falls victim to division again at the next inheritance, provided, of course, that there are children to inherit. In favorable economic conditions, continuous real division necessarily ends in a dwarf farm. In reality, however, the owner loses his economic independence due to the smallness of his property and must look for a secondary occupation elsewhere, which is only possible if the labor market is particularly favorable or if they find success within the so-called cottage industry. Such owners of dwarf farms can hardly be called peasants anymore as they live under similar conditions of existence as those in industrial workers' settlements. Only if the agricultural conditions are particularly favorable, for example if the land can be cultivated as a garden (Palatinate and the wine-growing areas) or if the conditions for livestock breeding are particularly good and can be exploited on a cooperative basis (Denmark and areas of the Rhine lowlands), is dwarf ownership still economically viable in and of itself. These are exceptions! In general, the end of real division is usually the buying out of the economically weak by their economically stronger neighbors, i.e. the formation of large estates or large landholdings. There are enthusiasts today who, despite these experiences in agricultural history, still advocate for real division. It should be pointed out to them that in English politics, real division was once deliberately used to destroy a section of the population, first economically and then also demographically. England ordered real division for the Irish peasants, but left the right of inheritance of the English peasants who had settled in Ulster. The success of this measure was quite satisfactory for England, and it would certainly have achieved its goal if the Irish who could no longer survive in Ireland had not found new and more favorable living conditions in the states of North America. The Irish in North America strengthened economically and were able to send financial support to sustain their fellow peasants in Ireland until England finally gave the project up.

Right of inheritance means that a son inherits the property. The heir, however, must compensate their siblings and other heirs. In general, the heir will only be able to pay off his siblings by taking on debts; a questionable measure for a farm in any case, because this debt is not taken on for the improvement of the property or an economic return. Things get particularly bad when the heirs in the city marry women who no longer have any connection with the land and press their husbands to have the inheritance paid out with no regard for the economic situation of the farm. The heirs who have left, for their part, generally still have enough peasant feeling of their own to not demand a payment that the farm could not easily bear. Therefore, the custom of inheritance, without protections against the market, generally leads to over-indebted farms. It is then really only a matter of time until the owner, with a white staff in his hand, leaves the soil of his fathers. But in places where peasant sentiments are still bound to the ancestral soil and the preservation of it is considered a sacred duty, the custom of inheritance very easily leads to a limitation in the number of children produced in order to avoid the dangers of inheritance payments. For a people, this state of affairs is more than life-threatening, indeed it is a certain end.

If, therefore, the peasantry is not protected by special measures, both real division and the custom of inheritance will sooner or later lead to the destruction of the peasantry in a state with a transactional monetary economy. For in this economy, land becomes a movable commodity, a circumstance which in history has always led exclusively to large landed properties, because only these can withstand the pressures of an unprotected market in the long term—unless the state seeks to destroy them as well through targeted taxation.

With regard to the free economic competition on the goods market, it should be noted that agriculture is a largely aleatory trade—dependent on chance. Whereas, for example, every industrial plant can more or less precisely calculate the process from raw material to finished product, it is precisely here that the unknown intervenes in the case of the peasant: nature often delivers the most surprising jokes. In industry it is possible to regulate the entry of raw materials into the processing cycle so that the sales market can more or less regulate the speed and quantity of the production of finished goods. For the peasant, however, a period of time is required here over which he has no control and which is determined by the growth conditions of the goods to be produced. If the growth conditions, with their many unpredictable aspects, do not depend on the market, then the conditions of the market can often not even be predicted because of the long time that the plants need to grow. Separately, there is the fact that we have some regions in Germany where nature simply dictates to the peasant what he can produce, as well as places where even the peasant with the strongest will in the world is not able to produce according to the sales market. For example, if a peasant can only grow rye and oats in his area, it does not help him much to read in the newspaper that wheat and barley prices are satisfactory, but rye and oats are in less demand.

These are all very tangible difficulties! It is only natural, however, that a versatile, larger estate will be able to cope with these difficulties more easily than a farm, which usually has to reckon with very limited economic opportunities. A larger estate is more likely to have access to money reserves and is also more easily able to offset the hardships of unfavorable sales markets through the diversification of its branches of operation. However, if they are deliberately neglected by the state and taxed too heavily, even large estates cannot survive in the long run, mostly because they run out of money to compensate their workers satisfactorily. The history of agriculture proves, however, that in such cases the large estates are able to keep their heads above water with a small number of workers by abandoning agriculture and introducing extensive livestock breeding on simple pastures (penetration of sheep breeding in England!), marking the end of the *latifundia*.[97]

[97] Editor's note: The *latifundia* were enormous agricultural estates that first

Therefore, freedom of movement in agriculture, or, to put it more clearly—the consideration of agriculture as a mere trade—inevitably destroys first the peasants and then the landowners, while mostly sparing the large landowners. It may also be said that liberal monetary policies in the commodity market do not harm the large landownership to the extent that it destroys the middle landownership and the peasantry. The individual landowner may be quite comfortable if the land of a people is completely transferred to the large estates—even if it is then passed on to small tenants—but for the people as such the lack of an independent peasantry is a serious loss of blood-related opportunities for rejuvenation. If the peasants of England who were dispossessed by the English nobility had not found new economic opportunities in the English colonies and if a new peasantry had not grown up in these colonies as a result, the British Empire would not have survived the World War of 1914–18. In Germany, the example of the English nobility was actually only followed by the Mecklenburg nobility and the nobility of the formerly Swedish Western Pomerania, but unfortunately without settling this peasantry in German colonies. With regard to the question of the freedom of movement of goods in the market, the common fate of peasants and landowners is definitely quite separate in this area. In all cases, however, unrestrained freedom of movement in economic terms is the best means of destroying a healthy peasantry, which on the other hand also means that it is a way of cutting the lifeblood from a people.

If we follow the financial approach to agriculture to its ultimate logical conclusion, we must eventually conclude that the ownership of an estate or farm only depends on the landowner's ability to make money. For example, Aereboe, a left-wing agrarian politician, coined the slogan "migration of the soil to the best landlord" in his work *Agrarpolitik (Agricultural Policy)*. From his purely financial point of view, it is logical and natural for him to take this idea to its logical conclusion and say (*Agrarpolitik*, page 516): "Neither the farm, nor the manor, nor the landlord may be protected from competition." Unfortunately, however, the case is such that external circumstances beyond the peasant's control often play the same role as efficiency, and so Aereboe's proposals would

---

developed as the Roman Republic expanded militarily out of its central Italian heartland. Profit-centered and based on slave labor, the practice was opposed by many of Rome's traditionalists, such as Pliny the Elder, who saw the small, free peasant farmer as the backbone of both Roman society and its military. The word remains in use to describe any large agricultural estate.

certainly drive many useful and industrious peasants from their homes and farms. If, moreover, these things are considered from the point of view of maintaining the good hereditary stock of our people—i.e. in the family-law mentality of the Germanic peoples—the only harsh verdict that remains is that such teachings, even if probably unintentional, are really nothing more than an invitation to squander our best national blood value. People-conscious agricultural politicians, such as Fuchs in *Deutsche Agrarpolitik vor und nach dem Kriege* (*German Agricultural Policy Before and After the War*; Stuttgart 1927), are therefore right to speak out against unrestrained free movement.

While it is relatively easy to demonstrate the family-destroying effects of liberal economics on land ownership, the knowledge of which is generally more widespread today, very little attention is paid to the culture-destroying effects. As says Sokolowski in *Die Versandung Europas (The Sinking of Europe):*

> No war with its devastations, no devastation by force majeure are dangerous to cultural advancement as long as man cultivates and cares for the earth for its own sake. Only the mobilization, the transformation of landed property into an economic object, into a justifiable thing, robs it of that steadfast permanence and security without which its cultivation and advancement are inconceivable. It cannot even occur to a man who has his seat on a piece of land that he or his successors might, for the sake of some economic advantage, vacate the carefully cultivated property. There must be no value in the world for which he would be willing to sacrifice or abandon his ancestral seat!

Or do we seriously believe that the German people could have ever overcome the damage of the Thirty Years' War if the agricultural system of that time had not been subject to policies that offered an incentive to entrepreneurs who wanted to try their hand at building something lasting? We cannot imagine that with today's absurd views on roots and soil-boundness (which have received a legal basis through the German Civil Code) that a German culture can be kept alive for more than half a century![98]

---

[98] For example, the Gracchi were undoubtedly the first to lay the axe to the root of Rome's greatness, for they planted the seed of later insecurity in the Roman land

Recently, there has been one movement in particular that claims to want to heal the increasingly obvious damage to our land law. This is the movement of the land reformers. But the land reformers also distort things, because they base the moral right to land reform on the concept of land rent. What to make of this land rent theory has already been explained above in detail.

Even if we did not have to work out any guidelines here on how to help our peasantry, the question will probably arise in the reader's mind and so we will answer as follows: all peasant laws are good if they limit the mortgage burden of the farm, declare the indivisibility of the farm, legally determine the right of inheritance, and ensure that the payment to the heirs who leave the farm is only made within the framework of the farm's economic viability. Prussia was undoubtedly on the right track with the pension property legislation that began in 1886. In any case, peasant family law is the key to understanding the prosperity or decline of peasant families.

3

The history of agriculture clearly teaches us that there are fundamental laws whose unconditional observance or non-observance leads to either the life or death of the soil-rooted peasantry. One example: Rome! We often hear that in ancient Rome it was not the economic freedom of movement that actually caused the uprooting of the Roman peasantry, but the insufficient protection of domestic agriculture and the influx of foreign grain. G. Ferrero took this view in *Größe und Untergang Roms (Greatness and Decline of Rome),* which subconsciously projects today's means of transport and traffic conditions to that time—an absolute fantasy for Rome and Greece. Even into the nineteenth century, the nature of the roads and the means of transport prevented a larger city from being able to feed itself exclusively from its hinterland. The waterways were essential for the nutritional survival of such cities. But in ancient times, the shiploads were relatively small, and the dangers of the journey very great, so that the transport of grain by sea was not only a thankless business, but also one that brought no appreciable profit. So when we often hear today that Rome's famous grain fleets destroyed the

---

and agricultural order, which was founded on permanence.

Italian peasants, such an assertion is based on two false premises. Neither were the means of transport of the time such that the growing Rome could have fed itself from its own hinterland, nor were those grain fleets of any significance for the Italian domestic grain market. The case is exactly the opposite—because the Romans could not feed themselves from their hinterland, they had to solve the question of food by sea, both by equipping special sea fleets and by rewarding those shipmasters who loaded grain. Many a Roman statesman was forced to consider Rome's foreign policy from this point of view.

In the Roman Empire, peasants were uprooted because they were taxed too heavily after they had become free. This exodus from the countryside created the famous large-scale Roman land holdings (*latifundia*), from which Rome is said to have perished (according to a frequently mentioned quote from Pliny: *Latifundia perdidere Italiam*—the *latifundia* have destroyed Italy). Rome undoubtedly also perished from the depopulation of the countryside, but its large landholdings were not primarily the cause, they were rather the consequence of a land exodus movement that had its origins in the senseless taxation of the peasants.

In Greece, the situation was similar during the Hellenic period. But for those of you who are more "modern," you can see the proof of this phenomenon's eternal repetition in English history. Perhaps most revealing in this respect is Dutch agricultural history. In Holland, the development of the national economy led to the complete devastation of the province, so that the state—which was increasingly reliant on the financial economy—logically had to inevitably collapse and lose its position as a world power. But in Dutch Friesland, the peasants there had preserved their old property laws and family protections. From Friesland, Holland was again settled by peasants from the eighteenth century onwards. There is probably no more brilliant proof of the ability of family inheritance laws to preserve the peasantry.

In ancient times, attempts were made to compensate for downward development by creating hereditary leases. The same proposal is reappearing today. However, it will not stop the wave of destruction against the still well-adapted, blood-valuable hereditary tribes of our people, nor will it promote the settling down of others. For it is the nature of things that in a state which is devoted to an unrestrained financial economy, the tenant peasant will never be able to consistently pay his annual rent. Misfortunes in the family or on the farm, bad harvests, bad weather, and all the other difficulties that the peasant has to face with his hands tied behind his back will always bring him into years of need, forcing him to have his rent debt deferred. It is then questionable whether favorable conditions during the following years will allow the leaseholder to pay off the deferred debt. History teaches us that such a thing is rare. Once the leaseholder is in debt to the state, he is no longer a peasant, but a tiller of the soil—bound to the soil but toiling for the state. All land rent which is raised solely from a financial point of view creates either soil-bound tenants or tenants who abandon their land in poverty.

Of course, I am aware that in certain cases the leasehold has been a blessing. But the cause of this blessing was less the leasehold itself and more the other circumstances under which it was carried out.

It would not have been necessary to mention all of these facts if the majority of people today, both peasant and non-peasant, still had natural relationships to the land, as our grandfathers did and as Bismarck in particular always emphasized about himself. "Experience has led me away from the delusion about the Arcadian happiness of a landowner incarnate, with double-entry bookkeeping and chemical studies," he said regarding his childhood on the Kniephof rural estate.[99] If I wanted the reader to understand this proposal of the *hegehöfe*, some fundamental questions of German agriculture must be clarified first. We have enough well-intentioned proposals of this kind in Germany today, but they mostly increase confusion and are unable to resist the determined advance of all opponents of agriculture.

The experience of history tells us quite clearly that the actual cause of the downfall of all formerly important states was their adoption of a state attitude hostile towards the peasantry and, by extension, towards its land. It must be considered sheer madness if our people recognize this truth but do not draw conclusions from it. We must be indifferent as to whether this fits in with the current doctrine of economic development. Sokolowski writes:

> The rise of human civilization proceeds as long as the best forces devote themselves to the cultivation of the soil, the decline begins

---

[99] Editor's note: At the time this book was written, Kniephof was located outside the town of Jarchin, in Pomerania province (within the Weimar Republic's Free State of Prussia). During the Second World War, the area was occupied by Soviet forces, who, through mass expulsions and executions, eliminated the region's entire German population. Today, Kniephof is a ruin on the outskirts of the Polish village of Konarzewo.

> as soon as the culture of reverence of the land for its own sake dwindles—the strong and energetic turn away from it and go other ways.

Before our eyes, Mussolini is demonstrating to us how to intervene in the wheel of history in order to save our people from ruin.

The core of all of these questions, however, is ultimately neither the customs duties, nor the internal market, nor whether the labor of agricultural workers is the cheap or expensive, nor the most appropriate agricultural labor machines, nor anything else that is mentioned in this context for the betterment of agriculture. The key point is and remains the attitude of the people and their leaders towards the nation's land, and with their relationship to the idea of dynastic succession in relation to land ownership.

Either: Land is a matter of satisfying needs in the sense of an individual's gainful employment. Thus, land has become exclusively a matter of the economy. Once this has been thought through, it is only a matter of arithmetic to decide how to secure the highest possible pension. The relationship of the landowner to his people is thus also regulated by the calculator. This is today's conception of agriculture! It is served today by books on agricultural management and agricultural policy, which logically limit the management of agriculture to the question of the struggle for markets and the protection of production—it is an attitude which results in the Polish laborer, or even (as once happened before the war) the Chinese coolie,[100] being preferred on German estates because this labor is cheaper and more convenient than German labor. It is an attitude which chips away the peasantry because it has the effect of inhibiting production, and which therefore logically leads to "grain factories" (the Russian Soviets have already realized this idea), the culmination and perfection of this conception.[101] It is an attitude which,

---

[100] Editor's note: A coolie (*kuli* in German) was an indentured servant of Asian descent, most commonly Chinese and Indian. They were used as cheap labor on agricultural plantations, in resource extraction, and in the construction of infrastructure. They played an important role in the economic development of the British Empire, and to a more limited extent, that of the United States. Their role outside the Anglosphere was limited.

[101] It was quite logical that Stresemann, an ardent liberal, also demanded grain factories for Germany—i.e. for large estates that managed exclusively according to the principles and considerations of commercial profit, and thereby similar to Russia. Unnecessary or disingenuous, however, was the outrage of our

with a serene countenance and a thoughtless, uninhibited complacency, kills the last vestiges of German culture, because all culture emerges from the peaceful growth of creativity that is rooted in the soil. But peaceful growth means nothing to the advocates of grain factories, because unfortunately it does not factor into the balance sheets of agricultural double-entry bookkeeping. It is an attitude that knows how to turn the most flourishing landscape into a desert, even if instead of grains of sand, treeless beet or grain fields stretch for miles; it is an attitude that turns the refreshing biodiversity of woodland communities into a soul-killing uniform forest with impeccably aligned rows of trees. And this attitude is then shocked to find that today instead of old folk songs being heard in our villages, only the droning and squawking of gramophones or radio loudspeakers can be heard.

Or: Land is both the breadwinner of the German people and the healthy foundation for the preservation and multiplication of its good blood; it is thus part of family law and is granted state protection. This is an attitude that respects the peasant just as much as the settler or the large landowner, each according to their agricultural peculiarities and national economic needs; it is an attitude that takes care to ensure that every generation can take root and is able to harmonize with its surroundings. It is an attitude that, for example, is able to keep an old avenue of trees alive, because its picturesque, sinewy appearance pleased father and grandfather. It is an attitude that knows how to integrate every technological achievement of the time into the people's way of life, based on the rootedness and style of successive generations that is cultivated out of blood and agriculture, and so sensibly and sensitively molds things and styles without the glaring dissonance that destroys the aesthetic of the people's way of life. Overall, it is an attitude which serves the ways of life of man as well as agriculture and which, out of a healthy attitude towards existence, stands firmly grounded on the realities of this earth, just like, in contrast, it correctly views finance and the economy to be its servants—the servants of its own race and of the people.

A small example quickly shows us the importance of this either-or. Whoever manages his estate exclusively according to the yield calculation and only allows the mathematics to decide his policies, must,

---

agricultural leaders about this, because for years they have been following similar liberal lines of thought which would have inevitably led German agriculture to where Stresemann was proposing.

among other things, commit to eradicating the entire wildlife population of his estate and, if possible, also of its surroundings, because he is not able to justify normal levels of wildlife damage to agriculture in purely mathematical terms; only in special cases can enough profit be achieved from wild game or from proceeds generated by hunting licenses to compensate for or even exceed wildlife damage. The "devastation" of nature becomes quite apparent here from a purely calculative point of view. What an abundance of life, on the other hand, can a peasant with a connection to nature carefully nurture out of his woodlands if he knows that his actions are according to his forest way of life and that he need not allow it to be raped by the ruinous effect of pure yield calculations!

This either-or is unconditional! In this question, the German people still have their future fate in their hands. But the either-or demands a clear and unambiguous decision, before which everything else must be subordinated. In any case, rhetoric does not help, and edifying lectures or conscientious statistics about the vital necessity of the peasantry for our people even less so. May the books on the history of Germanic peoples not soon write the final line on the history of the German people! For whether or not Wall Street graciously allows us to call ourselves Germans or the German Reich, that has nothing to with the death of the German nation.

V

THE *HEGEHÖFE*

"Only nobility that sits on inviolable ground develops the full-fledged spiritual freedom that, in every situation of life, dares to act and advise exclusively according to conscience."

1

Perhaps some readers will want to ask the question from the outset: Why *hegehöfe*? Is it not possible to achieve what must be achieved in another way? For example, by state subsidies to those families who submit to specific conditions and demands that are to be expected in this context, as well as by making suitable housing available (garden cities[102] could point the way!) to these families? The answer to this can only be: no!

For it is doubtful that the city, even the garden city, is able to influence the soul of the growing youth in such a favorable way that a generation of leaders with a truly mature nobility of soul can emerge from it. The German soul, with all its warmness, is rooted in its native landscape and has, in a sense, always grown out of it. The importance of the German countryside—with all its trappings of millennia-old tradition and civilization and with all its subtle, imponderable influences for the development of the German soul—should be made clear by the following: the German people, the people of poets and thinkers, have

---

[102] Editor's note: Inspired by Edward Bellamy's 1898 utopian novel *Looking Backward,* the garden city was an urban planning movement in the early twentieth century that sought to develop self-sufficient communities which combined the benefits of rural and urban living, typically as part of a concentric city plan.

indeed given up a very large share of blood to the population of the North American states, but hardly any important thinkers or poets born on American soil have emerged from this share of blood.[103] The view that the landscape physically shapes the race or the people, however, must be emphatically countered here. This is not the case, nor do we have sufficient evidence that it could be so, with perhaps the only exception being natural selection indirectly modifying the humanity of a region over long periods of Earth's history. Rather, the environment shapes a maturing youth in such a way that they can never completely get away from the experiences of their childhood in their later mental development.

Whoever takes the natural landscape away from the German soul, kills it. Even the best-designed garden city is not a landscape in this sense. The restlessness of the city dweller, who seldom finds a permanent place in which he can grow spiritually in his sea of stone—as well as the all-too-early independence of young people brought about by urban life—cause the soul to atrophy and give undesirable encouragement to a way of thinking that is focused on externalities.

Ernst Hasse is quite right, "The country is the home of the individual. Truly great individuals and 'heroes' have always come from the countryside." The city, on the other hand, with few exceptions, produces *massenmenschen* (mass-man).[104] In order for Germany to survive, however, it needs "heroes" who are firmly self-confident. The city dweller who has grown up with all the trappings of the metropolitan experience may be "quick" and "bright" (at least that will be the impression he gives at first), but he will seldom possess those gifts which,

---

[103] Darré, as a born Argentinean-German, is quite clear about the many reasons for this phenomenon. Among them, it is only worth mentioning here that it is hopelessly impossible to instill an understanding of German fairy tales and legends in a child growing up in the appalling sobriety of the American environment. Every child who has grown up "over there" knows how its monotony and colorlessness affects the mental development of a child from the very beginning. It is a different matter when the German man in America is able to maintain the landscape according to his nature in a relatively large, closed settlement—Blumenau, Brazil comes to mind as an example. Such landscapes are, of course, not monotonously American, but, for all their lasting foreignness, still have a somewhat German character, and the children growing up in them have a different mental development than those in the rest of America.

[104] Editor's note: For Nietzsche, the *massenmenchen*—weak, insecure, decadent human beings—were the antithesis to the *übermensch* (over-man)—the ideal, superior man that humanity should aspire to be.

in pivotal moments of history, provide a leader with the inner guiding star necessary for correct action.

From Swedish peasants in Finland, I once heard an uprooted person (it was the usual urban intellectual, with a lot of mental agility but little depth) described as having lost his "inner sense." A quite excellent judgment! For if we look at the life stories of the great leaders of our people, it becomes obvious that they—mostly against all sense and understanding of time—knew how to obey an inner feeling, more precisely an "inner sense," with the same somnambulistic certainty that a healthy mother possesses when she senses (without having to call upon the powers of reason) the suffering and pain of her helpless infant. This "inner sense," perhaps the most divine gift of true humanity, only grows in direct contact with Mother Earth; undoubtedly developing exclusively in the manifold world of energies that all life in free nature so extensively sends out to each other and against each other, and whose powers we are only slowly now being able to grasp by experimental means. In any case, such an "inner sense" and its possibility of developing in direct connection with nature should be assumed for the Germanic—these things may be different for other races.

After all, what do we know about the living conditions that a healthy body—not to mention a soul—needs to maintain its health? On closer inspection: very, very little! A quarter of a century ago, animal breeders built stables for their cattle and pigs that seemed to be true miracles of hygienic and managerial practicality, with the end result being that breeding had become increasingly difficult due to previously unknown diseases and disorders (epidemics, birth problems and much more) appearing in abundance. At first, it was all blamed on the fact that highly bred animals were more sensitive than the wilder breeds. But on closer inspection, although this convenient explanation did, of course, contain a grain of truth, it was not entirely correct. Then, a well-known breeder decided to lead his animals out to pasture in God's great outdoors and house them there in simple wooden sheds. Although he experienced some losses at first, the problems he had complained about until then—especially the birth problems in the herds—soon disappeared almost simultaneously. Today, in animal breeding circles, we only laugh about those perfectly hygienic animal stable "coffins" from the beginning of this century. Are we not currently on the same path with our human dwellings as the animal breeders mistakenly took half a century ago? I cannot find much difference between the "cement coffins" of pig breeding, which animal breeders today reminisce about with quiet horror, and the "cement cubes" of the oriental-Asian-modern architectural style of Dessau Bauhaus.[105] Why do you think the healthy frontline soldier during the World War of 1914–18 never fell ill in the cave-like life of the trenches—which smacked all hygienic principles in the face—while twenty-four hours of leave at home were enough to conjure up all kinds of illnesses that were not even remotely likely outdoors? In any case, this is what happened to me during my four years of frontline life, almost all of which took place at focal points along the Western Front, where decent shelter was very rarely possible—other healthy comrades experienced this as well.[106] Was it really only stupidity that prevented the Germanic tribes of the Migration Period from settling the conquered Roman cities with their non-inheriting sons? Was the resistance that the Saxons put up to King Henry I when—because of the Hungarians—he forced them to establish and live in city-castles really only thoughtless resistance to change, as we have been taught so far? Rather, it seems that our science has not yet been able to answer these questions, that we have misinterpreted the traditions of history, and that we are therefore still blindly passing by things whose decisive importance for the physical and mental health of our people is unfortunately not cancelled out by our ignorance.

Whoever wants to develop nobility in the true and actually German sense of the word must transplant the families chosen for this purpose out of the cities and into the countryside, in conditions that enable a lineage to take root. It all depends on the roots of the nobility!

---

[105] Editor's note: The Bauhaus Dessau, also known as the Bauhaus Building Dessau, is a building complex in Dessau-Roßlau in the modernist Bauhaus style. The building's construction was completed in 1926 and would serve as the school building for the Bauhaus School of Art, Design, and Architecture. The school was visited by Paul Schultze-Naumburg in 1932 with National Socialist members of the local municipal council, all of which were fiercely critical of degenerate modern architecture. Shortly after the visit, the decision was made in favor of closing the school but against demolishing the building. It would serve as the *gauführerschule* (*gau* leadership academy) for the Magdeburg-Anhalt region until March 7th, 1945, when it was damaged during the Allied bombing of Dessau, which nearly annihilated the city.

[106] Franz Schauwecker occasionally draws attention to this fact with wonderment in his war novel *Aufbruch der Nation (Rise of the Nation)*: "'You'll get sick if you sit in the wet grass for too long,' said Herse. 'Out here it doesn't do much harm,' Albrecht replied, standing up. 'Here you stay healthy. I didn't expect that before either.'"

We no longer have nobility in the German-Germanic sense at all. For nobility in this sense belongs to the land as the gardener belongs to the garden. Uprooted Germanic nobility is no longer nobility, neither in its essence nor in the sense of the word, see Chapter III, Section 1. The vast majority of those who still sit in the countryside as nobility want to earn money from their land, so in essence they are nothing more than industrialists, tradesmen. Whether they evaluate the land in terms of coal or in terms of cabbage does not matter, because both amount to the same thing, namely, making money. For true nobility, however, the only decisive factor is whether or not they recognize that the land is the guardian of the family and the line of succession.

Only when nobility can grow into the landscape of its homeland, unburdened by economic concerns, is it able to develop genuine, outwardly and inwardly mature leaders. Working on their fathers' soil, struggling with the forces of nature, and caring for and nurturing plants and animals in various seasons generates a very specific soul force, precisely that "inner sense" of which we spoke above, which is like a part of nature itself—rooted in it and grown out of it. In this way, agriculture influences the soul in a way that allows it, in turn, to be influenced by the creative power of the racially-conditioned human being. The result is a growing together with the soil, shaping the nobility's actions and attitudes, and providing a natural integration into the nation; for out of the soil, true nobility experiences homeland, people and state.

But only a nobility rooted to the soil through successive generations is able to cultivate a home culture based on traditions and beliefs that have a sufficiently decisive effect on the soul life of a growing young person. Does anyone today have any idea just how beneficial the effects of the mysterious magic of reverent home traditions—as well as the trappings of a home inherited from one's parents—are on the soul lives of young people? Does anyone seriously believe that the enigmatic, life-warming, fairy-tale soul of our people can be kept alive in today's latest-style home furnishings, which may be impeccable from a hygienic point of view, but ultimately look like hospital facilities? Make no mistake about it! At the most, it can be stated that the worldly experiences of a youthful spirit have different effects according to the racial disposition of the person concerned. But in today's racial literature, the possibility of the environment influencing a youthful soul is occasionally denied altogether, with references made to Hebbel (the bricklayer's son from Dithmarschen) as a kind of star witness. It must be countered that although Hebbel grew up in poor and oppressive circumstances, he otherwise spent his youth in the healthy purity of a rural environment.

Another circumstance must be taken into account in the question, "City or country?" Every city—garden city as well as the stone-box agglomerations—does not have a basis in the laws of life. It is today, as it has always been, a product of transport possibilities, to an extent even a prisoner of transport development. Every city is like a polyp that sucks its nourishment from its surroundings or, if the means of transport and the road network permit, from even further away through these far-reaching arms. If, however, this influx of food stops for any reason, the city becomes as helpless as a fish left out to dry. In such a case, the city cannot keep itself alive on its own—it must always be helped from outside. The existence of the city is based on parasitism. Every parasite dies as soon as one deprives it of the basis of its nourishment. If, therefore, a people wants to create a nobility built on roots and permanence—if, therefore, it wants to develop future-conscious policies with regard to its valuable human hereditary stock—then a people cannot build its nobility on, of all things, the shaky and insecure foundation of an urban home. This should be obvious! This in no way suggests that an attempt should not be made in cities to promote the adaptability of certain families. However, this will always remain a purely local urban matter and, moreover, will probably only be possible in certain cities with any real success.

If, however, the nobility settles on estates which employ suitable measures to prevent them from being lost to the families, then, as experience shows, even a people's hardest times of need will not affect its ability to bring forth valuable blood. Such difficult times then have the same the effect as a violent storm in the forest, which makes the rotten and decaying things obvious and tears them down, thus giving the healthy more air and light to flourish.

It is therefore my conviction that the creation of a new German nobility is not feasible without the *hegehof* idea or one similar to it, at least not as a long-term institution.

There is no getting around this realization, no matter which side you want to tackle the task from.

2

What size should the *hegehöfe* be? This question cannot be answered at all in the form of uniform size specifications or a model template, at least not for estates within the borders of the German Reich. How many hectares of land someone owns or what yield he generates from this property is a question that must be subordinate to another—whether there is a healthy relationship between the size of the property and the degree of obligations towards the state. It should be noted, however, that in this context, "duties" and "taxes" are two quite different concepts!

If, however, we want to answer the question of the size of the property by taking as a basis the extent of the owner's duties towards the people as a whole, then we should at least put the yield or the potential yield of the property in the foreground when assessing things. The mere comparison of land sizes with each other—as is unfortunately very popular in Germany today—makes no sense and should be described as gross nonsense because it causes unnecessary antagonism amongst professional colleagues and popularizes completely wrong ideas in non-peasant circles. For example, in the marshlands of the North Sea there is many a "peasant" who, despite owning far less land, can reap as much from his farm as many noble landowners in southern Germany. And vice versa, in the Geest region of north-west Germany there are "estates" whose vast land ownership does not take away the fact that many farms in the granary of Bavaria can match them in terms of yield.

The core mission of a *hegehof* should be the preservation of the family settled on it. It should be able to carry out this task as independent of conditions in the country as possible. Thus, as a minimum extent of area, a *hegehof* should be a self-contained economic unit in such a way that it is able to satisfy the living needs of the families settled on it, including the servants, even in times of economic hardship. In addition, however, it should provide the owner with a pension in times of tranquility, which is needed to support himself and his family and to pay the contributions due to his professional association.[107] If we add to this some woodland as a "savings box" and for a few other more spiritual reasons, we arrive at a farm size which, depending on the soil and climate, can be considered a large farm or a small to medium-sized estate. This would be the

[107] Taxes will be discussed further below.

minimum amount of area for a *hegehof*. It is therefore clear that the size of the area of the different farms will vary: the very different soils of Germany and the very different climatic conditions (in Germany alone we have about a dozen climatic zones that are quite different from each other) mean that it is virtually impossible to harvest the same overall yields from areas of the same size. Old, still soil-rooted peasant and landowner families—provided they are physically and morally fit—could apply to have their farms included among the nobility, so that their previous property becomes a *hegehof* if it is of the minimum size. This proposal stems from my belief that our best blood is still to be found in these soil-rooted people and that this blood would therefore be kept alive most easily in this way. But this is not to say that our entire peasantry and all the landowners in Germany should be turned into *hegehof* noblemen.

Such a balanced and well-rounded economic basis, determined by the nutritional needs of a family, gives a property, if it is a single estate, an external unity that has often been admired by reliable assessors of the landscape. They may not be castles or eye-catching manor houses, but they are not ordinary farms either. They are still frequently found in north-western Germany and southern Germany, and even more so in Denmark and Scandinavia, and such a sensitive observer and assessor of the landscape as Paul Schultze-Naumburg could not help but to give them the designation of "noble estates" in *Das Bürgerliche Haus (The Bourgeois House;* Frankfurt am Main, 1927, page 30).

This should provide a clear indication of the minimum size of the *hegehöfe*. We have not yet established an upper limit. In general, however, the demand for a well-rounded and self-contained economic unit also limits the upper limit to a certain, albeit somewhat elastic, extent. We do not have any region in the territory of the Reich that permits the uniform cultivation of a closed large estate from a central farm. In Germany, existing large estates are almost always a multiplicity of independent entities that are either managed by tenants or are under the direction of more or less independent administrators, who in turn are united under a head administrator. If, therefore, it is demanded that the *hegehöfe* be managed under all circumstances from a central point that unites all the farm buildings in the area, then their size is thus more clearly limited than it would appear to the non-peasant at first glance.

The difficulty in determining this outer limit lies in something else. We have many estates in the Reich that originally developed from a number of estate units or farms (*bauernlegen*![108]), but which over the course of time grew together to form a self-contained estate unit, with the farm buildings of the former estate units being used as the so-called *vorwerke* (outworks). This is particularly true in Mecklenburg and the formerly Swedish Western Pomerania, but can be found throughout the whole of eastern Germany. The peasant calls any building erected for reasons of economic expediency outside the actual farm and its immediate land area a *vorwerk*. The *vorwerk* as such cannot be excluded from the concept of a uniform and self-contained estate, because in most cases its establishment or non-establishment does not arise from the discretion of the owner, but rather from situational constraints such as the landscape, the position of the estates in relation to each other, or other circumstances.

In principle, the *vorwerke* cannot be forbidden for purely economic reasons, even in the case of a *hegehof*. Just imagine an estate whose land stretches over a narrow but very long strip of terrain, and even a non-expert can clearly see the expediency of outlying infrastructure. On the whole, however, we will have to demand that the management of a *hegehof* be carried out from a farm. Self-contained farmland must remain a characteristic of the *hegehof*. If we allow for *vorwerke* in the *hegehöfe* without any restriction, then the danger can arise that under the cloak of the *hegehof's* family law protections, giant estates are once again reassembled by simply making every estate that somehow falls to a *hegehof* a *vorwerke*, and thus part of the *hegehof*. Questions such as that of the outlying infrastructure should be answered on a case-by-case basis by special committees where agricultural advisors are adequately represented. In the interest of fairness, the committee will primarily have the task of understanding the *hegehof's* genuine economic situation, whereby existing unfavorable circumstances in *hegehöfe* can be considered and mitigated. Furthermore, exemptions would be made for estates that have obviously grown together and form a close unit and who would suffer a significant disruption to their hitherto well-rounded economic unit by the removal of the *vorwerke*.

I would like to propose an exception to these basic rules in such cases where ancestral seats (which are already a series of lineages in one

---

[108] Editor's note: *Bauernlegen* (peasant laying) was a practice in Germany between the fourteenth and eighteenth centuries where landlords would expropriate or purchase small peasant-run farms, often through the use of intimidation or force, in order to farm the land themselves for profit.

family) must, for their economic preservation, have an estate which exceeds the permissible property size of a *hegehof*. It would be contrary to the intention of our creation of a new nobility if such manors—which have grown into their present state in one way or another—were to be excluded from family law protection only because they do not correspond to the established guideline size. It would also be contrary to our intention if such estates were to be included among the *hegehöfe*, but were nevertheless handed over to inevitable economic decline through the allocation of insufficient manor lands. In the case of such an exception, each case must be investigated with regard to whether it really is a matter of inherited family property, and furthermore, whether the family sitting on it is still physically and mentally eligible for the new nobility, and finally, whether the ancestral seat in question is really an expression of well-developed civilization—which is worth protecting and whose protection is also recommended out of a respect for the works of past German generations. The increase in land ownership that such an ancestral seat brings with it when it is designated a *hegehof* can be compensated for with an increase in responsibilities within the framework of the noblemen's self-governing institutions.

3

A necessary prerequisite of the whole *hegehof* idea is, of course, that the *hegehöfe* are excluded from any market freedom of movement, because this would contradict the meaning of the whole system; they do not necessarily have to be unsellable. It will have to be demanded that any nobleman on a *hegehof* may not dispose of any land and soil. Whoever wishes to convert a farm, an estate, or a manor into a *hegehof* and receives permission to do so must either sell the land that cannot or may not become *hegehof* land, or pass it on to heirs, who in turn can apply for the establishment of their own *hegehof* if the area is large enough.

If we look at, for example, Theodor Häbich's *Deutsche Latifundien (German Latifundia*; Königsberg Preußen 1930, second edition), it is quite evident that many noble families still own huge estates today. For example: in Brandenburg, the von Arnim-Boitzenburgs own 14,126 hectares; in Silesia, the Imperial Counts Schaffgotsch gennant Semperfrei von und zu Kynast und Greiffenstein own 27,668 hectares; in East Prussia, the Counts Finck von Finckenstein-Schönberg own 20,887 hectares; in Württemberg, the Princes Thurn und Taxis own 17,085 hectares; and in Baden, the Princes von Fürstenberg-Donaueschingen own 16,374 hectares (all of which, however, is mainly forest property). There is no doubt that such estates do not meet the standards of healthy land distribution among a people that is called the *Volk ohne Raum* (people without living space). The owners of such estates will hardly be able to escape the inevitable reorganization of land ownership—on the basis of my proposal, these families would have the option of avoiding being completely uprooted by transferring parts of their large estates to *hegehöfe*. I am far removed from any kind of "expropriation" mindset, for reasons that will be mentioned below. But the fact that the distribution of land in today's overpopulated German Reich no longer conforms to morally justifiable principles is easy to see. For a renewal of the nobility, it would be appropriate to divide the excessively large estates where a single member of a family now lives, into *hegehöfe*, on which several members of the same family could then take root. These *hegehöfe* could perhaps be formed according to proposals from the previous owner. If there are no longer enough members of the family in question to fill the farms created in this way, it is conceivable that the old owner could fill the *hegehöfe* (within the framework of the principles of the *hegehof* idea) with his friends' families or, at a minimum, he can retain a decisive influence on the filling of the farms.

If we take the *hegehof* out of the cycle of free movement of goods, this circumstance forces us to pay separate attention to the labor question on the *hegehöfe*. In a later section it will be explained why every heir to a *hegehof* must receive a thorough and specialized agricultural education. Nevertheless, it is not the nobleman's task to exhaust himself in the exercise of his agricultural occupation, quite the contrary! Because of this, workers are necessary to provide assistance on the *hegehöfe*.

The value of the agricultural labor force for the nation as a whole does not lie primarily in the relationship between agricultural labor and its moral and health-related benefits to the laborer. Rather, an agricultural labor force only becomes valuable to a nation when it also becomes rooted to the land. Care must therefore be taken to ensure that the workers' families can also take root on the farms. Their remuneration cannot, therefore, follow the needs of today's soulless labor market, but must be regulated according to moral principles. The *artaman* communities, which are fortunately becoming more and more recognized today, could be useful in drafting plans for this; they are probably in the best position to judge these matters at the moment. For the rest, it is not our task here to determine in detail how to regulate the relationship of the *hegehof* nobleman to his workforce; only in principle will it be mentioned here that it can, of course, never be a relationship between a master and a servant. A moral working and service relationship among freemen must be found in the field of the division of labor.

4

How can new land be won for the *hegehöfe*? For it is not only families already located in the countryside that are to be made noblemen, but also proven leaders who are not endowed with land. This blood is to be preserved for the people on the *hegehöfe* so that this principle is upheld: Leadership by blood, supplemented by merit.

We must emphatically warn against any thought of expropriation by the state. In the German-Germanic sense, nationalization is only morally justified in certain institutions that all citizens have no choice but to use, and where it would therefore be immoral for individuals to exploit everyone's needs. The nationalization of the railways by Bismarck, for example, was moral in this sense. Such moral reasoning cannot be put forward to demand the redistribution of all land in the German Reich, even if we refer to the old Germanic margraviate, which is usually misunderstood.

From the German point of view, the soil has two tasks: it is to preserve the generations settling on it and to ensure the nourishment of the entire nation—it thus fulfills both a blood-duty and an economic task. The demarcation between these two tasks would be a matter of responsible German state management. But the beneficiary of the land will always have to regard himself as a trustee of the general public, to which the general public, for its part, will necessarily object if the beneficiary does not fulfill his moral obligations. What remains decisive for both parties is their subordination to a moral idea. As you can see, this is quite different from the social democratic position demanding the nationalization of all land ownership for the purpose of "fair distribution of income;" in plain language: fair food distribution.

Furthermore, any linking of land with family-promoting and, therefore, civilization-promoting ideas only makes sense if the continuity of the investment is assured. There can be nothing more dangerous for

German-Germanic civilization than undermining the belief in the continuity of land ownership. But this is exactly the effect of all expropriation plans. Land laws which are only created to temporarily satisfy covetous or distressed factions by transferring landed property will always devastate confidence in the permanence and inviolability of property. For who can assure the beneficiary of the new order that further "improvements" made by the state will not drive him away from the land he has won? Even maudlin reflections on the sad fate of the urban "dispossessed" do not change these facts.

Nevertheless, the fact that a change in the distribution of land ownership must occur has already been mentioned. But this change will have to be based on a moral idea that is clear and obvious to all sections of the people, for only such a common understanding would give the change the necessary consistency. Such a moral idea could be, for example, the blood-based regeneration of our people.

Expropriation plans are therefore out of the question. However, a German state governed in the German sense could obtain a pre-eminent right to land or facilitate the establishment of *hegehöfe* through monetary subsidies. Donations from the people or from dedicated foundations could also raise the necessary funds. It is conceivable, for example, that a town or a municipality could acquire a *hegehof* for one of its proven sons or his descendants. There are numerous ways to realize the idea of a *hegehof* without compulsory expropriation.

I am also not proposing the division of all large domains into *hegehöfe*. On the contrary, careful consideration should be made as to whether the domains would be better allocated towards the national bread supply, i.e. whether they could be given over exclusively to the fulfillment of economic tasks of national interest. For the bread supply of our urban population cannot be ensured by *hegehöfe* and farms—large estates will always be necessary for this. Here, the domain receives a task from the people. A German—I repeat, German—state leadership would thus have in its hands, perhaps in conjunction with granary facilities, a very simple option for securing the nutrition of our urban population and for making it independent of the world economic grain market. The oppressive power position of the urban centers would otherwise increase with every kilometer of new road development and could never be sufficiently mitigated with protective tariffs, which in any case make the foreign relations of the Reich cumbersome.

5

We turn to the question: who is actually supposed to oversee the *hegehöfe*?

For this purpose, I propose to unite the new nobility into an *Adelsgenossenschaft* (Noble Cooperative) who would supervise the *hegehöfe* and would be responsible for the granting of fiefs, in the sense of so-called hereditary fiefs.

Solving this task may seem easier than it is. First of all, we should refer to certain historical experiences with fiefs. The early medieval fiefdom was a custom of non-German origin, but it essentially was a combination of Gallo-Roman and German institutions. Gallo-Roman vassalage (liegemen), German allegiance, and Roman land lending merged into a unified entity. The medieval feudal lord was obliged to render knightly and courtly service to his liege lord on the basis of the Germanic concept of mutual loyalty and received the use of the feudal estate as remuneration. We could describe the feudal property system as a civil servant's salary on a natural economic basis, which it undoubtedly was originally. All of Western Europe adopted the feudal system. But while in England and France the feudatories succeeded in bringing the state under the conditional sovereignty of a uniformly directed state leadership, in Germany they slowly transformed the state into a so-called feudal state, actively opposed a uniform state leadership, and finally broke up all coherent state association. This was the beginning of a trend for the German people, which General Krauß aptly condemns in his book *Der Irrgang der Deutschen Königspolitik (The Misguided Course of German Royal Politics)*, a sentiment already conveyed in the title of this book. As long as the feudatories were only enfeoffed with land—as was the case up to the ninth century—and the feudal property thus represented a kind of civil servant's salary, they had no meaningful influence over the state. However, things would change when the feudatories and the associated sovereign rights became hereditary and the king was forced to continue lending the fiefs that fell to him after the death of the feudal lord—essentially a kind of compulsory loan. This obligation to lend, from which England and France exempted themselves, was the state-destroying feature of the German feudal system. Instead of the feudatories being entrusted with specific tasks on a case-by-case basis, the privileges that became hereditary with the feudal estates led to more and more state power slipping out of the hands of the German head of state and passing into the hands of the feudatories. This development benefited all kinds of people, but unfortunately not the people the feudal system had originally favored—namely, the common peasant freeman. Thus, on the one hand, the unified state was broken up and, on the other hand, the old German idea of self-government was not promoted. The seeds were sown from which the later sovereign rulers would develop.

From this we learn that a system of hereditary fiefs, compulsorily lent, without any obligations on the feoffed, and without the right of objection by the sovereign must be prevented for the sake of safeguarding the integrity of the state. However, I consider it wrong to give the state a completely free hand in the dispensation of the *hegehöfe*. This would hardly guarantee the long-term continuity integral to the *hegehof* idea and would also create the dangerous possibility that undesirable attempts to influence the Noble Cooperative would occur with the aid of state power.

However, I believe I can propose the following: just as the nobles are united in the Noble Cooperative, so also do the *hegehöfe* become the property of the Noble Cooperative. However, this Noble Cooperative would not be a cooperative in the modern sense, but in the sense of the old German corporation. In the old German corporation, the multiplicity of individuals that it was composed of were not irrelevant, but actively shaped the inner life of the association and regulated it through a self-developed corporate (social) law. Freiherr von Schwerin writes in *Der Geist des Altgermanischen Rechts (The Spirit of Ancient Germanic Law)*:

> The corporation and its members did not relate to one another as third parties, but were bound together by legal rules governing the relationship of the whole to its parts. Therefore, the rights of the members to the assets of the corporation were not rights to another's property. The corporation partitioned itself, as it were, with the members' rights to the corporation's assets divided in such a way that the authority of disposal remained with the corporation, while the use remained with the members; the right of use was again only membership-based and, by definition, could only be due to a member.

The nobleman on a *hegehof* is a member of the Noble Cooperative in this sense. He bequeaths this membership and with it the use of the *hegehof* to a son or, if he is denied this, to another male member of his family—provided that the heir meets the minimum requirements of body, mind, and morals laid down by the Noble Cooperative. In special cases, a daughter may be allowed to take over the inheritance if there is no longer a male heir or if the heirs in question do not meet even the minimum requirements set by the Noble Cooperative, which are interpreted broadly.

As is well known, the institution of the "inheriting daughter," i.e. the inheritance of a hereditary seat to a daughter if a male heir (better: son) is no longer available, is an ancient custom among Indo-European and Germanic peoples. In England, this custom has survived to the present day—when the male line dies out, feudal property and titles of nobility are passed on to a daughter; according to Dibelius, there are today twenty-six peeresses in their own right. But it is precisely the English experiences with these inheriting daughters that force us to recommend this custom for the *hegehöfe* only with reservations. Galton, the great English eugenicist, has made investigations into the offspring of these inheriting daughters. On the basis of the results of this investigation, he feels compelled to draw attention to a certain "sterilizing influence" of the inherited daughters, and he proves that they have often had a disastrous effect on fertility. Galton concludes that it must involve a genetic predisposition to childlessness and that this is probably the cause of the sterilizing influence. I will dare to doubt this conclusion of Galton's—I believe that I can give a different explanation for the sterilizing influence of the inheriting daughters: if a country gentleman has only a few children and there are no sons among these children, it would seem (provided, of course, that no sickly woman had been married) that the male stock of this family has already fallen prey to a degeneration of some kind. Therefore it would be natural, even if not absolutely necessary, that this degeneration—which manifests itself in a lack of procreative power—is passed on by the heir's daughter, so that even a husband capable of procreation cannot change much about that fact. Therefore, we will not reject a daughter's claim of inheritance without proper investigation, perhaps only accepting their claim under the stipulation that their existence as sole heir clearly arises from chance (due to the loss of sons in war or through misfortune or the restriction of the number of children a family can bear, which is sometimes necessary for health reasons, and many other such examples) and not from an inherent inferiority in their paternal line.

These are the rights of the nobles, given to them in order to best secure the idea of family rootedness, as well as to bring the idea of family succession to the fore.

However, the right of disposition for the *hegehöfe* remains with the Noble Cooperative, which thus also retains the right to object to the inheritance of the *hegehöfe*. The Noble Cooperative shall determine whether the heir proposed by a nobleman is worthy of this inheritance. In order to not cause any misunderstandings stemming from today's ideas of cooperatives and cooperative systems, it should be pointed out once again that the noblemen are the Noble Cooperative, so the question of the inheritance of a *hegehof* is solved on the basis of pure self-governance.

After all, the state leadership of the German Reich must be granted a right of objection; on the one hand, for educational reasons—in order to keep the Noble Cooperative conscious of state sovereignty and to fill it with a sense of state responsibility—and on the other hand, to prevent attempts to influence it by power-hungry or ambitious families and to guarantee the self-governing body full independence from malicious and influence-hungry members. Accordingly, I propose that each confirmation of inheritance must be submitted by the Noble Cooperative, substantiated and supported with details, to the Reich leadership for countersignature and only becomes legally valid after confirmation by the state. If both parties cannot agree, the Supreme Court of the German Reich shall, in its capacity as the most distinguished administrator of German law, adjudicate in a legally valid and final manner. In this way, the Noble Cooperative is able to do two things: firstly, imbue a noble spirit onto the question of succession, and secondly, consult established views on the matter; simultaneously, the German state remains confident that things will not develop in a direction that is undesirable to it.

Of course, there should be no "compensation" for the non-inheriting sons in any sense. This would contradict the idea of the entire system. However, we should consider the possibility that the non-inheriting sons could retain the right to reside on the *hegehof* where they were born, at least until they became professionally independent. Additionally, we should also consider the possibility that non-inheriting sons could be guaranteed retirement homes in the form of foundations administered by the Noble Cooperative, into which they could buy their way into over the course of their lives by means of small payments. Under such circumstances, we might also contemplate the custom, which is not necessarily noble, of considering the youngest son to be the preferred heir. This form of succession—the minorate—has appeared since the

Middle Ages in certain parts of Germany as a peasant system of inheritance (ultimogeniture), which is contrasted by the noble system of inheritance by the eldest son—the majorate (primogeniture). Agricultural history shows us that the peasant minorate has been of excellent effect wherever circumstances did not permit or did not make it advisable to allow the non-inheriting sons to remain as dependents on the paternal inheritance. It was then usually relatively easy for the peasant to either give the non-inheriting sons a good lifetime education or to support them in a new settlement somewhere else. The number of children was never restricted, even on smaller farms. One stipulation of the minorate, however, is that in principle, the youngest son of the first wife is the heir. It is thanks to the establishment of the minorate, for example, that the German peasantry in Russia—which today is arguably being destroyed by the Soviets—increases in population and settles new lands surprisingly quickly.

Of course, taxation of the *hegehöfe* in the current sense of tax collection must cease. For the land of the *hegehöfe*, the *scholle* (soil clods),[109] should be tended and cared for—not exploited for profit. The *hegehöfe* should bear fruit for the German people in every respect, not be merely a financial resource.

However, this should by no means be understood in the same sense as Early Medieval "immunity." This had its roots in the late Roman Empire of the Caesars. There, the imperial estates were free of fees and taxes and were therefore called "immune." The term was transferred to the Franconian "royal estates"[110] and then, with the granting of such royal estates, also passed on to the vassals enfeoffed to them, who thus became, in a sense, "immunity-lords." The church and the secular landowners later received the same rights by royal prerogative and also became immunity-lords. The immunity-lords were entitled to a certain limited jurisdiction, which over the course of time resulted in jurisdictional disputes with the royal courts, from which the immunity-lords ultimately emerged victorious. They thus created their own jurisdiction alongside the royal one, and the result was the landed sovereign or territorial lord that emerged in the twelfth and thirteenth

---

[109] Editor's note: Soil clods, also known regionally as *ackerscholle*, *scholle*, or *klute*, are lumps of soil 10 to 50 cm in diameter that occur in arable farmland on loamy and claylike soils when the land being worked by a plough or cultivator is too wet or too dry.

[110] The royal estate itself, however, is of Frankish origin.

centuries, the *dominium terrae*. Roman immunity transplanted to Germania was thus the real cause of the destruction of German imperial unity.

Tax exemption does not mean exemption from all taxes for the *hegehöfe*. Rather, funds required by public authorities are raised on the basis of an agreement between the public authorities and the Noble Cooperative; the funds are then collected by the Noble Cooperative. The individual nobleman must therefore pay only the taxes which he needs to sustain the self-governing body of the *hegehöfe*; aside from that, he will also pay the amount that the administration of his self-governing body has agreed to pay in their negotiations with state leadership. This is then levied from him by means of a payment proportional to the earning capacity of his property. Here, I follow lines of thought which, on the one hand, are old German, but which, on the other hand, I essentially owe to the book by Edgar Julius Jung: *Die Herrschaft der Minderwertigen, ihr Zerfall und ihre Ablösung* (*The Rule of the Inferior, its Dissolution and Replacement*; pages 189-196, first edition, Berlin 1927).

* * *

In conclusion, allow me to briefly mention the following: I imagine a *Bauerngenossenschaft* (Peasant Cooperative) alongside the Noble Cooperative, based on the same principles and endowed with the same rights. The difference between the two is not of a fundamental nature; rather, the difference lies in the degree to which a peasant is expected to perform somewhat less than a nobleman. The peasant's farm will generally, though not necessarily, be smaller than a *hegehof*, but it will be clearly larger than the property of a small settler. The physical, mental, and moral requirements for the peasant heirs will be more shaped by aspects of peasant expediency—in this regard, agricultural or tribal idiosyncrasies can and should be given special consideration.

The self-governing bodies of the Noble Cooperative and the Peasant Cooperative would work side by side on equal legal standing and would be represented together externally as members of the agricultural profession, the Landstand, in the Chamber of Professional Estates of the German Reich, where the nation's professional estates coordinate their economic tasks with one another. The next section will show us what will be required so that this can be guaranteed. Thus, despite the fact that the

Noble Cooperative and the Peasant Cooperative operate side by side independently of each other, they are still members of one profession and represent their economic concerns jointly and uniformly to the outside world. The thousand-year-old stratification of our people into nobility and peasants will have thus been overcome, and the link to the Germanic system of division of tasks between nobility and peasants will have been reestablished.

I would like to mention at this point that this could be considered the realization of a plan that the racial hygienist Lenz made years ago under his proposal for "peasant fiefdoms" in Baur, Fischer, and Lenz's *Grundriss der Menschlichen Erblichkeitslehre* (*Outline of Human Heredity Theory*; second edition, volume II, page 230, Munich 1923). This proposal by Lenz is unique in its clear, creative design, and it speaks to Lenz's keen understanding of human development when he places racial hygiene at the core of his plan and "everything else is made more or less secondary."

In the same way, small settlers, rural workers, agricultural civil servants, and, if necessary, also the non-agricultural rural workers can be united into similar self-governing cooperatives which can then be incorporated into the Landstand, which would represent them in the professional chamber. Thus, according to Germanic custom, these newest self-governing bodies are also incorporated into the spheres of duties of their fellow workers, the nobility, and the peasants. For the representation of the interests of the agricultural professions in relation to the non-agricultural professions concerns the Landstand's five or six parts in quite the same way. How the interests of these individual parts of the Landstand should be regulated amongst themselves is a question whose answer does not belong here.

In this way, the interests of agriculture are protected in relation to the other professions, a circumstance which, given Germany's central position in the Europe, is not entirely without significance.

VI

Outline of the Nobility's Structure and Governance

"The German future belongs to the Germanic people's state, founded on nationality and leadership, which: as a powerful unity is able to defend the German right of self-determination, as a plurality grants free range to the diversity of Germanic life through broad internal self-governance, and as a non-partisan constitutional state based on the rule of law effectively protects the freedom and personal integrity of the German people against arbitrariness and breach of law by authorities."

Walther Merk

1

A cooperative, organized in the old German tradition as was presented in Chapter V, Section 5, cannot exist without trained self-governance. However, true self-governance only exists when the costs of governing operations are drawn from the cooperative's own resources without subsidies from the state. In all other cases, self-government becomes merely a pretense. The balance of rights and duties is the fundamental law of all viable state-building; this applies not only to the state as a whole, but also to its parts.

Under such circumstances, the Noble Cooperative is inconceivable without far-reaching legal powers—this circumstance requires special attention, for the Noble Cooperative has legal power only if it is able to legally enforce valid judgments. This logically leads to a corporate law that enjoys judicial protection against both the state administration and individuals, just as conversely the nobleman must be legally protected against abuses by his Noble Cooperative.

However, this must not be understood as the Noble Cooperative being entitled to its own court. Laws and courts must remain exclusively in the hands of the state. The Noble Cooperative only has the right to enact administrative statutes in accordance with the laws of the Reich, in accordance with common law, and limited to the purposes of the Noble Cooperative as recognized by the state. Only when the law and the courts remain firmly in the hands of the state is extensive self-governance possible without the state running the risk of its structure being weakened or even destroyed.

The genuine old German self-governing bodies were undoubtedly very powerful living entities, perhaps even a little too independent. A good self-governing body should relate to the state (if we want to revive old German principles in modern state garb) like an organ to an organism, that is, a body-part to the body-whole. Every highly developed living body has reached its advanced level of development through the separation of tasks (i.e. through the division of labor) on the one hand, and on the other hand through the strict standardization of everything related to the cohesion of the body parts and their relationships to one another. Anyone who wants to advocate for self-governing bodies must be clear about these things. This consideration should be made here first, so that it is clear from the outset that the following proposal for a self-governing structure for the Noble Cooperative never disregards the idea of state sovereignty, which is safeguarded in every respect. It should be emphasized in particular that state sovereignty is not understood here as state power. The idea of state sovereignty is only safeguarded when the state leadership and administration, including the means of power at their disposal, abide by the verdicts of an independent supreme court, i.e. remain servants of the whole.

Any self-governance that does not build itself up from its own resources, that does not bear full responsibility for its own actions, and that does not have its offices administered by fully responsible and unsalaried representatives is no longer self-governance by its very nature, but at best an imitation of the concept of self-governance. We should remember that all correctly managed self-governance automatically promotes genuine leadership (the men of true grit and mettle, as we like to say), while self-governance that is managed poorly drives away these genuine leaders and instead promotes the chatterers, the vain, and the strivers, where they are then able to puff themselves up and dominate the limelight, without, however, actually doing any useful work.

2

A book could be written about the construction of the self-governing body that is the Noble Cooperative. The reader will not hold it against me if, for the sake of clearly implementing a basic idea, detailed legal, legal-historical, historical, moral, and ideological explanations are avoided here. What follows below is a draft in the form of a basic outline drawn with a few brief strokes: at a minimum, the essential points have hopefully been taken into account.

The Noble Cooperative is the sum total of all of the *hegehöfe*, and thus also the sum total of all the noblemen and, importantly, of all the retired noblemen as well. The Noble Cooperative administers itself through the House of Nobles, which in a sense represents the superstructure of the whole.

In order to carry out an efficient distribution of labor, the Noble Cooperative would rely on groupings of *hegehöfe* united by region, tribe, or some other territorial unit, which can be called "Gau."[111] In doing so, a template-like allocation of territories can be avoided and the special features of tribes, environments, and the like can be taken into account as much as possible. The Gau is administered by the Chamber of Nobles.

Again, within a Gau, the *hegehöfe* which lie together in a district or otherwise belong together are united to form a Landschaft and administer their special tasks and affairs in the *Rat der Edelleute* (Council of Nobles). We thus obtain the following breakdown:

Noble Cooperative = House of Nobles

Gau = Chamber of Nobles

Landschaft = Council of Nobles

---

[111] Editor's note: the etymology of "Gau" appears to come from the Gothic *gawi*, meaning region or land, and the Old High German *gewi*, meaning district or region. It is roughly equivalent to the English "shire." The plural is "Gaue." At the time this book was written, the NSDAP was divided into thirty-three regional associations called "Gaue," with borders roughly matching the Weimar Republic's states and the provinces of Prussia. Like many other proposals in this book, a version of the Gau administrative system would be implemented during the NSDAP's time in power—the regional associations would later serve as units of civil administration; the Reich was divided into forty-two Reichsgaue in 1939.

All healthy self-government is characterized by its bottom-up structure with corresponding divisions of tasks, not by the reverse, see Chapter II, Section 1. We therefore begin with the Landschaft.

Landschaft = Council of Nobles

The noblemen and retired noblemen of the *hegehöfe* united in a Landschaft form the Council. Noblemen and retired noblemen have a seat and a vote in the Council. After their appointment, the candidates for *hegehof* inheritance sit on the Council with the right to observe and consult, but without a vote, in order to be trained as early as possible in the tasks of self-governance. They have no vote in order to adhere to the principle that only those who are feoffed with a *hegehof* (or were once feoffed and have departed honorably) belong to the nobility—not those who have merely been nominated for a *hegehof*. The Council has the task of answering and settling all questions of self-government in its local district.

The Landschaft has a chancellery whose administrative structure is left to the Council and which is exclusively subordinate to it; its name is the Council Chancellery. The Council's chancellery should be located in the most suitable place available in the countryside in terms of transport and postal services. Its structure and size should correspond to the scope of the tasks being performed—anything from an office on a conveniently located *hegehof* to a country house in a strategically located place, all possibilities can be considered.

However, it remains an open question whether the placement of the Council's location should be a pragmatic decision, e.g. whether it should be in the location of the Chancellery, or whether the Council should meet in alternating *hegehöfe*: the former is recommended for reasons of convenience in the facilitating of the business and conduct of the Council meetings, the latter for reasons of familiarizing the *hegehöfe* with one another and keeping them together—reasons which anyone who knows about and is experienced with life in remote rural districts will be able to understand without explanation.

The Council is led by the Alderman, who is supported by two assistants—the council assistants—one of whom manages the treasury and the other, the correspondence. Their term of office should probably be one year. The election of the Alderman shall take place publicly in the Council by acclamation and shall be decided by majority vote. Aldermen shall bear full responsibility for their actions, for which they shall be granted certain privileges in return. To ensure that he is truly and fully responsible, the two council assistants are not assigned to him by the Council, but are chosen by him from the council members. His election takes place publicly because of this responsibility, for he must know who trusts him and who does not. It is only fair that the assistants are not simply assigned to him, but that he is able to choose them according to he can trust rely upon.

The Aldermen and assistants shall vouch with their honor the honesty of their management. The course of business of the chamber is directly subordinate to the Aldermen.

Gau = Chamber of Nobles

The Chamber is not merely an intermediate administrative unit towards the next higher administrative level (the House of Nobles), but is an intermediate grouping interposed for reasons of expediency, standing between the Council and the House. The Chancellery of the Chamber is an intermediate administrative unit, but not the Chamber itself. The two must be kept clearly apart. Accordingly, the Chamber cannot be formed from deputies selected from the Landschaft Councils of its Gau, but rather from the nobility on the *hegehöfe* of its Gau.

Before the composition of the chamber is explained, a brief clarification should be included here: strictly speaking, as has already been pointed out, the Noble Cooperative should only be composed of noblemen, not retired noblemen. However, the restriction to noblemen would be inexpedient for reasons which have already been indicated, but which will be dealt with in more detail below and in the following section. Here only this much will be said—if a nobleman is forced to become a retired nobleman due to old age, this extends the time between families at a *hegehof*, a circumstance which is questionable with regard to supplying a people with a healthy abundance of children. If, however, the noblemen were required to become retired noblemen after reaching a certain age, then the time of successive families is regulated very favorably. Still, healthy noblemen would be placed in an unbearable, or at least a very unpleasant, situation. For handing over the *hegehof* to the successor would not depend on the nobleman being old and weak, but rather on the successor becoming marriageable.

For these reasons, retired nobles should be left with their full voice in the noble community, allowing their life experience to be utilized where it can have the greatest effect—within the local Landschaft and, as will be shown, in the House of Nobles. In these two places, the retired noblemen can always use their life experiences beneficially, indeed, they can impart on the noble community the necessary trait of steadfastness.

The Chamber itself, however, remains reserved for nobles, for the task of the Chamber will mainly be the handling of locally determined day-to-day issues; a business which, according to experience, is always best mastered by men who are in the prime of their years.

The meeting place of the Chamber should be pragmatic. In accordance with the fact that the nobles of a Gau are the Chamber, each *hegehof* receives a chair in the Chamber Hall. The retired nobles can take part in meetings in an advisory capacity, but without a vote, while the heirs can take part merely as guests. How often the plenary assembly of the Chamber should meet need not be discussed here. It would be expedient to elect an executive committee to deal with the day-to-day business. This Chamber Committee elects the Chamber Elder, called the Elder for short, from among its members. Similar to the Alderman, the Elder is fully responsible for the performance of his duties and therefore has the right to assemble the Board of the Chamber Committee from his closest associates among the nobles of the Chamber Committee. In addition to the Elder, the Committee Board will also be appropriately composed of: the Deputy Elder or Speaker, who, among other things, represents the Chamber Committee in Chamber meetings, which the Elder presides over; the Chamber Provost, who essentially manages the office administration and appoints a member of the Committee to serve as the Accounting Manager (Treasury); and the Superintendent of Education. Other offices may be held by members of the Committee. If necessary, other noblemen who are not members of the Committee may also be entrusted with occasional special assignments. All offices are unpaid honorary positions. Each nobleman shall vouch with his honor for the honesty of his conduct while in the position. Each nobleman shall bear full responsibility for the performance of his duties. With increasing responsibility, a measure of increased power must go hand in hand in such a way that the assumption of each self-governing office entails special duties and privileges in balance with one another. Only in this way is it possible for self-government to give genuine leaders an incentive to self-select. In this way we consciously incorporate the noble custom of the old English state ethos: equal rights for all, greater power for those who assume greater responsibilities.

The pragmatic nature of the questions of the Chamber's location, whether there is a necessity for a boardroom, and many other factors make it advisable to grant the Chamber its own assembly building. The Chamber Chancellery should be housed in or attached to this assembly building. The development of the Chancellery is left entirely up to the Chamber, which also hires and dismisses the officials of the Chancellery as it sees fit. Since the Chamber Elder is constantly changing, an older and proven civil servant should be appointed as the Chancellery Administrator, because otherwise the business of the Chancellery would suffer from a lack of continuity. Similarly, the management of finances will be entrusted to a treasurer from the civil service who will work directly with the Accounting Manager. Presumably, the Chancellery will also be divided into various other administrative branches, because we must bear in mind that genuine self-governing bodies must handle many responsibilities on their own which today are exclusively—and very unnecessarily—managed by the state alone; these responsibilities would be impossible to manage without a well-structured and well-managed Chancellery.

What has been discussed here applies exclusively to the self-governing body of the Gaue. However, the nobleman is not only a nobleman, but also a farmer, and therefore his professional self-governing body must also be briefly mentioned here.

In this way, what was hinted at the end of the last section can now be carried out, namely the close welding together of all the rural professions into a unified Landstand. This is only possible, however, if all the professions establish independent internal self-governance even as they carry out their professional self-governance together.

The professional self-governing body of the *hegehöfe* united in the Landstand is the Chamber of the Landstand, the Landstand Chamber. Its model could be today's Chamber of Agriculture, insofar as this still has features of genuine professional self-governance. All noblemen, peasants, small settlers, agricultural civil servants, and soil-rooted agricultural laborers, and, if applicable, also the non-rooted agricultural laborers (provided they are of German origin) of a district are members of the Landstand Chamber, so long as his profession has granted him full membership status on the basis of its cooperative corporate law. In other words, a member of the Landstand Chamber is anyone who has been granted permission to establish a household by the Landstand after an examination, irrespective of whether the person concerned makes use of the permission to establish a household or not. In this way, we are following an old German principle whose extractive value with regard to nurturing high-quality and constructive humanity deserves to be widely respected by those of us dedicated to the racial improvement of our people; at the very least, its advantage lies in the fact that among each new generation on every *hegehof*, the chaff is continuously—and to a certain extent, passively—separated from the wheat.

The details of how the Landstand Chamber is to be structured in detail and how it must be administered so that the noblemen, peasants, and small settlers are not outvoted by the superior number of agricultural workers and civil service officials, as well as how the principle of the balance of rights and duties can be maintained, is not a matter for this book, which is why it will not discussed here.

However, this much needs to be said: the Landstand Chambers of the Reich are united in the capital of the Reich in the Reich Chamber of the Landstands (the Reichslandstand Chamber), which facilitates the uniform cooperation of all Landstand Chambers. The Reichslandstand Chamber is the professional representation of the entire Landstand in relation to other professions and the Reich leadership. Consequently, it also sends representatives to the Chamber of Professional Estates of the Reich, where the professional issues of all German estates are discussed.[112]

In summary, the individual provincial professions are completely independent in their self-governance; each profession is divided in the same way, even if the scope of tasks is not always the same, like the Noble

---

[112] A Reich Ministry of Agriculture, or the present Reich Ministry of Food and Agriculture, will not become superfluous as a result. Even if the Reichslandstands Chamber and the Landstand Chambers of the Gaue take over some of the current tasks of the various ministries of agriculture, special public and administrative tasks will always remain with the Reich Ministry of Agriculture. The proposal was only to abolish the word "ministry," which is ugly to the German ear. Better would be: *Reichsamt* (Reich Office), for instance, *Reichsamt für Landwirtschaft* (Reich Office for Agriculture). Our word "minister" comes from the Latin "*minus*," meaning lesser, like magister from "*magis*," meaning more. In Roman imperial times, a minister was a freeman who was a domestic servant. The professional chamber of the Reich is, of course, subordinate to the management of the state. For wherever the economic interests of professions come into conflict with the demands of the common good, only the power of the supreme state authority can reconcile the differences to uphold common good and prevent the splintering of the nation for selfish reasons by individual professions.

Cooperative into local, Gau, and Reich representations. The Reich representation is in direct contact with state leadership. In practical terms, however, the individual provincial *hegehöfe* join together to form provincial Landstands to defend their interests uniformly and jointly against all external interests in the Chamber of Professional Estates of the Reich, and this through leaders who have the confidence of their professional comrades.

Noble Cooperative = House of Nobles

The House of Nobles is the sum of all nobles and retired nobles.

In accordance with the old German cooperative idea that we have adopted, a general assembly must be demanded, which could be called a Nobility Conference. The realization of Nobility Conferences as actual assemblies of all active and retired noblemen is likely impossible for reasons of space, but the idea must not be dropped altogether because of this and we must develop some other solution. Perhaps the following idea could resolve this: Nobility Conferences as general assemblies of all members of the noble community do not take place, rather, matters of particular importance are considered by the responsible Landschafts of the individual regions who thereupon commission and instruct representatives that then meet and form a Nobility Conference. The Nobility Conference is thus a representative assembly of the Landschaft Councils that meets in special cases to discuss questions of fundamental importance, and which would be independent of the leadership of the House of Nobles described below. The Nobility Conference can also pass resolutions and, given a supermajority of votes (about four-fifths of all those voting counted according to the votes of the individual Councils behind the representatives), can under these circumstances force the leadership of the House of Nobles to take the resolution of the Nobility Conference into consideration. The discussion of the matter is then continued in the House of Nobles, where the specifics of the resolution are worked out in detail. This legislation is then sent to each Council. Voting there takes place via a simple tabulation of votes from within the individual Councils. The principle of calling a plenary meeting of the Noble Cooperative on occasions that require the Nobility Conference is preserved by allowing the Nobility Conference to take place without being constrained by the limited space of a meeting hall.

In order to avoid the cumbersome workings of Nobility Conferences as much as possible and to only make use of them for really fundamental matters, the House of Nobles is generally led and managed by the Noble Assembly.[113]

The Noble Assembly is equivalent to the Chamber Committee, except that it is, of course, considerably more important. Its composition is based on three features: (a) It shall receive two elected representatives from each Landschaft, a nobleman and a retired nobleman; (b) It shall contain all the members of the Board of the Chamber Committee (Committee Board); (c) It contains up to a certain number of the most senior retired noblemen, as long as they are physically and mentally able to attend a Noble Assembly.

Regarding point a: the direct delegation of two representatives from each Landschaft to the Noble Assembly ensures the closest possible cooperation with agriculture, strengthens the unity of the nobility's ideas, and prevents any undue influence from the Chambers. There is a reason for the provision that one nobleman and one retired nobleman must be sent from each of the provinces—it prevents the retired nobles from exerting too much political (or even only psychological) influence on the nobles in the local Council, which could eventually lead to the exclusive nomination of retired nobles to the Noble Assembly and thus making senility a danger to both the Councils and the Noble Assembly. This policy also prevents the exclusive delegation of nobles and ensures that the retired nobles of each Landschaft retain a certain level of influence on the Noble Assembly.

Regarding point b: Even if, in general, the Chambers only serve to relieve the Noble Cooperative of some of its manifold tasks of self-governance, political interplay nevertheless requires that the Chambers be strongly represented in the Noble Assembly. The best way to achieve this is to make the members of the Committee Board also members of the Noble Assembly, with the restriction that they are not eligible for election to the Board of the Noble Assembly.

Regarding point c: This proposal stems from two considerations. Firstly, it must somehow be assured that the retired noblemen retain their participation and a feeling of co-responsibility for the affairs of the Noble Cooperative until their end; the prospect of one day being able to directly participate in shaping the direction of the Noble Cooperative as part of a

---

[113] The word *adelskapitel* (noble chapter) would also be correct here, but its foreign origin makes it unsuitable for a German nobility.

kind of council of elders will be an incentive for many retired noblemen to not become stagnant in their old age. Secondly: It must be ensured that the Noble Assembly—which is charged with the most important aspects of the actual management of the Noble Cooperative—also remains the guardian of its traditions. Since the execution of self-governance is reserved for the young noblemen from the Chambers, a permanent council of elders within the Noble Assembly could help ensure the continuity of the whole noble idea. Education in the respect of tradition can develop a spiritual strength in the members of a state or a corporation—a strength that is often required to withstand difficult stressors inherent to political life.

To carry out its tasks, the Noble Assembly elects a committee, the Noble Council, by first electing its leader—the Noble Master, and his deputy—the Herald, in a continuous run-off election until the final result is achieved. The Noble Master and the Herald are the leaders of both the Noble Assembly and the Noble Council. The members of the Noble Council are the Noble Lords; their number will be determined by experience. In the same way as in the Chambers, the Noble Lords are each appointed as the head of an administrative branch.

Just like the Chambers, the House of Nobles has a chancellery, the Noble Chancellery, which ensures the cooperation of all Chamber Chancelleries. We may imagine the headquarters building of the Noble Chancellery to be very extensive, with many different administrative branches as well as their offices and secretarial rooms. Such extensive infrastructure is necessary because having a well-thought-out and efficiently structured Noble Chancellery is a vital prerequisite for the health of the entire self-governing system, given the considerable assets available to the Noble Cooperative and its wide-ranging scope of tasks.

The House of Nobles should operate an assembly building in the Reich capital, purposefully combined with the Noble Chancellery, serving both as a meeting place and for dealing with social and other tasks; the furnishing of lounges for the members of the Noble Assembly and the furnishing of accommodations for the Noble Lords will have to be considered.

The Noble Assembly is a legally-binding decision-making body within the framework of the internal laws of the Noble Cooperative. Amendments to the statutes, on the other hand, are the exclusive prerogative of a Noble Conference—each amendment to the statutes only acquires legal validity through confirmation by state leadership.

Disputes of this kind, between the Reich and the Noble Cooperative, shall be settled by the Supreme Court of the German Reich; both the Noble Cooperative and the state, after the expiry of a sufficient interim period, shall have the right to appeal and request a new decision from the Supreme Court. This provision is necessary, because otherwise we run the risk of initiating an ossification of circumstances out of a respect for the Supreme Court; conversely, we make it possible for the Supreme Court to correct a judgment that may over time prove to be incorrect without damage to its reputation.

The Noble Master is the immediate and sole responsible liaison for all matters between the Reich leadership of the German People and the Noble Cooperative.

Summary

Local *hegehöfe* are grouped together in a Landschaft. The professional (agricultural) and social self-government tasks are managed by the Council of Nobles. The Council is the sum of all noblemen and retired noblemen of a Landschaft. The Council is led by an Alderman and his two council assistants. The actual administrative tasks are carried out by the Council Chancellery.

Several Landschafts together form a Gau. The professional (agricultural) self-governance tasks of the Gau are assumed by the Chamber of the Landstand, the Landstand Chamber. The social self-governance tasks of the Gaue are assumed by the Chamber of Nobles. This Chamber relies directly on the noblemen of its Gau, who in turn are the Chamber. The Chamber is led by the Chamber Assembly, which elects the Chamber Committee to take care of the day-to-day business, with its board members, the Elder, the Speaker, and the various department heads. The Chamber has a headquarters and an administrative building, the Chamber Chancellery. The Chamber Chancellery relies directly on the Council Chancelleries and overlaps them.

All nobles and retired nobles together are the Noble Cooperative. The House of Nobles manages the social self-governance tasks of the Noble Cooperative and represents the nobility externally. The plenary assembly of the Noble Cooperative is the Noble Assembly. The Noble Assembly relies directly on the Landschafts. To deal with the day-to-day business of the house, the Noble Assembly elects the Noble Council, after first electing the Noble Master and his deputy, the Herald. The members of the Noble Council are the Noble Lords. The House has an assembly building and an administrative building, the Noble Chancellery. The Noble Chancellery is based directly on the Chamber Chancelleries and overlaps them.

Special remarks

The English nobility acquired their power in the English state only through centuries of actively performing duties related to statecraft. The *raison d'être* of the majority of the English nobility is statesmanship. However well-known these things may be to us, it is not generally understood that the English nobility could only achieve this high level of involvement in affairs of state by restricting the free peasantry, i.e. by repressing and living off the rent of their tenants. Here we come up against a difficulty in our *hegehöfe* concept, because we do not want to have a rent-collecting nobility; on the other hand, we do not demand in any way that the nobility be merely the first servant of their *hegehöfe*, that is, that they limit their activity exclusively to agriculture on their *hegehöfe*. Treitschke is not wrong in saying, "There is either a political nobility or none at all." But he also says on another occasion, "Political bodies that bear no real responsibility for their actions either go wild or they lapse into slumber."

We must therefore give our nobility the opportunity to make an impact in the field of statecraft without turning them into a rentier aristocracy. Perhaps the following proposal will point the way forward:

If we have in Germany a Chamber of Professional Estates, it is only logical that a representative body which discusses the public and non-public questions of state governance can also be created. Whether this popular representation is composed purely by election or by partial election and partial appointment by the head of state is of no importance to us here. The only thing that is essential is that in such a representative body, a group of Germans meets expressly for the purpose of discussing questions fundamental to statecraft and dealing with affairs fundamental to statecraft, for all professional questions would be dealt with by the Chamber of Professional Estates. No matter how capable a person may have been in life and in his profession, no matter how much he may enjoy the confidence of his electorate, he is not necessarily a statesman in the true sense of the word, for this is a matter of active involvement. In many cases, even those that have the qualities of a born statesman frequently lack training, or at least the necessary confidence, to move onto the dangerous ground of statesmanship.

Therefore, it is conceivable that a certain percentage of seats in this representative body are life-long (we might say perhaps: one third) and are filled by the professional estates according to their discretion and a pre-determined allocation of seats—the appointment to such a seat then remaining with the selected person for life. Although each professional estate exclusively determines who receives the life-long seats granted to it, the estate is not in a position to remove a person from his seat after the appointment is made, so long as he is not guilty of a dishonorable act.

If we now secure for the Noble Cooperative a certain and influential number of seats in this percentage of life-long seats—in accordance with its inherited leadership qualities—and stipulate that these seats must be filled by the descendants of noblemen who did not inherit a *hegehof* and have passed the age of thirty (irrespective of the profession to which they had hitherto devoted themselves), as well as that the Noble Cooperative would be responsible for the salary and livelihood of these delegates, then we have ensured that the Noble Cooperative will be closely integrated into this representative body and assured its participation in all questions of statecraft. This need not exclude the possibility of sending noblemen or retired noblemen from case to case.

Our people will only benefit from such a representative body if there are not just men whom they have chosen and those whom their leader has trusted enough to nominate, but also those who—free from economic worries—have made their life's work the familiarization and comprehension of all questions of internal and external state governance; men who, because of the longevity of their seat, are unbiased by the trends and the opinions of the day. In this way we obtain men who are able to think through the question of state governance with the same rigor as they would have if they were discussing the very fate of the Reich in the heart of Europe.

Where states are ruled by a nobility, they have the advantage of leveraging the governance experience that develops in their ruling families and is passed on from fathers to sons. This is the source of the so often admired steadfastness of such rulers in all matters of statesmanship. The only possibility of achieving something similar by other means is probably to be found only in the plan, roughly outlined above, of a representative body that could be called the Upper House, in which a portion of the members are able to see the occupation of statecraft as their life's work. The rest of the members of the Upper House, on the other hand, are elected and appointed from active life on the basis of extraordinary achievements, thus linking the Upper House more closely with living reality. In this way, one part of the Upper House assures the German Reich with a continuity of leadership and experienced statesmen, while the other part is entrusted with stimulating an awareness of the practicalities of the daily struggle and the questions of the day. In this way, the members of one part do not become disconnected men "from the green table"[114] who are alienated from daily reality, and the other members, who come from active life, are prevented from overestimating the importance of their previous professional experience—instead, their colleagues teach them how to view the questions of the Reich from a great and statesmanlike perspective.

The Chamber of Professional Estates could be called the Lower House. Upper House and Lower House—a very clear and concise division of state government that is comprehensible to even simplest person.

* * *

It would be significant and undoubtedly successful if the Reich decided to have a very specific percentage of its Foreign Office civil servants come from the ranks of the non-inheriting sons of noblemen, whose upkeep and facilities the nobility would have to provide—no privilege without obligations! The civil servant would of course be paid by the state. In a similar way, all other professional estates should also be authorized to take on, as it were, sponsorship for young candidates in the career of the Foreign Office from their circles. Indeed, this could even be made obligatory for the professional estates. For the prosperity of every professional estate depends on the skill of the Foreign Office of the Reich. Therefore, the best that a nation possesses in terms of statesmanship

---

[114] Editor's note: A decision made *am grünen tisch*, meaning "at the green table," describes a decision made by bureaucrats or negotiators with little relevance to reality or practice. In Christian liturgical colors, green is considered neutral and is thereby suitable for negotiations. In depictions of the signing of the United States Declaration of Independence at the Pennsylvania State House in Philadelphia, green tablecloths are shown being used. The Cabinet Room table at the British Prime Minister's residence is also green. The color remains popular for negotiation tables in nations with a history of English or German rule.

certainly belongs in the civil service of the Foreign Office. However, experience has shown that this is only feasible if enough funding is available so that the applicant's paternal or father-in-law's finances can be disregarded; the profession of foreign service cannot be limited by the traditional concept of frugality.

* * *

The question of who regulates new admissions to the Noble Cooperative is solved by having the Reich leadership and the Noble Councils have an equal say in this. If estates, cities, tribes, or regions want to see some deserving man admitted to the Noble Cooperative, perhaps at the same time donating the necessary *hegehof,* then they turn to the Reich leadership, which would then pass the case to the Noble Cooperative; the interested party could also contact the Noble Cooperative directly. If the Noble Council believes that it can give its approval and if the Reich leadership also agrees, then there are no more difficulties standing in the way of admission. If, however, the Noble Council believes it must refuse approval, it will first present the reasons for this to the Reich leadership. If, however, the Reich leadership insists on the admission, i.e. if it rejects the reasons of the Noble Cooperative, the Noble Council passes the matter on to the Noble Assembly. If the Assembly backs the Noble Council, but the Reich government still insists on admission, the case comes before the Supreme Court of the German Reich for a final decision, where it is conclusively settled, and both the Reich government and the Noble Cooperative submit to the decision. In this way, the nobility retains the ability to keep itself free of undesirable people, just as the state is given assurances that this right will never degenerate into an arrogant separation of the nobility from the people. For any caste-like separation would be contradictory to the sensibilities of both our nobility and our people.

* * *

Despite the strict standardization of the main leadership in the House of Nobles, the proposed structure of the nobility is still quite flexible and its overall form is very suitable for adapting to the most varied circumstances potentially caused by regional or tribal idiosyncrasies. However, such a system always carries the possibility of developing its own idiosyncrasies. Even if the diversity of the German character and its spiritual life was not in the least an impetus for the particularly highly developed German civilization, the danger of fragmentation does easily arise from it. A special task of the House of Nobles will be to establish an intellectual connection between all nobles as firmly as possible. First and foremost, a Noble Journal is recommended in the form of a weekly or monthly magazine that is sent to every *hegehof* and which stimulates the desired intellectual connection. The ability to speak freely in it should be the basic right of every nobleman and retired nobleman. Only in this way is it possible to preserve the liveliness of the content and to avoid the decline of the Noble Journal into a paper of indoctrination, which, as is well known, is always a great risk when public life is in a state of external and intellectual tranquility.

* * *

Courts of Honor: a nobleman who does not protect his honor is no longer a nobleman in our sense. The sanctity of his honor must be the nobleman's moral guide. Therefore, the whole *hegehof* idea is inconceivable without a Court of Honor and a Council of Honor.

As a matter of principle, even duels must not be eliminated. Anyone who does not have the courage to defend his honor with a weapon (if necessary) does not belong in the nobility. It must, however, be ensured that in every case that a weapon is used among noblemen, there was a real reason to do so. Therefore, it should be stipulated that every duel may only take place if it is approved by a Supreme Council of Honor at the House of Nobles. Ruffians do not belong in the nobility! In order to stamp them out, it would first have to be determined whether the challenger or the challenged have disregarded noble comportment in the creation of their quarrel. A legitimate nobleman of true vigor must not be expected to respond with a weapon to the undignified behavior of a fellow nobleman; in many cases, the undignified person must be punished, but a weapon must not be used.

The establishment of a Supreme Council of Honor at the House of Nobles is also necessary for other reasons. The judicial training for the Judges of Honor in the local Courts of Honor will generally not be sufficient to fairly judge issues with such far-reaching legal consequences; for example, what an expulsion from the Noble Cooperative entails for the person concerned. The establishment of a Supreme Council of Honor would make it possible to correct hasty lower court decisions. For educational reasons, it might be demanded that the summaries and minutes of every Court of Honor or Council of Honor meeting be submitted to the Supreme Council of Honor at the House of Nobles for examination and safekeeping. Otherwise, it could very easily happen that, although the individual nobleman is protected against attacks from within the cooperative by its internal law, independent spirits or other loners could be targeted by a local clique out of revenge, envy or other unfriendliness via the Courts of Honor.

* * *

Any scenario that could breed Junkerism is to be avoided. The term Junker means the non-inheriting son of a nobleman who receives nothing from the inheritance of the eldest, but who has the right to live unmarried on the inheritance until the end of his life. Therefore, we will have to demand that the non-inheriting sons of the *hegehöfe* can claim a right of support only until their professional training is complete, with the right expiring upon the completion of their training. Precautions can be taken to ensure that this provision is not abused by idle sons. For example, it would be advisable to have the support costs borne not by the father, but by the whole Gau; on the one hand, so as to not "punish" the bearing of children and to distribute the burden of raising children, and on the other hand, to inspire the interest of the whole Gau in the promotion of its gifted sons and to make it difficult for the incompetent to take advantage of their parents' blindness.

Moreover, the non-inheriting sons could perhaps buy into a kind of retirement home over the course of their lives by means of small payments, which would always ensure them a carefree old-age residence, be it with or without family. In this way, a certain attachment to the old homeland could be maintained, which always benefits the whole. I can think of several reasons why it is not appropriate to grant the non-inheriting sons a life-long right of residence for themselves and their family on the *hegehöfe*.

3

Things should be judged differently when it comes to daughters. As is well known, unmarried women from good families who are independent in their occupation or position in life have always played the role of disrupters—even destroyers—of order in history. More heroic ages than ours have not been able to cope with this. In most cases, education and customs are of no help.

If we were to propose the same for daughters as for sons, we would most likely experience quite unpleasant surprises; at a minimum, a preference by our daughters for the unattached professional life could set in, which would be of no use to anyone and which would probably bring about a kind of modern *hetaera*[115] economy—towards which we are currently heading into due to the independent nature of our modern daughters and women. However, we should not presume that women will ever give up the opportunity to work freely, a privilege that they have long fought for.

As with the sons, the daughters of the *hegehöfe* shall have the right to be trained in an occupation that suits them. The support expires with the completion of their vocational training. For reasons of general morality, however, it must be demanded that the Noble Cooperative provide proper accommodations for its working daughters—be it in the form of a bursa (university cooperative), as exemplified by the Viktoria-Studienhaus in Berlin-Charlottenburg, or by placing them with families. All this can be done and arranged in such a way that the freedom of the individual professional woman is not restricted. The present circumstances of our working and independent daughters is impossible for our people to maintain in the long run for moral reasons.

The possibility that professional daughters could buy into retirement homes should also be considered. However, the seat in the retirement home must be earned and saved for—this must also be the case for sons—and must by no means be a common end of life scenario for people of noble birth. For this reason, retirement homes do not have to be built exclusively on the savings of their dependents.

* * *

A brief word about the noblewoman. A man is born a nobleman or appointed one by virtue of his own special achievements in the service of the German people. A woman becomes a noblewoman through courtship

---

115 Editor's note: the *hetaerae* of ancient Greece were highly educated, often independent women who provided entertainment, companionship, and sexual services to men.

by a nobleman, i.e. it is up to the woman in question whether she wants to become a noblewoman or not.

Therefore, the question of what tasks noblewomen are charged with has nothing to do with the academic question of the position of women in public life. Those who become noblewomen do so consciously with an understanding of the tasks expected of a noblewoman—the tasks of the housewife and mother. If they don't want that, they don't have to become a noblewoman. The decision is up to each individual woman.

Because the noblewoman on a *hegehof* has to manage a clearly defined and rather firmly delineated number of tasks (which run alongside that of her husband's, but hardly intersects with his), she does not belong in the self-governing body of the noblemen. Instead, the noblewomen should have their own self-government, which facilitates their distinctive tasks. The noblewomen of a Landschaft can unite to form a *Frauenschaft* (women's society), like the Councils of their husbands. Building on this, they can then join their Chambers and have high-level representation in the House of Nobles. The details of how the women in the Chambers and in the House of Nobles interact with the self-governing body of the Noble Cooperative and cooperate with it is a question which does not have to be discussed nor answered here. Let it be left to experienced women!

VII

The Basic Ideas of Breeding Duties and Marriage Laws

"The German Reich will never rise again if good German blood does not rise again in it."

Ruedolf

1. Introduction

"I am annoyed when I see the pains taken to make pineapples, bananas, and other exotic plants thrive in this harsh climate, while so little care is taken for the human race. Say what you will, man is more valuable than all the pineapples in the world. He is the plant that must be cultivated, that deserves all our toil and care, for it forms the adornment and glory of the fatherland."

Frederick the Great[116]

There is no doubt that if Frederick the Great had the misfortune of being our contemporary, the ranks of his historical enemies would certainly have been supplemented by a group of Germans who would have viciously condemned him for his audacity in wanting to adapt plant breeding techniques to the human race. For today, it is part of the intellectual accessories of the absolute idealist to consider the adaptation of any breeding policies (as have been applied in the animal or plant world) to man as an expression of material worship, "materialism" in the

116 Compared works of Frederick the Great in the translation by Friedrich von Oppeln-Bornikowsky, published by Reimar Hobbing, Berlin 1913, volume VIII, pages 266-7.

most unpleasant meaning of the word.

Such a hostile attitude against the transfer of breeding concepts to human beings generally goes back to ideological concerns. A few things will be said about this in the following pages, because we very well cannot create a nobility if it is not subjected to some type of breeding rules.

The fact that today's Germans consider any effort to associate questions of breeding with those of the public good to be the opposite of idealism is in itself an intellectual curiosity, because for centuries what these Germans now condemn was considered by our people to be an expression of custom and morality. It is perhaps even more strange that this is happening in a nation where, for example, a hundred years ago, no apprentice craftsman could rise to the rank of master craftsman unless he could produce proof of his unobjectionable ancestry, nor could he ever reach his master's rank if he chose a woman of unknown or undesirable origin as his wife. Not only the nobility, but also craftsmen and Germanic peasants deliberately practiced breeding in Germany until the nineteenth century. It is surprising to find the old traditional German marriage laws filled with wisdom about the interdependence of blood and civilization, especially in those cases where the Germans consciously created a blood barrier—for example against the Slavs. All this knowledge seems to have been lost to our people today, and we have carelessly gotten to the point where he who acknowledges the necessity of observing such things runs the risk of attracting the antagonism of precisely some of the best of our people.

The opposition today often stems from a certain agitation about the word "breeding." But applying this word to human reproduction is not something new that is being adopted from animal or plant breeding! No, in earlier times the word "breeding" was used for all living things; only later did its use almost disappear with regard to human beings, while very much surviving with regard to animals and plants.

The derivation of the word *zucht* (breeding) is accordingly quite clear: our word *zucht* is related to the verb *ziehen* (to pull/drag/grow). One of the meanings of *ziehen* can be seen in the German phrase "*das und das ziehen*" (to grow this and that), meaning "to cultivate." Derived from the same root are: Old High German *zuhtîg*, meaning pregnant or bearing, which in Middle High German was still called *zühtic*, meaning well-bred (in the sense of fertile or fruit-bearing). The etymology of the word *ziehen* being connected to the concept of breeding can readily be traced to its

Germanic original form: Dutch *tucht* and Old Frisian *tocht*, meaning fertility or procreation, and Gothic *ustauhts*, meaning consummation.[117] This explains words such as *züchten* (breeding) meaning chaste in Middle High German. A "chaste" virgin was therefore not a woman who completely ignored sexual matters, but a woman who remained aware of her "duty to breed."

For our ancestors, the concept of breeding applied within the framework of acceptable possibilities related to the procreation of all things. Accordingly, the opposite of breeding in this sense was *unzucht* (fornication). "Fornication" referred to all acts of sexual intercourse which grossly violated the limitations set on sexual intercourse by the people's moral views and customs. It should be noted that the word "fornication" has been understood in different ways over the course of German cultural history. For example, to our ancestors, having a child out of wedlock was not unchaste if there was nothing indecent in the parentage of the child; such behavior was perhaps unseemly, possibly even immoral (at least in the eyes of the Christian Church), but by no means unchaste. In contrast, today, for example, the production of an illegitimate child by a married person is punishable via the Civil Code, since an illegitimate child is grounds for divorce, and is thus, strictly speaking, considered fornication.

The ancient connection of the word *zucht* with child-bearing, however, becomes clearest from a third word: *notzucht* (*stuprum violentum*). Significantly, this word is today mostly used incorrectly, as it is understood to mean any "rape." Nothing is as conclusive of the fact that our people have lost their natural connection to the word *zucht* as the incorrect use of the word *notzucht* in public life (with the exception of lawyers, of course). In common law, *notzucht* is the term used to describe the violent gratification of a sexual desire against a respectable woman or an innocent girl. The violation of a disreputable woman or girl was fornication, but not rape. Today, the average person will not understand the subtle difference between fornication and rape. But anyone who knows that marriage was originally largely a breeding concept—and that it essentially represented a protection of blood—is not surprised that our ancestors developed two different terms to describe a sexual aberration (fornication) and an act that endangered the purity of the offspring (rape); it is not surprising either that our ancestors also judged the acts very

---

[117] Wieigand, *Deutsches Wörterbuch (German Dictionary).*

differently. Whoever forcibly violated a virgin (which, by the way, a free woman was understood as being, because the unfree woman was a *dirne* (harlot), from the Old High German *diorna*, which is related to the Old High German *diu*, meaning servant) or a respectable woman, was—in accordance with the thinking of our ancestors—directly violating the blood heritage, which was close to the heart of the family as well as that of the national community. Rape created the possibility that a bastard, i.e. a child of inferior descent—a so-called *kegel*[118]—would be born in secret and was thus an act that related to the property of the family or the people, namely to their blood heritage. Incidentally, the Germanic did punish the violation of unfree girls or women, no matter what their reputation; but in this case not because of a danger to the hereditary stock, but because of the flaw in the perpetrator's character revealed by the deed—this was considered fornication and not rape. It is therefore not surprising to find the provision that rape is punishable with execution by the sword in Article 119 of Charles V's 1532 *Halsgerichtsordnung (Procedure for the Judgment of Capital Crimes)*.[119]

---

[118] The *kegel* was a child born of inferior parentage, either in or out of wedlock. In general, it was understood to mean the offspring that the master of the house conceived with unfree women or girls, while his offspring conceived in marriage were *kinder* (children) in the true sense of the word; the expression "*mit kind und kegel*" (with bag and baggage) derives from earlier times when the *kegel* grew up together with the children in the father's house. *Kegel* were, of course, also the offspring of unmarried freemen with unfree girls or women. In contrast, children born out of wedlock whose parents were freemen on both sides were not *kegel*, but *winkelkinder* (corner child). There was no stigma attached to these children, but in general they could not claim the same inheritance rights as their father's legitimate children. For example, in 1375, the entire Holstein knighthood asked their count to recognize the *winkelkind* of the last lord of Westensee, but the count refused for political—not moral—reasons. Until modern times, illegitimate children of the nobility were considered equal if the mother was of the same rank; the situation was similar with regard to the attainment of full membership in a guild or the granting of full legal capacity within the free peasantry. As you can see, these concepts have nothing to do with our modern notions of illegitimacy and marriage. A *kegel* could be born in a marriage and a *winkelkind* could only be born illegitimately, which is why the *kegel* never attained the legal capacity of the necessarily illegitimate *winkelkind*. Only the Church, in a centuries-long struggle, has brought things to the point today where a child is no longer judged according to its parentage, but according to whether or not he or she was born in a sexual union approved by the Church.

[119] Editor's note: The 1532 *Halsgerichtsordnung*, also known as the Constitio Criminalis Carolina, is generally accepted as being the first criminal and civil legal code in Germany. It was based in large part on the criminal code of the Bishopric of Bamberg, which was in turn based on Roman law.

We can see that the word "breeding" was based on the intention of striving for perfection through a sexual union centered on procreation, in other words—sexuality was regarded as a conscious means of furthering human development and of safeguarding the best of human existence, see Chapter III, Section 1.

Breeding is the applied knowledge of heredity. It is completely irrelevant whether this knowledge (that there is indeed a heredity of physical and mental predispositions and that people are therefore hereditarily different) was acquired through a belief in a family's divine origin (or some other corresponding ancestral origin) or through observation of human life or through both—as was obviously the case with our forefathers—or whether it was established in an erudite manner with modern devices such as calipers, measuring tapes, magnifying glasses, experiments, and arithmetic. The fact that up to the nineteenth century, the entire social structure of our nation was based on class equivalence in marriages clearly proves that our people have been imbued with the idea of breeding (in the most original sense of the word) for one and a half millennia—and this in spite of Christianity, which makes the circumstance even more remarkable. By filtering which relatives and women were eligible for marriage, each generation consciously practiced breeding. It also irrelevant whether the breeding goal was deliberate and had a material, so to speak, realistic target image (selection model) and was thus subject to racial evaluations, as is more or less clearly indicated in the demarcation ordinances against the Slavs—or whether the goal was only indirectly present via the selection of mental and physical advantages of more immediate importance (for example, with the evaluation of a woman's competence as a housewife, etc.). In either case, they were aware of the significant role that women played in passing down the hereditary traits vital for the future of the family, and, based on their knowledge and ability, tried their best to prevent any damage to the institution of marriage, which determined the future course of the family, for good or bad. So if, until about a hundred years ago, no apprentice craftsman—to say nothing of the nobility and the urban patrician class—could become a master craftsman without proving that he was born of a "legitimate marriage," and that the same was true for his four grandparents, this proves that the whole of German civilization was consciously built on breeding for a millennium and a half—a breeding concept to which the legal system was subordinate to just as much as it in turn was conditioned by it, and which must be called the eternal rock on which the civilization of the German people rested. It is therefore either simple thoughtlessness or gross ignorance of the history of German civilization and customs when Germans today protest against the hereditary scientific evaluation of our people on the grounds that it is spiritually degrading to use the word "breeding" (this "animal" appropriate concept) in connection with the German people.

By combining breeding objectives with class privileges, the old German marriage law acted like a filter which only allowed performance-tested blood to produce fully legitimate children; it also provided a safeguard that protected the tested blood to such an extent that times of struggle and privation did not have a negative effect on the founding of families or the number of children produced. This old German marriage law was the bulwark that protected valuable German humanity and kept sub-humanity out of the German social order by considerably limiting its possibilities for reproduction—sometimes even making it impossible. It must be emphatically pointed out that the present victory of "sub-humanity" (which the American Lothrop Stoddard wrote about in his well-known work *The Revolt Against Civilization, the Menace of the Under Man,* which discussed a question being considered by today's geneticists, namely the root causes of the excessive growth of inferior and undesirable populations—i.e. human races that have an unfavorable influence on the German social order) has only become a problem for the German people as a result of Hardenberg's decision about a hundred years ago to embark on a path that was bound to end in the current dismantling of all restrictions on marriage. Read what Freiherr vom Stein, with a clear understanding of the causal connections, proclaimed to the German people regarding these insane measures:

> It is convincing that our present condition is solely the consequence of having turned away from that time's German views on marriage, thus creating the subsoil upon which inferiority of all kinds could thrive. If we today declare the "demographic struggle of the races" as the reason for this decline, we are confusing cause and effect.

Every legal system has not only an educational effect, but also an effect on the breeding of the people as a whole, even if the individual person is not always aware of this. The social order is the living expression of the legal system. To use an analogy from natural history—the social order burns up as fuel the intrinsic values of the people. In this sense, it is less important that something is being burned up and more important what is being burned up. This "what" determines the "how" of the social order, and is directly dependent on the legal system. It can therefore be said that the legal system has a significant and decisive importance on the inherited values of a people, since it determines which human values are promoted and which are inhibited or even eradicated.

The legal structure, however, is an expression of a worldview. We therefore get the following chain of causes and effects: worldview—legal system—social order—breeding—manifestation of human physical characteristics. Applied to our people, this means that: Christianization and late Romanism changed the worldview of the Germanic peoples, thus shifting their legal conceptions in an un-Germanic direction; it is, as explained above, quite logical then that both German-Germanic civilization and the Germanic appearance of the German people are now being displaced by increasingly un-Germanic elements.

Wildhagen, in his excellent *Der Englische Volkscharakter (The English National Character)* points to the selective and thus formative power of the English social order, which, building on the foundation of Old Saxon law, has been shaped by English history without undergoing any significant change. However, Wildhagen underestimates the value and importance of race. For it is not the case that every development of a thousand years of English history and what is now the English social order had to result in the Englishman as he is today. It is rather the case that the English were able to give their political life a legal system which, through its objectives and its selective effects, created a social order that, so to speak, automatically kept the original Germanic humanity of the Anglo-Saxons alive. This allowed it to largely keep its Germanic spirit alive in surprisingly good condition right up until the present day, responding to external stimuli in a reasonably consistent manner.

Anyone who leaves his plants in a garden and abandons them will be surprised to find that in a short time all of his plants will be overgrown with weeds, i.e. that the appearance of the plant population has changed fundamentally. Therefore, if the garden is to remain a place of plant development—i.e. if it is to rise above the harsh forces of nature—then the creative will of a gardener is required. A gardener that, with a caring hand, nurtures (whether by making suitable living conditions available or by keeping away harmful influences or by both measures together) what should be nurtured, and, with a cutting hand, weeds out anything that might rob the higher-quality plants of sufficient air, light, and sun. This is exactly how the old German legal system was applied to the Germanic people, whose weeding and nurturing undoubtedly arose out of the Germanic people's ideological blood consciousness, and which created the conditions for the existence, preservation, and advancement of the Germanic people.

We are thus faced with the realization that questions of breeding are not trivial political matters, but that they must be at the center of all considerations, and that their solutions must come from the spiritual and ideological attitudes of the people. We must even say that the spiritual and moral equilibrium of a people is only achieved when a well-understood breeding mentality is at the center of its civilization.

This results in two things for us. Firstly, that we cannot treat the breeding duty of the German nobility as simply related to the creation of the new nobility proposed here, but that we must consider it as part of the broader breeding mission of the whole people. And secondly, that we have to consider the ideological core of the question. We want to first touch on the ideological part of the matter here, even if only briefly.

This topic also falls into two parts that need to be kept separate: the question of *whether* a person should breed is purely ideological, whereas the question of *how* to breed is only conditionally ideological, because the *how* is closely linked to the empirical laws of heredity, which we have no choice but observe. We shall see that the failure to distinguish between the *whether* and the *how* has led to a *rattenkönig*[120] of conceptual confusion.

For those of us who promote a German-Germanic civilization, there can be no doubt about the *whether*, because civilization cannot be maintained without the concept of breeding. The answer to the question of *whether* is therefore a resounding "yes." However, anyone who promotes a German-Germanic civilization and nevertheless believes that he must deny the *whether* must at least give explanations for his attitude, because his assertion is in clear contradiction to the totality of the experiences of German civilization and customs. Unfortunately, these experiences are usually not taken into account, and thus the situation arises that demands are made for an ideologically German attitude or

---

[120] Editor's note: a *rattenkönig*, or "rat king," is a group of rats whose tails have been knotted or glued together by a variety of means. While technically possible in nature, most examples of rat kings are largely considered to be hoaxes. In German folklore, rat kings are considered to be bad omens associated with confusion and sickness.

stance that simultaneously denies the importance of breeding, which invites into the discourse thoroughly un-German concepts about the direction and development of Germanism, absolutely confusing the whole matter. It is possible that one day there will be a so-called Germanism that will no longer have anything to do with any kind of breeding—we basically have already come a very long way towards this state of affairs; for today's very un-German moral life, like a foreign rice that has been grafted onto a native plant, still draws its energy and strength from old German ideas and is already producing very un-German blossoms. Evidence for the existence of a genuine German-Germanic civilization or custom without any inherent breeding concepts is nowhere to be found in the entire course of German history, or at least it has not yet been found.

So if we affirm *whether* and now turn to the *how*, we are unfortunately faced with the realization that we are now entering a discourse in which a deplorable amount of confusion prevails.

The *how* more or less assumes the hereditary inequality of human beings. It is now necessary to make some kinds of classifications within the flowing inequality in order to find any sorts of boundaries and designations. This has also been done, and it has been agreed that certain groups of people who are self-consistent in their identity and heredity should be called *rassen* (races). Unfortunately, the word *rasse* is not very well chosen for us Germans, because our historical word for ourselves is actually *art*, meaning "kind," (*arteigen*, meaning "intrinsic," *unartig*, meaning "wicked," *aus der art schlagen*, meaning "to differ from the rest," and so on). For reasons of scientific etymology, however, *art* and *rasse* are not interchangeable. *Rasse* is therefore a term introduced into science for reasons of expediency, and which makes it possible to establish certain classifications within the manifold manifestations of human inequality, which can then be judged and evaluated.

It has become apparent that what we call human civilization and what essentially constitutes history has obviously been dependent on and is still is to very specific races. From this, the concept of race stepped out of the purely scientific realm and became a tool for evaluating people in terms of civilization and customs. In the field of racial studies, this doctrine was expanded, and in applied racial studies, attempts are today being made to evaluate the findings of racial studies and utilize them for the betterment of human society.

The procedures for this evaluation should be quite simple. If it can be established that this or that race exclusively or predominantly creates civilization, and that this civilization's condition and existence depends on the race in question, then the task is basically very simple—the race to which the desired or conserved civilization is bound with must be preserved and advanced. Strangely enough, this simple conclusion is reached by very few, and those who make demands based on this conclusion even fewer. A large proportion of racial scientists, and with them a correspondingly large audience, want to avoid the assessment of natural phenomena (including race)—which is necessary for natural science—and relegate themselves exclusively to questions of ethics. But this means avoiding taking a stand because you no longer can or are not willing to do so. This mixing of the purely empirical, natural-scientific standpoint with an unempirical one, which is concerned with the ethics of race, produces a great confusion; the confusion is increased by those who also mix in ideological concerns without separating them according to *whether* and *how* (see above). A few things need to be said about this.

The difficult question of the relationship between the spiritual and the material cannot be dealt with comprehensively here, but we must at least touch on it. Although there are no empirical facts from which we can conclude that the spirit is able to simply suspend the laws of nature, many people—even those who are adherents of the doctrine of heredity—proceed as if this was a fact, as if there were a dominion of the spiritual over the material that is not bound to any law of nature. Now we can well imagine—though not prove—that the human soul could one day free itself from the laws of nature in the afterlife; but for this world it is true that the soul can only shape the natural world by observing its laws. Let us use an example to illustrate this. The architecture of a building is an expression of the architect's spirituality. This fact, however, in no way cancels out the laws of physics, the enforcement of which is carried out by the building material. The architect, for all his spirituality, cannot simply disregard the laws of gravity, the durability of his stones, the effects of the weather, and so on. The architect is merely a person who masters the building material through his spirituality. The building depends on the mastery of the material by the spiritual, but the laws of nature cannot be disregarded simply because a person possesses spirit.

Regarding the racial question, similar misconceptions about the relationship between spirit and material are currently in vogue. This confusion of concepts has clearly arisen in the public discourse since Clauß wrote his two well-known works: *Die Nordische Seele (The Nordic*

Soul; Halle 1923) and *Rasse und Seele (Race and Soul*; Munich 1926). But Clauß is not responsible for the resulting confusion. He too wanted the soul to be evaluated as a racial characteristic and thus strove for the spiritual assessment of race, but he did not seek to dispute the physical restrictions of race and the underlying material laws. Even his pupil, Friedrich Wilhelm Prinz zur Lippe, in his book *Vom Rassenstil zur Staatsgestalt (From Racial Style to National Character)*, certainly does not reject the physically-restricted laws of nature with regard to the question of race. For example, he expressly says: "Each soul can only manifest fully in and through a body appropriate to its kind." Nevertheless, Clauß's ideas had an effect on certain circles of people who believed that the affirmation of the existence of racial souls allowed them to disregard the physical laws of race.

Now it is not to be claimed that things are as simple here as in the example of the architect. But the following must be said: opinions regarding the essence of the soul belong to metaphysics, and are therefore ultimately a matter of faith. No matter what a person believes to be the essence of the soul, we are by no means entitled to simply overlook the laws of nature. We certainly have similar cases where we know nothing of the essence of a thing but must nevertheless observe the laws of the physical world within which and through which the unknown thing functions. We do not know, for example, what gravity is, what electricity is.[121] Our hypotheses about them may be very different, but in all cases we must take into account and investigate the laws of their effects on the material world. The scrupulous separation of questions of spirituality from those of empirical research into the laws of nature has proven its worth in physics—for example, wherever it was necessary to make the essentially incomprehensible indirectly comprehensible and, above all, usable through its behavior in the material world. It is precisely this last point that should give us food for thought.

C. Schleich stated in *Von der Seele (From the Soul*; Berlin 1926) that the possibility certainly exists of increasing our understanding about the incomprehensible soul by means of our current knowledge, in a way similar to that which is done in physics. He understood the body as the tangible material expedient of an incomprehensible, or at the very least intangible, force—precisely the soul or some other vital power—formed

[121] Editor's note: Written in 1930, this book precedes major scientific developments in the theory of general relativity and electromagnetism.

in order to overcome the material resistances of this world and the effects of the other beings living in it. Ludwig Klages once said the same thing in a slightly different form, "The soul is the sense of the body and the body is the appearance of the soul."

In direct connection with this intellectual doctrine, although hardly starting from it, Clauß, already mentioned above, transfers the same ideas to the study of the human races, writing:

> Through the movement of the body, through its mode of expression, or through the way it responds to external stimuli of every kind, the mental processes that have led to these actions become an expression in space thus—the body becomes the soul's means of expression. According to this, the soul is not the body, but it possesses it.

Clauß then used the different physicality of the human races to draw conclusions about an equally different spirituality. He says the following (paraphrased): the physical appearance of every race on Earth is the means of expression of racially-different or differently-tinted souls. He thus shifts the crux of the racial question—and thus also of heredity—from the material to the spiritual. There is no doubt that Clauß thus made a highly noteworthy contribution to the knowledge of German spiritual life and enriched the field of humanities research. It must also be noted that, philosophically speaking, his approach does not necessarily contradict that of the scientifically-minded racial researchers. For if, with the so-called psychophysical parallelism, spirit and material are ultimately regarded as simply two different ways of looking at the same reality, then it is logically necessary that the laws of heredity—of both the natural world and of the spiritual—behave in the same way.

We can leave such questions to the philosophers!

Unfortunately, the above-mentioned books by Clauß and Prince zur Lippe have had an effect on a wide audience which was obviously not foreseen by the two and hardly intended, but which very much concerns us here. A portion of the readership believes that when it comes to race, they can ignore the scientifically-proven facts of heredity as well as racial theory in general—any affirmation of the influence of the physical laws of race on questions concerning the further development of the German people is summarily dismissed as a view caught up in material thinking, i.e. as materialism; they stamp themselves as "idealists." A man who says, "It is possible that electricity is not a material thing, so I don't need to adhere to the laws of nature when building electrical machines" is just as "idealistic." We would like to see the machines of this idealist running!

Whether we look for the source of the laws of heredity in the material (that is, in the body), or in an unknown elemental force, or in the soul, we are nevertheless obliged to observe the material laws of heredity, for experience shows that they do exist. The observance of the laws of heredity in the creation of a human child has as much to do with the different theories about the soul as, for instance, the different theories about the nature of electricity have to do with the manufacturing of electrical machines—namely, nothing. Since materialism is the doctrine that regards matter as the only thing that exists, it is clear what mistake the above "idealists" are committing when they deride as "materialism" the idea that physical laws in the human body may be soul's means of expression.

But this question could also be considered from a completely different point of view. If we do not accept Clauß's "racial" souls, but presuppose a single spiritual or fundamental force, parts of which act as individual souls in every human being, then we arrive at this conclusion: the soul as part of a divine elementary power, pure and perfect in itself, has human bodies as its worldly means of expression, which follow physical laws during the soul's existence on Earth—a limitation that we must accept as God's will. Consequently, a soul can only express itself fully and purely in a perfect body, for every imperfect body clouds the soul's appearance or somehow inhibits its possibilities of expression. Accordingly, it is our mission to strive for the perfection of the human form in order to produce the most comprehensive availability of possibilities of expression for each individual soul; we would therefore want to free our people, as it were, from all bodily impurities which could tarnish the individual bodies and thus also their souls. In the long run, this goal is only achievable through the observation of the laws of heredity and by eradicating the undesirables.

With these remarks, I in no way want to give an ideological (philosophical) explanation of the soul. But, I do want to show how thoughtlessly and inaccurately the terms idealism and materialism are used today in all questions concerning racial science. As long as the union of the two parental hereditary genotypes (a very much material fact) is necessary to give life to a child, even those who are exclusively sworn to the "spiritual" will not be able to avoid admitting that a human being is bound to material laws. Additionally, this connection to physical laws must be willed by God, for otherwise God would hardly have established it in the first place. Whoever does not want to acknowledge a connection to material laws should at least be consistent in his standpoint and also fundamentally reject the laws of heredity for the human race, as Bruno Goetz has honestly done in *Neuer Adel* (*New Nobility*; Darmstadt 1930, page 148):

> The New Nobility, on the other hand, whose mystery is the sacred marriage of the ensouled spirit of light with the earth mother, cannot inherit itself solely through blood. It is no longer the ancestral blood as such that is divine, but only the spirit-incarnated blood, the spirit-incarnated body. The spirit blows from whence it will and produces sons for itself in all flesh and blood that motherly cherishes and bears its seed.

It is very strange: people who fundamentally deny any heredity of spiritual qualities nevertheless—just like us ordinary mortals—always portray a Christ, a Mephisto,[122] and so on, in quite definite corporeality, even though this is unjustified from their point of view. They seem to simply be unable to reach these basic conclusions: that certain characters are regularly associated with corporeality; that science has proven the hereditability of physical traits; and that spiritual dispositions must also be hereditary.

Since Kretschmer's *Körperbau und Charakter (Physique and Character*; Berlin 1926), science has been familiar with the fact that physical, mental, and spiritual characteristics of human beings are closely interrelated and to a certain extent interdependent.[123] But many still do not want to draw

---

[122] Editor's note: Mephisto, short for Mephistopheles, in one of main demons of German folklore. He first appears in the sixteenth century legend of Faust, where the eponymous main character trades his soul in exchange for unlimited knowledge and material gain (the Faustian bargain). The demonic figure appears in many subsequent works of literature.

[123] A very nice contribution to this idea, which also emphasizes the dangers of urban life and is particularly recommended to non-agriculturist readers, is Stieve, *Unfruchtbarkeit als Folge Unnatürlicher Lebensweise: Ein Versuch, die Ungewollte Kinderlosigkeit des Menschen auf Grund von Tierversuchen und Anatomischen Untersuchungen auf die Folgen des Kulturlebens Zurückzuführen (Infertility as a Consequence of an Unnatural Way of Life: An Attempt to Alleviate Unwanted Human Infertility Based on Knowledge from Animal Experiments and Anatomical Investigations on the Consequences of Civilized Life)* (Munich: J. F. Bergmann, 1926).

conclusions on heredity from these results.

Our ancestors knew the truth even without the science of heredity. Mathilde, a granddaughter of Widukind (the Saxon duke deposed by Charlemagne) and the wife of Henry I—the progenitor of the Ottonians—repeatedly said that in her opinion, only a noble lineage guaranteed a noble way of thinking; in other words, that the soul is absolutely bound to the physicality of a dynasty. In German history, we can easily convince ourselves of the truth of these words—there we are clearly shown that only good blood lends to the permanence and continuity of good disposition.

What these medieval families knew in their instinctual blood-derived understanding—what their "inner sense" told them without needing to consult their intellect for an explanation—is confirmed to us today in the most intellectual terms by leading scholars and geneticists. K. Bauer says in his readable work *Rassenhygiene* (*Racial Hygiene*):

> It cannot be emphasized often enough that, in spite of all the external influences on a currently living individual resulting from changes in their environment, it must remain clear that external conditions only have an influence on the realization of the individual's disposition in the present—never on the preservation of the disposition for the future. No education, no matter how favorable the external conditions may be, can make a human child anything other than what it possesses in hereditary endowments, for man can always only realize that which he already possesses according to his disposition.

And so he declares two moral commandments to the German youth: "Become what you are according to your dispositions!" and, "Preserve what you have according to your dispositions!"

But the majority of our people and—what is actually even worse—a large part of our nobility still think completely differently from the traditions of German cultural history, from the views of our ancestors, and from the voices of scientific reason. In his essay "Genealogie als Wegweisung: Statistik als Prophezeihung" ("Genealogy as a Signpost: Statistics as Prophecy," Baltische Blätter (*Baltic Magazine*), February 1930), Eduard von Stackelberg tries to enlighten his fellow nobles by showing them this juxtaposition:

> If our knighthoods[124] still form a living body, they must exhibit the two characteristics of life—separation of the foreign and admission of the suitable. It no longer makes sense to exclude a "Mr. Neumann," whose mother, grandmother and great-grandmother were called Altenhausen, who belongs to the Dorpat Corps[125] and fought in the trenches of Verdun—while including "von Altenhausen" among his own, who is fifteen-sixteenths Semitic-Slavic, studied in Moscow, and in the *Berliner Tageblatt*[126] rips down everything that is German and everything that is Baltic.

In comparison with Stackelberg's statements, the two following phrases from our history and our science seem like a scornful side note regarding the average thinking of our nobility and our people: "There is nothing more precious on this earth than the seeds of noble blood." and, "No medicine can turn corrupt seeds into good ones."

Today, instead of breeding people, we merely reproduce people. We are amazed that German customs dwindle more and more. But the general public in Germany is already too cowardly (because it ultimately is a question of cowardice!) to analyze these issues and determine their root causes. Or is the thinking capacity of the German people already so severely diminished that it can no longer recognize the causes? Having large numbers of children alone is of no use to us—it depends entirely on the quality of the genetic inheritance of the children. But if we could ask our children what they actually have to say about these things, they could only answer: "We are becoming fewer and fewer!" and, "We are becoming more and more inferior!"[127]

---

[124] This refers to the Baltic knighthoods, see von Dellingshausen, *Die Baltischen Ritterschaften (The Baltic Knighthoods)* (Langensalza, 1928).

[125] Editor's note: The Dorpat Corps was a Baltic German student union at the German-speaking Imperial University of Dorpat (Estonian: Tartu). It produced a disproportionate amount of prominent thinkers, writers, and leaders. After Estonia's independence in 1919, the university was renamed University of Tartu; the German student union continued to operate until the Soviet expulsions of the German population in 1939. It was reconstituted in 1959 by descendants of Baltic Germans in the *Curonia Goettingensis* student union at the Georg August University in Göttingen (Lower Saxony).

[126] Editor's note: The *Berliner Tageblatt (Berlin Daily Magazine)* was one of the most influential liberal newspaper in Germany. It was shut down by German authorities in 1939.

[127] These two answers were taken from a work without remembering the author or the title of the book. When writing this book, it was not possible to find the

And thus our current customs stand condemned—they are useless! That is the truth! At least have the courage to admit that it is the truth, and that no amount of fine speeches about a "faith in Germany's future" will help us surmount this, even if they are delivered in frock coats, top hats, and by official decree; and we are helped even less by maudlin sentimental reflections on the wickedness of modernity and the superiority of the pure and noble German soul.

Let us return to the morality of our forefathers, which was successful in keeping German civilization alive for a millennium and a half. Let us educate our women again in the well-understood old German concept of breeding. To our ancestors, a "chaste" woman was not a woman who had no conception whatsoever of sexual matters, but a woman who consciously prepared herself for the idea of one day becoming a mother and raising a large flock of children. For these women, childbearing was not the exercise of a right of self-determination, but a responsibility to their descendants; their life's purpose was to serve their family—their task was to preserve, advance, and multiply the species. These women understood the concept of breeding and it was their pride. They did not feel degraded to the status of "broodmare," as is the silly objection of modern people who apparently understand the highly praised "personal freedom" of women to mean only the freedom to savor all the pleasures of "bed mates" as they see fit and as unrestrictedly as possible. The pride of these women was to become the progenitor of a noble family and to receive confirmation of their own worth in their noble sons.

"There is no finer honor for children than this,
To be born of a noble and brave father,
And to marry into nobility.
But I will not praise the man who is overcome by desire
And casts his lot with the base,
Getting pleasure for himself but leaving his children in disgrace."

Euripides, *Heracleidae*

It is not the case that by adopting the ideas of breeding we are introducing something animal or unworthy of man into our new nobility—we are simply resuming the best spiritual and moral traditions of our ancestors,

---

author in question in time.

and refining them with the knowledge and discoveries of the field of genetics. With this we have averted all suspicion of "materialism."

2. Animal Breeding as a Source of Knowledge and Guidance.

This sub-section is not so much intended for amateur heredity researchers as it is for readers who are either experts in the fields of race and genetics research or who have already become well-acquainted with these questions in some other way. Animal breeding—in this respect differing from plant breeding—is a subject matter which is very similar in essence to human genetics theory, in particular the theories regarding the racial improvement of our people (although, of course, with certain key differences). Animal breeding is better established than human breeding science, so naturally some things have already been more clearly ordered and structured in former than in the latter, where the solution to the problem is itself much more complicated.

For this reason, a short sub-section is inserted here in which questions related to racial improvement are compiled and arranged on the basis of animal breeding points of view. It is not the intention that human breeding should be carried out in exactly the same way as animal breeding, but rather that the expertise of animal breeding should be used—purely in an advisory capacity—to show how the issues related to racial improvement could be approached from an animal breeding-trained point of view, and also to achieve a greater clarity in the field to be dealt with.[128]

Breeding means: to generate offspring, which, if possible, increase in value over time through thoughtfulness and with well-planned application of the available resources.

The means of breeding are twofold: (I) Breeding selection, and (II) Measures for the evaluation of breeding selection and its results, including: (1) Breeding, (2) Nutrition, and (3) Demeanor and care.

I. Breeding selection: This is based on the planned utilization of the laws of reproduction and heredity. Its task is the application of a

---

[128] In particular, material was borrowed from the latest animal breeding work and theory, with the structure largely followed. This includes the work of the Director of the Animal Breeding Institute at the Berlin Agricultural University: Dr. Kronacher, *Züchtungslehre: Eine Einführung für Züchter und Studierende* (*Breeding Theory: An Introduction for Breeders and Students*) (Berlin, 1929).

purposeful breeding selection process, i.e. utilizing for mating and reproduction only those individuals which possess the hereditary traits necessary for the desired physical and performance dispositions in a pure (or as pure as possible) manner, thus generally only producing offspring with such dispositions.

Breeding selection employs the knowledge of the following two fields of study: (1) Laws of reproduction: to discuss them in more detail here would take us too far from the central topic,[129] and (2) Laws of heredity: these too can only be briefly mentioned here. This is understood to mean the following—the hereditary factors from which the outwardly visible characteristics of a human being (which, like all growth, can be inhibited or promoted by external influences) emerge are the same in ancestors and descendants, even if they are grouped differently in the individual descendants from the paternal and maternal lines, which are expressed in the same way. The course of this hereditary transmission from parents to offspring is subject to certain laws, which we have understood better since Johann Mendel and which, in honor of their discoverer (whose research was rediscovered by chance in 1900), are summarized under the term Mendel's laws or Mendelism. Mendelism is therefore the doctrine that deals with the way in which hereditary traits are transmitted from parents to their offspring.

II. Measures for the evaluation of breeding selection and its results:

1. Breeding: This is the most important task after the selection of the breed and begins at the moment of fertilization of the egg. The aim of breeding selection is to create a set of circumstances in the fertilized egg (i.e., the sum of the paternal and maternal genetic material coupled together in the egg) where, given the appropriate developmental conditions, a living (human) being arises whose physical body (constitution) is of high quality. Or, to put it another way—to shape the development of the fertilized egg in the womb as well as its further post-birth development in such a way that its genetic make-up is able to develop to the greatest health and perfection possible according to its nature. Essentially, in the case of human beings, we will have to understand this as: all that is necessary and correct for the protection of the mother and the child during pregnancy. This can be further described

---

[129] However, it should be noted that no German should be granted full citizenship in the future German state who does not have at a minimum a clear basic knowledge of the anatomy (study of the body and its parts) and physiology (study of the life processes in the body) of reproduction.

by the terms obstetrics, obstetric care, infant care, and well-managed nursery care; in essence, it is today part of the fields of social policy and racial hygiene. The realization of these objectives can be achieved through the appropriate education of young women before marriage, the provision of a healthy environment for the pregnant mother, and a well-trained and responsible medical and nursing staff.

2. Nutrition: this is an essential part of all breeding. If we use the modern experience of animal breeding as a basis, we are tempted to say that this question is at least as important as the things mentioned in the previous paragraph. However, we generally have the impression that this fact has hitherto received little attention from the medical world, not much more attention from those concerned with the reproductive and genetic health of our people, and least of all from those endeavoring to research race. The appearance (not the genotype) of every race can be modified by nutrition up to a certain limit unique to each race, for good or ill. Animal breeding has shown that the way in which the young animals are fed has a lasting influence on and determines the performance of adult animals.[130] Whoever desires high-performance German offspring will therefore have to make sure that they pay attention to the question of nutrition, since even the best hereditary dispositions will never develop satisfactorily with unsuitable nutrition, let alone be expected to perform at a high level.

3. Demeanor and care: this includes all those measures which do not concern internal possibilities of influence, i.e. nutrition—concerning instead with the external possibilities of influence on the growing body.

---

[130] And it seems to be similar with humans. The English and Scandinavians—whose legendary demeanor and poise in all circumstances is well known—claim that their morning porridge of oats with raw cream protects them from neurasthenic phenomena (i.e. diseases resulting from nervous weakness). In fact, for example, in the English thoroughbred horse (an animal who has a genetic predisposition to great nervous sensitivity), deprivation of oats triggers neurasthenia, which has an immediate depressing effect on the animal's performance in a race and on the effects caused by the race. Whether the stomach and intestines are accustomed in their youth to work vigorously and to extract nutrients even from food that is more difficult to access—or whether they are pampered in their digestive work by puree, white bread, and other easily digestible foods—plays a decisive role in later health, which even affects questions of reproduction. At any rate, this has been established in animal breeding, and it is difficult to see why these natural laws should not apply to humans; see also: Blendinger, *Die Bedeutung der Spätreife für den Menschen (The Significance of Late Maturity for Humans)* (Rennslingen, 1930).

These external possibilities of influence are in turn divided into two main parts:

a) Possibilities of influencing the body: These are quite varied – they begin with healthy sleeping quarters, concern clothing appropriate to a race or people, personal hygiene, and extensive exercise or physical training in fresh, unpolluted air; these include all factors related to the home and its impact on the soul and health, as well as many other questions that the reader can imagine. For health plays a decisive role in all questions of breeding. Health is the root of all performance. After all, the following principle also applies to animal breeders – disregarding the state of a breed's health is the best way to initiate its runaway degeneration. Unhealthiness eliminates any breeding value.

No race can be kept healthy without a healthy environment suited to it. The animal breeder says in this case – a breed must be given the most favorable living conditions in every respect (which may include, for example, environmental conditions which are obviously beneficial, such as coolness, dryness, heat, the possibility of reaching the highest speed of movement, etc.) if it is to continue to be bred to its full potential. This can also be expressed in this way: a race cannot be bred in an environment not suitable for it.

b) Possibilities of influencing the spirit, both the mind (intelligence) and the soul (demeanor): These are fewer than is generally accepted today, because spiritual and intellectual education can only develop or strengthen what already exists – it can never conjure up nor invent what does not already exist.[131] It is true that the superstition of the age now ending quite seriously believed this, but it must be emphasized that it was an attempt to put the cart before the horse. These attempts cannot be better realized by closing our eyes to the facts of heredity and describing our head-in-the-sand mentality as "idealism"[132] in a grandiose and unjustified manner. Perhaps it is advisable to quote Günther's *Platon als Hüter des Lebens (Plato as the Guardian of Life):*

---

[131] Compare Lenz, *Über Die Biologischen Grundlagen der Erziehung* (On the Biological Foundations of Education), second edition, Munich 1927; and Mickermann, *Kind und Volk* (Child and People), Freiburg 1924.

[132] In this field there is often so little sense that we must, for example, welcome with special pleasure a book like Ziegler's, *Magna Charta einer Schule* (Magna Carta of a School), Darmstadt 1928 – which at least makes an attempt to incorporate the theory of heredity.

> It was Plato who gave the Greek word "idea" its philosophical meaning and who with his teaching became the founder of idealism; who endeavored throughout his life to recognize the essence of the idea and the hierarchy of ideas; who finally granted the realm of ideas an irrefutable validity. This same Plato, this idealist, also conceived the idea of selection.

Nevertheless, we may ascribe an important role to influences on demeanor, even if we remain aware of the fact that the boundaries drawn for human races cannot be transgressed. Unfortunately, official German education has so far paid little attention to these things, apart from a few old and venerable Prussian schools and some southern German ones. There will be more to say about this in the final section of this book.

3. The *Hegehof* Marriage

On a *hegehof*, only the monogamous marriage makes sense.

Every self-reliant household requires responsible management of the household's internal operations. Since the man, even if he is legally the head of the household, must seek his professional career outside the home—be it in the fields or in public business—he must hand over the management of the inner workings of his household to someone else, and depending on the situation, this is typically the woman. This is why (in the two final sections of my book *The Peasantry as the Source of Life of the Nordic Race*, I have explained all this in more detail) we find the following among the Indo-European and Germanic peoples, whose civilization is based on a peasant domestic economy: the woman had supreme authority over the household management;[133] while this woman occupies

[133] Only one person can give orders, especially in a closed economic area. It must be said that the duties of a Germanic wife are often misjudged today because people project today's ideas of the duties of a wife to those times. In today's households, the only thing that matters is that the immediate family doesn't goes hungry, something that any reliable cook can do without a housewife—whereas in those days it was important that everyone was cared for. This task may seem easy, but in order to appreciate its full gravity, we have to be aware of the huge scale of household economies of that time, which, by the way, remained pretty much the same until the beginning of the nineteenth century. The households of that time consisted of the family's relatives, the servants, the domestic workers, and often also tradesmen. If someone wanted to manage such a huge household

an apparently unfree position in public law, it was in reality a very independent position through the so-called *schlüsselgewalt* (power of the keys).[134] The manager of the house was the wife. Since the whole institution only made sense if its permanence was ensured, people married with the long-term in mind and with an understanding of what kinds of tasks were to be done by the housewife and wife. Accordingly, in terms of linguistic history, our word *ehe* (marriage) is directly connected with *ewig* (eternal) in the sense of *ohne ende* (without end).

The marriages of our ancestors were not individualist affairs as they are today. We cannot return to their conception today because we have become more individualist (i.e. more selfish) and because we have taken away the domestic basis of our marriages and thus deprived the wife of a large part of her life's work in the sense of the old idea of marriage—we have lost all this only since Hardenberg. It was Riehl who, not quite fully understanding, clearly saw the disaster developing once the domestic basis of urban marriage had in principle been withdrawn. Riehl predicted two things about this development—firstly, the ever-increasing alienation between town and country, because estate ownership and peasantry could not exist without a domestic economy and thus without the housewife in the old German sense (i.e. the gulf between urban and rural women would become deeper to the extent that only the urban married household would move away from actual domestic aspects); and secondly, that the morality of urban marriages would continue to decline and open the way for an ever more unrestrained conception of female self-worth, quite simply because the housewife would find less stimulation and less responsibility in the household, which would make it easier for ever more lower quality women to marry, as well as giving the higher quality ones foolish ideas because of a lack of stimulation.

Nowadays it is often claimed that the original position of the German-Germanic wife was something very depressing for the female soul. This was certainly true for women who lacked the aptitudes and gifts to

---

as a self-supporting body, then this was an organizational and leadership activity of the highest order, which not only required a well-rounded personality, but above all a purposeful will.

134 Editor's note: in German family law, the "power of the keys" refers to the concept of wives having the right to make financial and management decisions for their household. In the Middle Ages, married women wore a keychain as a symbol of their rights.

manage a household,[135] but was hardly true for the healthy woman of Germanic blood—at least during the Middle Ages it was certainly not the case. For the strikingly pronounced gender roles of the Germanic are quite contrary to such an assumption. The sexual organs, with their influence on desire and will, already ensure that in a marriage where the man is a man and the woman is a woman and both belong to the same race, each of them gets their effort's worth. Where the masculinization of the woman is to be observed in her views, dress, behavior, and occupation, this speaks against her naturally feminine nature. In such cases—if the cause is not obviously un-Germanic blood—we can say (without having to be a trained doctor) that the glandular activity of the woman in question is somehow lacking.[136]

Our forefathers believed these things with much more conviction than some of today's people. As Schwann writes in *Vom Staate (Of the State):*

> The old view was that procreation created the man and the woman, but that the "personality" was only born through marriage. Only the procreative human being was considered a whole human being. Until this stage of development was reached by the individual, the human being remained diminished. The *kind* (child), the *fräulein* (young lady), and the *herrlein* (young man) are still used today in southern German dialects. The non-procreating woman is diminished to a *fräulein*, just as the man who allows himself to be diminished ends up as a *männchen* (little man) or *männle* (manlet) or *herrle* (little lord) and falls under the slipper.[137] But above all, what remained in the living language was the person that did not possess the ability to procreate, that did not make use of it, or even abused it: that person—the wench!

---

[135] In particular, this can be expected in women who are partly or wholly descended from nomadic ancestors, since nomadism requires the skills of cooking and manual labor, but has nothing to do with running a proper household.

[136] Compare Eberhard, *Geschlechtscharakter und Volkskraft, Grundprobleme des Feminismus* (Sexual Character and Popular Power, Basic Problems of Feminism), Darmstadt and Leipzig 1930.

[137] Editor's note: "Under the slipper" (*unter den pantoffel gerät)* refers to an old German wedding tradition where the bride and groom would try to step on each other's foot. Whoever managed to do so first was said to be in charge of the marriage. Women typically wore slippers on their wedding way. Therefore, the phrase "under the slipper" refers to things non-dominant or effeminate.

Accordingly, we can also answer all modern-day questions about "companionship marriage" and "timed marriage" (a word—*zeit-ehe*—which, because of the origin of the word *ehe* (marriage) from the same word root as *ewig* (eternal), is like linguistic nonsense) and how these "important things" are all called "modern" by simply completely eliminating them from the *hegehof* idea.[138]

For purely economic reasons, the *hegehof* already demands a marriage based on permanence. But it demands it even more for moral reasons! "All morality emanates from the woman, exists in the woman and through the woman, ends with the woman," says G. Melzer in *Volk ohne Willen (People without Will),* thus succinctly and sharply outlining the responsibility of the German woman, and in particular the noblewoman, who after all is supposed to set an example for the people. "If it were possible to open the history of the souls of countless men and read therein about the influence that women have had on them for good or for vice, we would be astonished at the abundance of actions, noble and good, bad and criminal, which can be traced back to the influence of women. It is a fact that in many things, especially in ideals, the man is dependent on the guidance of the woman and she is burdened with infinite responsibilities in this respect," writes Countess Spreti in Noble Journal. Countess Spreti is only stating what G. Ferrero tried to prove regarding the history of Rome in his book *Die Frauen der Cäsaren* (The Wives of the Caesars; Stuttgart 1921).

But we only need to open our eyes and examine our circle of acquaintances. Whether a careless tone prevails in a family or a moral one, whether a person feels a sense of cleanliness in moral matters or feels a more or less restrained pleasure in the obscene, in every case a person will be able to observe that the woman of the house sets the tone. Only where visibly inferior racial traits assert themselves in the man may the influence of a virtuous woman fail in the long run to set the tone and an attitude arises that can no longer be called virtuous. Men of good blood in the German-Germanic sense have never been able to escape the influence of a virtuous woman. From our point of view, it brings a man's character into question when a virtuous woman is unable to exert any influence on him in a moral sense; German history proves this at every turn.

---

138 The whole "sexual misery of today" basically only proves that our time is no longer dominated by men, but by *männchen* (little men).

In short, the *hegehof* can only be a moral example to the German people if it sets an example of marital morality.

If it is true that the family and its continued existence is a primary requirement for the sustainability of the state and people through the millennia, then *hegehof* marriages have a primary duty to heed this truth.

4

Above, in Chapter VII, Section 2, we discussed the tasks summarized under the term "racial improvement." The aspects of the breeding concept discussed in Part II and the measures for evaluating the results of breeding selection can be integrated without difficulty into the *hegehof* concept and can be dealt with directly or indirectly by the self-governing body of the noblemen. We do not need to consider them here!

However, the situation is very different with the tasks of breeding selection mentioned in Part I. In Germany, we have distanced ourselves so thoroughly from the breeding ideas of our ancestors that even the simplest matter of course in this area has the potential of being misunderstood. This must therefore be given more attention.

The beginning of all refinement is the creation of the most perfect possible offspring. This makes it clear that, in essence, all procreation is like the setting of a course which over time will have a decisive influence on the future of the people as well as that of every family. If we want to "refine" those who are to come—and that is, after all, the purpose of our creation of a new nobility—then our main focus should be on the choices of the spouses on the *hegehöfe*.

However, this in no way means that we simply abolish the moral concepts that have developed in our people. For good reasons, it is said above in Chapter VII, Section 2 that breeding is nothing more than striving for the ideal offspring through thoughtfulness and the well-managed use of the available resources. In this draft for the establishment of a new nobility, it has already been emphasized several times and in no uncertain terms that the sense of family, family tradition, as well as of a family based on permanence—which is connected with the *hegehöfe*—are the foundations of a nobility. We have also said that only monogamous marriages could be valid on a *hegehof*, so we must now clarify this idea further. What we mean is that an aspirant to a *hegehof* can only become a nobleman if he takes certain requirements into account when choosing his spouse and if his wife—the future noblewoman—fulfills certain minimum requirements in bodily and mental qualities and is, so to speak, able to provide non-objectionable genetic material. For even more stringently than for the general public, the choice of new noblewoman determines the compass direction, in a favorable or unfavorable sense, of the genetic material of her respective *hegehof* family—a direction in which it will continue to move towards in the future. We do not want to hide the fact that this confirms a terrible truth for all those who, out of a moral and Christian feeling (and also quite rightly from a German-Germanic point of view), reject every form of "harem" and want to see monogamous marriage protected and preserved as the moral foundation of our people.

However, we not only reject any flirtation with forms of marriage other than monogamy, but also fundamentally reject any manipulation of the concept of "equality,"[139] i.e. any kind of caste demarcation within the nation. In general, everything that is connected with the concept of caste is to be rejected.

5

The concept of caste. Caste division is only morally justified where two very different races live together in the same territory and one rules over the other. The essence of caste is the separation of blood; it is therefore a measure to prevent inferior blood from seeping into that of the master caste. Historical examples of castes can be found in India, where the blonde-haired, blue-eyed, long-skulled conquerors of northern European origin encountered a black-haired, brown-eyed, short-headed indigenous population of undoubtedly inferior civilization, from whom they had to close themselves off; it is therefore logical that in India the term caste is linguistically related to the term color.

Today, there are eccentric individuals in racial studies who seriously envisage a caste-like division of the German people. Insofar as such efforts don't stem from confusion with the concept of class, such ideas overlook the fact that sooner or later all caste formation is followed (and must be followed) by civilizational torpidity if the ruling caste does not

---

[139] Editor's note: In nineteenth century German marriage law, the concept of "equality" in marriage was the preference (or in some cases, requirement) that both the husband and wife belong to the same class.

find ways and means to continuously renew itself. If it cannot do this from external sources, or even from lower castes, then it will either die one day from exhaustion of numbers or from losing the will to live (compare Sparta for the first, and the predominantly Germanic nobility of pre-1789 France for the second). It will inevitably renounce the self-preserving morality of its civilization and confine itself to the preservation of existing conceptions, thus allowing the torpor to set in. This is such a striking phenomenon in India: the castes exist, their differences are clear, but each caste is frozen in itself, in the worn-out tracks of its civilization's expressions.

If a people, living together in the same national territory, is allowed to intermarry without restraint, then crossbreeds will undoubtedly be born—purely by chance—of quite excellent dispositions, as the most favorable possible dispositions from across all of the people's racial components came together. These are *übermenschen* (over-men), whose development—as far as disposition and quality are concerned—has long been explained to us by the theory of heredity; and which, as Reibmayr was probably the first to point out in *Entwicklungsgeschichte des Genies und Talents (History of the Development of Genius and Talent),* are a necessary and natural consequence of all genetic combination, a consequence which can neither be consciously bred nor is in any way a sign of the health or creativity of a people. Generally speaking, they are the result of a gamble with a people's hereditary dispositions wherein the misses so outnumber the hits over the course of time that the value of the whole phenomenon for a people is more than doubtful, because it is essentially an anomaly of the people's genetic value; nevertheless, may we be graced by many "over-men" in the context of our human history.[140] Everywhere in nature, the principle applies that where all things compete against one another, the more highly developed species or breed is defeated by the simpler one—in the same way that no highly developed garden plant is able to prevail against weeds unless it renounces its special developments,

---

[140] Just to be clear, the term "over-man" is not used here in Nietzsche's sense. Nietzsche used the word "over-man" to designate "a type of the highest well-being," in contrast to "modern man." For Nietzsche, the physiological prerequisite of the over-man was great health—far more than what Hans F. K. Günther has today set up as the target image and selection model for the *Nordichen Bewegung*. Here, on the other hand, "over-man" should be understood to mean the special human being who surpasses usual or average humanity, for example Leonardo da Vinci, Michelangelo, Goethe, Shakespeare, Friedrich Wilhelm I of Prussia, Scharnhorst, Stein, Bismarck, and so on.

regresses, and in its regressed state takes up the fight against the weeds; in which case, however, it is still not guaranteed that it will prevail victoriously. Life is governed by the "law of the minimum."[141, 142]

Rank, however, should be evaluated quite differently if it is to be understood in the German-Germanic sense. Ammon describes the significance of rank very clearly:

> A state-organized community of people will be better able to survive the more it meets the condition that in each position there is the right person who is suited by his talents to fill that position in the best possible way. The highly gifted person, even if he has the lowest of origins, should be able to occupy a position appropriate to his gifts—even the very top rank of society—if there is no one who excels him in ability. A person born at the top should vacate his position if he does not have the ability to fill it in the way that is required to protect the interests of the general public. Here lies the most important social problem—for not only does the inner welfare of the people depend on the correct solution, but in the case of external conflicts, also their continued success in the very struggle for existence.[143]

Ammon came to these conclusions through a realization of the inequality of human beings—he therefore had to contemplate the idea of selection. It had become clear to him that even if human beings are unable to abolish the physical laws that determine the distribution of intellectual talents, they still had the duty of trying to control them. We cannot, for example, abolish the law of gravity when it suits us, but we can, for example, use the weight of falling water to operate a mill and thus directly serve the further development of our civilization. Tanck therefore correctly summarizes Ammon in these words:

---

141 See Darré's essay in the monthly journal *Deutschlands Erneuerung* (*Germany's Renewal*), issue 8, 1928.

142 Editor's note: Also known as Leibig's law, the law of the minimum states that growth is not governed by the total available resources—it is governed by the scarcest available resource (the limiting factor).

143 Otto Ammon, *Die Gesellschaftsordnung und ihre Natürlichen Grundlagen* (*The Social Order and its Natural Foundations*) (Langensalza: P. Tanck, 1928).

> The social order is based on inequality, and inequality is not something that can be abolished—it is inseparable from the human race, like birth and death. It is immutable like mathematical truths, and eternal like the laws that govern the courses of our planetary system.

Ammon wanted the people's division of labor to be organized according to the talents of the individuals concerned. He called for the formation of an institution which, on the one hand, carried out and fulfilled this task and, on the other, gave the distinguished people of talented and highly talented dispositions the possibility of producing offspring in greater numbers than would be possible with standard intermarriage—which the gifted person might not necessarily even achieve, let alone to produce a large number of offspring. It is true that Moltke said that "only the capable succeed." But not every capable person has succeeded and, given today's conditions in Germany, will likely not succeed in the future either, despite another quote from a less significant source: "free way for the capable." Many great leaders ultimately fail and perish, from Hannibal to Napoleon. Even the mightiest greatness can be marred by the smallness of others. Think of ostracism[144] among the Athenians! And ostracism can be found throughout history where the dissolution of states can be observed and the law of the minimum is allowed to have an unrestrained effect.

We can, therefore, be very well against any caste mentality and still advocate for the formation of an Ammonian institution. Harpf in *Völkischer Adel (Volkish Nobility)* says something very similar as well:

> The caste mentality—taken in the worst sense of the term—which used to be unduly popular in many circles, has fortunately received a strong blow sure to be of lasting effect among our people. It must be understood that we are not against stratification and class distinctions as such. On the contrary, they are and

---

[144] Editor's note: Ostracism in ancient Athens was the banishment of an individual from the city-state for ten years. Citizens would nominate individuals once a year for any reason whatsoever, from general dislike to disreputable behavior. If a particular individual received a sufficient number of votes, he would be ostracized. Capable individuals who quickly increased in influence through achievement would frequently find themselves ostracized as a "threat to Athenian democracy."

> remain necessary—as necessary as the gradient without which the turbine can do no work. A mass of people, economically and socially equal in all their components, would soon no longer be able to do any work, as if they were no longer powered—just as the turbine must stop without a gradient.

Kloß expresses himself in *Der Sittliche Gehalt der Arbeit (The Moral Wage of Labor;* Langensalza 1926) in a surprisingly similar way to Harpf:

> All egalitarianism ultimately means rigidity. The technician is quite familiar with this from his profession. An energy flow is an absolute prerequisite for getting work done. Without a gradient, the cycle of water that fertilizes our land and drives our water mills and turbines cannot be maintained. Stagnant water becomes swampy and putrid. Similarly, any flow, be it heat, steam, or electricity always requires a "gradient." There must be a driving "voltage." And this is exactly how it is in human life and especially in economic life. Here, too, all levelling leads to torpor. All levelling-out is at the expense of the better.

The words of Kloß, born out of economic thinking, are a confirmation of the law of the minimum that has long been recognized in the life sciences. Not least, the herald of a new era of humanity—Friedrich Nietzsche—also recognized the applicability of this law in the human sphere in *Also Sprach Zarathustra* (*Thus Spoke Zarathustra*). Nietzsche described all egalitarianism as flattening or as a form of higher Chinese mentality, compare *Wille zur Macht* (*Will to Power*), page 866.

The idea that the most able should make up the highest ranks of society and that the unfit must leave a position they have not mastered (a concept that is far removed from the idea that a person is simply born into an office by virtue of their birth, without having to first prove their ability to hold it) is thoroughly Germanic. It is revealing in every respect that this mentality has survived in England until recent times, despite the noble underpinnings of its society. Wildhagen explicitly draws attention to this in *Der Englische Volkscharakter* (*The English National Character*), as does Dibelius in *England* (fifth edition, volume I, page 140). Such a performance-centered mentality, in connection with the custom of marrying women without a dowry or inheritance (mentioned below), makes it unsurprising that England never entertained the idea that equality was based purely on things related to class and property. The German caste-like demarcation of rank, based on outward appearances rather than blood-proven breeding potential, has done as much harm to our nation as a whole as it has to our noble families individually. Treitschke says this quite clearly in *Drei Aufsäße Staatswissenschaftlichen Inhalts: Die Grundlagen der Englischen Freiheit* (*Three Reviews of Political Science Content: The Foundations of English Liberty*):

> Look at the English House of Lords, you admirers of Gothic almanacs and German barons, their "documented" ancestors were knights in a time when, according to the uncomfortable assertions of historians, our lower nobility did not yet have dynasty names—is it not a sight to pity? They have only twelve couples of medieval creation, while we have 196 from our century alone,[145] many of them of impure origin with royal paramours and such, with pedigrees stained by innumerable mismatches![146]

6

In summary—we affirm rank in the professional sense and thus also the rank-based division of the nation, so that the best of our people's abilities and talents can be brought to their appropriate place and can succeed there. We continue to regard rank as an enabler of marriage for those who have proven their abilities—but we reject any caste-like separation and accordingly also reject "being born into" a class without proof of the corresponding aptitude for that class (either in professional terms or as an equal marriage prospect), because then we have a caste rather than a class in the Germanic sense, and castes always lead to civilizational torpidity.

For our *hegehöfe*, this means that any sort of template for succession of the male heir is impossible; likewise, girls born on the *hegehöfe* can never lay claim to preferential consideration as future noblewomen, simply because they are the daughters of noblemen.

But another concern also guides us in this statement. Today, we no longer have the option of preserving the good blood in the upper classes

---

[145] Here referring to the nineteenth century.
[146] Compare also Dibelius, volume I, page 18.

alone—even if we wanted to do so and even if we disregarded the wartime and post-war profiteers and looked only at the families with good names and of good origin. The nobility, high nobility, lower nobility, and many good bourgeois former patrician families, have, through bad crossbreeding and imprudent inbreeding, been infiltrated by hereditary diseases and in many cases become as inferior in blood as any mixed family of the middle or lower classes. Today, in all strata of the population, the decent human being is virtually on the verge of extinction. Either we save this decent German and thus also his heritage in time and remain a German people, or we—along with our intellectual abilities—are erased from the history of mankind. If we do not create in our hoped-for future German state a morality that makes it advantageous for a prince, for example, to marry a healthy peasant's daughter of impeccable genetic value when no woman of sufficient genetic value is available in his class, then we can let ourselves be buried. It would then be better to refrain from the salon conversations about the genetic health of the German people and racial improvement, because such things would only breed healthy work horses for the supranational financial powers—not create healthy German people.

7

If the German people allocate a large part of their land to form the *hegehöfe* of a certain number of families, for no other purpose than to bring dynasties of exemplary leadership qualities into being again, then it is only right and proper if, in return, these families are required to pay very special attention to the question of succession on each *hegehof*, i.e. the question of the choice of spouse.

It would now be very simple to make certain basic demands on the designated male heir in order to mitigate the undesirable consequences of an unfavorable choice of spouse. We could say, for example, that only the son who meets the requirements that the Reichswehr[147] places on its junior officers can become a *hegehof* heir. The extensive experience that

---

[147] Editor's note: The Reichswehr was the small military force of the Weimar Republic, formed after the disbandment of the Imperial German Army. It would become the Wehrmacht in 1935 following the restoration of German national sovereignty.

the Reichswehr and the *schutzpolizei*[148] today have in the field of screening candidates makes it a possibility for these organizations to conduct appropriate screenings of candidates for the *hegehöfe*. If we add to this, with all necessary prudence, the aptitude assessments (American: tests) currently being carried out by the state and the professions, it can almost be said that we already have very effective aids at our disposal to prevent an unsuitable person from being selected as a *hegehof* candidate, i.e. as an heir. For selection remains the exclusive purpose of all breeding. Only by weeding out the substandard can the hereditary dispositions of a people or a noble class be slowly but surely cleansed of all inferiorities and brought to an ever more perfect uniformity and perfection.

But be warned against exaggerated selection standards among *hegehof* sons, at least in the first hundred years of the institution.

Two circumstances need to be taken into account in this regard. Firstly, family tradition, and secondly, the rootedness of a family to the land.

Our uprooted times no longer tend to place particularly high value on the importance of family tradition, when in fact its educational value is quite immense. A great deal could be written about these things, but it will suffice for the serious reader to refer to history's wealth of experience. Therefore, if possible, we should adhere to the following principle: the son of a nobleman also becomes his heir, even if he does not perfectly satisfy the minimum set requirements for a *hegehof* heir. For the next hundred years, only major inferiority, heritable diseases, and those diseases (for example, venereal diseases) that could be directly detrimental to a *hegehof* family should be sufficient justification to forego a son's succession to a *hegehof*. In all other respects, however, the most clearly suitable son should become the heir and, in the case of a minor physical or other inferiority, should be urged to approach the choice of his wife with particular attention and with a special sense of responsibility.

The rootedness of a family to the land does more than just play a role in spiritual and moral development, as was explained in more detail in Chapter V, Section 1. For example, the following is taught in animal

---

[148] Editor's note: A true national uniformed police force, a *schutzpolizei*, would not be established until 1936, when it was formed as a part of the newly-created Ordnungspolizei (Order Police). The main tasks of the *schutzpolizei* were the prevention of crime and traffic control both within Germany and, during the war, within the occupied territories.

breeding: the bloodline (i.e. the inherited traits of a family) is not always the only essential factor. Very often it is primarily the rootedness of the bloodline that is important in manifesting the best possible perfection in an individual. At this moment, we do not know the exact reasons for this fact, apparently because very subtle imponderables play a role in this and are difficult to determine. For example, we must simply accept it as a fact that Oldenburger horses can be bred well in Silesia and Latvia, but not in the greater part of the province of East Prussia—a person can come up with infinite examples of this; it must be expressly emphasized that experience has shown that almost every breed behaves differently in this respect, so there are no fixed rules for this matter. It should also be emphasized that this observation has nothing to do with any kind of "Lamarckism."[149] It is obviously a matter of influences on the so-called sympathetic nervous system, which, as is well known, regulates the course of life processes in the body, and where even minor disturbances are sufficient to trigger bodily imbalances, which then do not allow the individual to reach the most perfect possible physical development.[150]

---

[149] Editor's note: Lamarckism, named after zoologist Jean-Baptiste Lamarck, is the now discredited theory that living things can inherit acquired characteristics, such as muscle development, based on the use or disuse of the body parts in previous generations.

[150] The dowsing rod experiments carried out on students at the University of Halle by a team of geologists and doctors could perhaps one day shed light on this whole matter. In the experiment, students who showed a predisposition to dowsing were exposed to the most varied Earth influences and then immediately subjected to a detailed medical examination. These experiments were initiated by the paleontologist Professor Dr. Walther. As of this writing (1930), the experiments have neither been completed nor published. What has been said about them in lectures would be suitable to support the view that, although graded very differently—from person to person and perhaps also from race to race—the influences of this world have an effect of some kind on the whole physiological system of a human being, which can have an effect for the better or the worse and accordingly can influence the appearance of the human being when they affect a developing body. Perhaps these things are not so far removed from a possible explanation—if we take the basic laws of physics and more or less still possess rudimentary facilities for investigation, we already have the most important things needed to find an explanation. For if our sympathetic nervous system can be demonstrably influenced by physical effects, then these things also indirectly influence the whole life process of a human being. Editor's note: dowsing is a process, today largely viewed to be pseudoscientific, whereby an individual can determine the location of subterranean or buried water, metals, oil, or even individuals through some kind of unexplained sensing inherent to either the individual or a tool, such as a dowsing rod. Belief in dowsing continues to this day, particularly in Germanic countries.

The fact that nobility cannot simply be equated with good physical and mental health also fundamentally speaks in favor of son succession on the *hegehöfe*. History knows of many families that have repeatedly provided outstanding leaders with obvious incompetents in between—this presents us with a phenomenon that cannot be explained by Mendelism alone. Think, for example, of the Capetian House and its 609 years of eminent personalities from Louis the Fat to Louis XIV, or of the House of Savoy, which is also one of the most outstanding examples of the law of the bloodline—all the men look strangely alike, are of unlimited personal courage, immensely ambitious, devious, without remorse, not very pleasant people at all—but great rulers and leaders.[151] And then the Hohenzollern! For five hundred years, this dynasty represented true leadership and then, from the Great Elector to Frederick the Great, rose to such heights that it is difficult to find anything similar in history. And even this did not exhaust it, as in the nineteenth century it produced the most royal of all kings, Wilhelm I. We will therefore understand that nobility cannot just simply be equated with physical and mental health and that these factors alone cannot decide whether a family should remain on its *hegehof* land or not. The first king on Prussia's throne would certainly not have met the minimum requirements that the Reichswehr places on its officer candidates today. At the very least and in no small measure, we owe our very existence as a people to him and his descendants.[152]

The following fact also speaks in favor of a fundamental succession of sons on the *hegehöfe*: nobility and race cannot be equated, even though

---

[151] For more details, see Wahl, *Vom Führertum in der Geschichte* (On Leadership in History).

[152] Since the most erroneous opinions are currently circulating about Frederick I, we will quote here a word about him from his grandson, Frederick the Great, concerning the acquisition of royal dignity: "What in its origin was regarded by many as a work of vanity, subsequently turned out to be a masterpiece of politics. Frederick I thus removed his state from the dependence that the House of Austria held over the other German states. Through this act he seemed to be calling out to his successors—I have earned you a title, make yourselves worthy of it. I have laid the foundation stone, complete the work!" Just how much we today, as an empire, are the heir to Prussia may be read in Treitschke's *Einleitung zur Deutschen Geschichte im 19. Jahrhunderts Nachlesen (Introduction to Nineteenth Century German History)*. In addition, if we consider the millennia of attempts by Rome and other powers to de-Germanize Germany—we refer here once again to Chapter II—it becomes clear that the self-coronation of Frederick I (even if it may have been a power play in terms of international law) can also almost be regarded as the birth of the German people.

nobility is always bound to race and any nobility of non-Germanic origin is out of the question for the German people. But nobility also goes beyond race in that the race represents only the self-evident raw material from which a nobility can select individuals of the most rigorous quality in terms of breeding, performance, and leadership. Think of it like this—there is no doubt about the special suitability of oak wood for certain building purposes, but not every oak tree is suitable for the purpose in question; or like this—nobility relates to the race from which it has emerged like the grafted fruit tree to its wildling. Nobility is, in every case, a purpose-bred and sophisticated achievement within a race![153]

As you can see, it is advisable for many reasons to stick with the principle that the son becomes the *hegehof* heir. However, it is right and proper that the selection of the spouse in any given noble family should be subjected to particularly strict rules in order to breed *hegehof* nobility that is more and more genetically impeccable—thus we must gradually make the minimum requirements for *hegehof* heirs more and more stringent.

If a nobleman's young son is being considered for the *hegehof* but believes that he cannot submit to an arranged marriage, well, let him have this right—but in return he must give up his place on the *hegehof* to another; for the German people cannot afford to make a *hegehof* available to a nobleman merely for his pleasure!

8

If we reject the overly harsh selection of *hegehof* heirs, we necessarily comes back to this basic idea: inferior *hegehof* heirs should simply not be born, that is, ways and means must be found to marry our best German women to the *hegehöfe*. In the following we will speak mainly on the genetic value of the female half of the *hegehof* marriage, because for the

---

[153] This is indeed a damning verdict on most of the representatives of our present-day nobility, since they hardly have enough good blood left in them to even hold a candle to a predominantly Nordic peasant boy. It wouldn't hurt if some of today's racial purity enthusiasts thought about these things once in a while; without an awareness of this, they will quickly lose sight of themselves out of a sheer imagined likeness to God and also due to the fact that a pure Nordic race can only be recognized physically when it corresponds with a high level of performance.

male the case is somewhat different. Only men of above-average ability are to be enfeoffed with a *hegehof*—their usefulness to the nation and generally, though not necessarily, their relatively high genetic value is proven by this very ability. The whole *hegehof* idea only makes sense if we regard the *hegehöfe* as a reservoir of our best German blood, so that they become the sources of the national body's highest quality bloodlines. Depending on the situation, all that needs to be done is to base the enfeoffment of new *hegehöfe* on the male candidate's performance level; this population's performance level would then be maintained through subsequent generations of proper marriages. Indeed, the choice of wife remains the decisive factor for the performance level of all *hegehof* lineage.

This will only be feasible if we return our whole nation to Germanic principles, which have survived in England up to the present day and which have contributed in no small measure to the fact that the English upper classes—despite their inherited wealth and centuries of power—have not bred themselves down. It is due to the marriage of women without a dowry and their almost total exclusion from any paternal inheritance,[154] as well as assurances by the husband of their spouse's protection in the future (in the event of widowhood, etc.). The women are thus essentially married according to their own worth or according to the position of their father, so that either physical beauty (in the case of women this generally at least means good health), or intellectual merit, or indirectly their genetics (in that a gifted father usually also has a gifted daughter) are the deciding factors. The soundness of this principle is actually so obvious that every advocate for the racial improvement of our people on the basis of the results of genetics research should first demand the reintroduction of this principle as state law. But then, of course, the future of the woman must be guaranteed (in the case of widowhood or divorce) by the husband through a marriage contract, so long as she is the innocent party. This circumstance would eventually educate men on the importance of carefully considering their future wife beforehand, while also encouraging women to not to bring about any frivolous divorces which could imperil her future financial security under the marriage contract.[155]

---

[154] An exception to this are the "inheriting daughters" discussed in Chapter V, Section 5.

[155] Rather than a dowry, among the Germanic peoples it was customary for the husband to pay a morning gift (*denum matutinale*) to his wife. Among the Dithmarschen, a dowry was not customary for most of its history. In Anglo-Saxon

It is very difficult to create institutions which, on the one hand, do justice to the requirement that the *hegehöfe*, if possible, only ever receive our best women as *hegehof* wives but also, on the other hand, leave the *hegehof* candidates sufficient freedom in their choice of spouse.

At a glance, however, this task does not seem difficult, perhaps it would not even seem like a task at all. This would be the case if we still had a large number of healthy and genetically valuable women and therefore young *hegehof* aspirants had the option to choose from a large number of women quite freely. Unfortunately, things are not so!

Consider this: according to Winckel in *Frauenkunde* (Women's Studies), out of one hundred German women, only fourteen still possessed reproductive systems that have been medically certified as flawless—eighty-six are either flawed or sick. This fact should be contrasted with what E. Mann states in *Vom Eliteheer zum Schwertadel (From Elite Army to Sword Nobility):*

> The nation with enough women of childbearing age recovers from defeat in a few decades. On the other hand, the nation with a lack of fertile women will perish after a few victories. Bloody battles do less harm to the strength of the people than the loss of women in childbirth. In the bosom of the good mother from the good family lies the eternal value of every tribe, of every people.

The juxtaposition of these two points illuminates with full clarity the helpless situation in which we find ourselves as a people. In reality, however, the situation is far worse than it appears at first glance. These fourteen percent of women are indeed fertile, but do not necessarily represent the best of our people in other respects. It can be assumed with certainty that a large part of this fourteen percent carry non-German blood—especially Polish-Slavic blood, which is completely worthless to us, and that others may have pure German blood but are otherwise somehow burdened with undesirable hereditary traits.[156]

---

law, only Kent required a dowry.

[156] Literature which discusses issues of genetic health: Baur-Fischer-Lenz, *Grundriss der Menschlichen Erblichkeitslehre und Rassenhygiene (Outline of Human Heredity and Racial Hygiene)* (Munich, 1927). Von Gruber, *Hygiene des Geschlechtslebens (Sexual Hygiene)* (Stuttgart, 1922). Von Gruber, *Mädchenerziehung und Rassenhygiene (Girls' Education and Racial Hygiene)* (Munich, 1910). Grotjahn, *Geburtenrückgang und Geburtenregelung (Declining Birth Rates and Birth Regulation)* (Berlin, 1921). Muckermann, *Kind und Volk (Child and People)* (Freiburg im

The state of our women's hereditary health is so bad that I cannot help but come to the public with a proposal which I very well know could possibly arouse alienation and aversion in wide circles for reasons of sentiment or because it is something new. But the situation in this area has unfortunately become so serious that such reactions can no longer be taken into consideration—drastic measures must be taken if we as a people do not want to become extinct.

One measure, however, has already been tried. Responsible men have set up marriage counseling centers in several German cities (on the basis of genetic health research) in an attempt to at least avoid the most preventable divorces and pave the way for racial improvement.

With all due respect to the work done by them, it must be said at this point that these marriage counseling centers can do little for our *hegehöfe*. I derive the reasons for this assertion first of all from the history of animal breeding. Marriage counseling centers are, by their very nature, breeding counseling centers—whether we want to acknowledge this or not is irrelevant. People who enter into a marriage with the conscious intention of remaining childless (except perhaps in cases of venereal disease or some other serious inferiority of one part) do not need any actual "counseling," at least not counseling that is paid for with public funds. Counseling with the assistance or supervision of the state only makes sense in the case of marriages whose ultimate objective is progeny. However, any marriage that takes into account the value of the children to be produced is already breeding in the true meaning of the word. Of this we must be clear! So it need not alienate anyone if we consult the experiences of animal breeding history below.

At the turn of the eighteenth century, things were not looking good for livestock breeding on the mainland of north-western Europe, especially not with regard to horses. The many wars of Napoleon I used up many good horses, and many more were needed for military replacements. In many places, the peasant horses were simply not suitable for this purpose, and so Napoleon I developed a kind of breeding

Breisgau, 1921). Peters, *Die Vererbung Geistiger Eigenschaften und die Psychische Konstitution (The Inheritance of Mental Qualities and the Psychological Constitution)* (Jena, 1925). Schallmayer, *Vererbung und Auslese (Heredity and Selection)* (Jena, 1920). Siemens, *Grundzüge der Vererbungslehre, Rassenhygiene und Bevölkerungspolitik (Basic Pinciples of Heredity, Racial Hygiene and Population Policy)* (Munich 1930). Theilhaber, *Das Sterile Berlin (Sterile Berlin)* (Berlin, 1913). Ziegler, *Die Vererbungslehre in der Biologie und in der Soziologie (The Theory of Heredity in Biology and Sociology)* (Jena, 1918).

advisory center that was run by veterinarians—an idea that later spread and was eventually adopted here in Germany. The breeding advisory centers succeeded in preventing the thoughtless breeding of evidently inferior breeds. However, success plateaued at a certain level of breeding because there were no means for the state to force compliance with "advice." The stubbornness, laziness, thoughtlessness, contrarianism, etc. of the breeders impeded the work of this institution to such an effect that the whole endeavor had to be discontinued in the end. Nevertheless, the breeding advice centers had sufficient success and the idea of improvement through breeding had reached a wide audience. Later, it was decided to send civil servants to inspect animal breeding facilities, employing veterinarians equipped with the appropriate authority and tasked with carrying out all measures that were deemed to be necessary. The results of this nineteenth century program were initially satisfactory, although the general economic upswing of the time was very conducive to this result. Over time, a completely different difficulty emerged. After all, it was absurd to make veterinarians—a profession that derives its livelihood from sick animals—the guardian of the production of healthy animals. In addition to this, while the veterinary surgeon had vast knowledge of healthy and sick animals at his disposal, he was less qualified to judge a healthy animal with regard to its suitability for breeding. Moreover, the veterinary surgeons usually lacked the agricultural training to be able to judge the economic aspects of the breeding question. In the years after 1918, with the Prussian Ministry of Agriculture leading the way, it was finally decided to no longer leave the question of animal breeding to civil servant veterinarians, but to entrust it to people who had been specially trained for this purpose.

This part of the history of animal breeding history undoubtedly gives us clues for assessing the very similar situation of marriage counseling centers. There is no doubt that the fate of the marriage counseling centers will not be very different from that of the animal breeding advisory centers one hundred years ago. In the end, perhaps the marriage counseling centers will achieve even less. The human shortcomings that inhibited animal breeding play an even more important role in human marriage. In addition, there are imponderables of a different kind—the embarrassment, for example, of having to cancel an engagement if the marriage counseling center recommends it, with the person concerned not always able to tell the world the real and perhaps not at all shameful reasons for the broken engagement. In short, the marriage counseling centers will continue to be useful as long as it is necessary to at least avoid the most preventable divorces and to, in addition, give advice to those who want it, given the almost general public ignorance in the field of life sciences. But we cannot afford to continue the thoughtless waste of our best genetic make-up for another decade. Therefore, until the reorganization of our state involvement in this area, may the marriage counseling centers at least prevent the worst; beyond that, we cannot hope for much more from them.

We would hardly be offending our doctors if we were to say that their relationship to questions of racial improvement and marriage counseling centers is similar to that of veterinarians to animal breeding. A doctor should be exclusively responsible for the recovery of a human being. In addition, knowledge of the sick body and the identification of sicknesses are a quite different skill set from the knowledge of a healthy body with regard to its suitability for the nation.

What we really need, then, is a new class of specialists whose training will be not so far removed from that of doctors, but who will essentially take the healthy body as the starting point of their knowledge, because the health of an individual is the prerequisite for any sensible breeding concept. Furthermore, we will have to demand of this class that they not only master the laws of heredity, but also have an understanding of the economic side of social life in order to be able to base their advice on economic necessities. Today, we call members of such a profession eugenicists, but with few exceptions, there is no clarity or agreement on the educational background of eugenicists. Instead of the word "eugenicist," I would like to suggest the German word *zuchtwart* (breeding warden).

The breeding wardens would have to be state-salaried positions (like judges) with Reich headquarters, state offices, and local subordinate offices. In their hands, all questions concerning the heredity of our people would be brought together. They would have to cooperate in some form with every doctor in the Reich in order to be in a position to keep an exact genealogical record of every individual German, naturally in a form that would in no way be perceived as harassing or official.[157] It would also be

[157] This could be done very easily in the following way: Every newborn child is given a kind of family record book (with their birth date, a serial number, and so on) by the registry office or by a local registrar—this custom already exists at many registry offices. Every official event in the life of the person concerned (i.e. illnesses, court sentences, degrees, other education and so on) is reported by the

incumbent on these breeding wardens to take stock of our national heritage and conduct a systematic survey of the pedigrees of every German.

If we now assume that in the future German state of the Germans, the acquisition of citizenship is primarily a matter of blood and thus the concept of the German citizen is conditioned by blood, then we have a very simple way of helping the best German women marry the highest quality German men: by using the system of breeding officers and family registry books to continuously screen for the best German offspring. For the penetration of foreign blood into our national body would thus be made almost impossible, because the birth of a full-fledged German girl would be dependent on the civic qualifications of her parents, and their parents in turn. It is now a matter of bringing the best of the German blood to the best opportunities for procreation. By keeping together the good blood, while at the same time keeping away foreign or undesirable blood, this plan is the only way to carry out a successful purification of our national body. Stronger unity always means stronger defense and a rejection of the foreign, thus increasing the possibilities available to one's own kind.

Those who have understood me so far will also understand the following second proposal and find it natural, however strange it may seem in a vacuum.

On the whole, we can divide our young women into two main groups: firstly, those women from whom we desire offspring for the nation, and secondly, those from whom this is not desired because they are made ineligible by health or hereditary reasons. Both main groups can again be divided into two subgroups. Of the first main group, a certain percentage will always be particularly suitable for marriage. Likewise, from the

---

competent authority or doctor to the local registry office with the person in question's family record book serial number, which they could carry on their passport or other identity card. This registry office then forwards the information to the actual home registry office of the person concerned, where it is entered into his or her family record book, which is kept at this registry office and is not available for public, i.e. non-official, inspection. The individual German does not need to notice this meticulous recordkeeping himself. Nothing is required of him other than not losing his passport. Everything else is done without him. In this way, we would very quickly get a clear overview of the state of the German people's health and genetics. If, for example, a German wanted to marry, everything could be arranged between breeding wardens, because the family record book of the person concerned contained everything worth knowing and is open to the breeding wardens for inspection.

second main group, a sub-group will have to be formed of women whose marriage cannot be objected to in the case of assured infertility, and another sub-group whose marriage would have fundamental objections, for example, if their moral inferiority forbids granting them the distinction of marriage. For it is clear that if citizenship is based on the question of blood, marriage can no longer be a purely I-and-thou affair—the state must grant it only to the worthy. This granting is the expression of state confidence in the marriage.

We thus get two groups, each with two subgroups, into which every year groups of young women could be divided. From these groups, we can form four classes:

Class I: This class includes women whose marriage seems desirable in every respect. In order to exclusively and consistently gather only the best in this class, only a limited percentage of the group of women suitable for full marriage will be admitted to it—a maximum limit of about ten percent annually should be set. If it is possible to eliminate the dowry for marriage, as has been explained above, then it can undoubtedly be expected that the members of this class will successfully be married.

Class II: The rest of the women whose marriage appears desirable will be assigned to this class. This class will generally be the most numerous; because of this, the establishment of two sub-classes—IIa and IIb—may have to be considered.

Class III: Women will be assigned to this class if there are no objections to their marriage on moral or constitutional grounds, but their hereditary condition nevertheless requires the prevention of offspring. These women will be allowed to marry if the childlessness of their marriage is guaranteed (sterilization!).

Class IV: This class is for all the women of whom there are fundamentally serious reservations regarding their marriage—so that not only do we not want any offspring from them, but we must also oppose their marriage, because this would degrade the very idea of a German marriage. This includes all mentally ill persons, public prostitutes (whose pedigree clearly demonstrates their trade), recidivist criminals, and so on—these are only mentioned as particularly obvious examples. For reasons of consistency, all illegitimate children of unknown origin also belong here; these are in all cases extremely dangerous to the national body and should be subject to a separate evaluation. As the means of transportation develop, the danger of the unobserved introduction of unwanted blood through illegitimate children increases. Think of the big cities where today the colored student, the black "artist," the Hawaiian jazz band, the Chinese sailor, the Central American fruit seller, etc. are made to feel as comfortable as they do at home and accordingly tend to "perpetuate"[158] themselves in some way. Of course, in the case of illegitimacy of unknown origin, it is not necessary to generalize and these incidents should be calmly decided on a case-by-case basis. In some cases the child can be initially assigned to Class III and transferred to Class II in the event that she is found to be obviously harmless and of high quality.

The above does not apply to illegitimate children of perfectly known origin. They are valued in the same way as legitimate children.

This requires us to briefly consider the question of illegitimacy in general. It is said, "He who recognizes the illegitimate child, cancels the meaning of the legitimate one." But this is only true under certain conditions. We have already seen that neither the Indo-European nor the Germanic nor even our Old German law evaluated illegitimate offspring as such, see Chapter VII, Section 1. What was evaluated was the ancestry of the child, with the child following the "worse hand"[159] in every case, regardless of whether it was born in a marriage or not. In the Middle Ages, the Church fought against this. After its success in gaining influence over marriage, and especially since it succeeded in gaining recognition for marriage as a sacrament (sanctuary), it managed to exclude family and community members from the process and killed the old idea of marriage as a guardian of pure blood. The old terms "legitimate" and "illegitimate" became more and more indicators of whether or not the child was born in a marriage recognized by the Church. In any case, the fact is that this is the origin of our current evaluation of legitimacy and illegitimacy. In this way, illegitimate childbearing has become something like opposite-murder, i.e. a person is not illegally transported out of this world, but into it.

An argument can be made for what is actually moral and what is not, for whether the Germanic/ancient German or the ecclesiastical-new-age morality is the higher one. Making a judgment here is really not quite as easy as it seems. For the last one hundred years or so, we have removed

---

[158] See F. Brehm, "Der Rassenbrei in Mittelamerika" ("The Racial Mush of Central America"), *Nordische Blätter (Nordic Magazine)*, volume 5, number 4.

[159] Editor's note: In old German family law, a child belonged to the class of the lowest parent regardless of his/her legitimacy.

marriage from any form of family-promoting legal protections and made it a purely I-and-thou affair. Yes, we have happily reached the point where we now regard marriage and childbearing to be two different concepts, a distinction largely protected by the law. We can even be as callous as to say that marriage today is either merely an ecclesiastical concept or the legally sanctioned form of sexual satisfaction. From such a point of view, of course, any recognition of the illegitimate child nullifies the meaning of the legitimate one. But if we look at the question of the legitimate and illegitimate children from the point of view of racial improvement, then the case is quite different, for then it is first and foremost the value of the genetics (i.e. the ancestry) that decides, with the child's legitimacy or illegitimacy being a secondary question. In our centuries of German history, no century has had a truly fixed standard for what is moral and what is not—every century shows some deviation from the others in this question. I can therefore hardly be accused of frivolity when I say that from the point of view of genetic quality, we must adjust our evaluation of the suitability of illegitimate children (of known and unknown origin) in playing the role of future German mothers.

It is not necessary to decide here how many women of legitimate origin and how many illegitimate women of known origin are to be allocated to each of the four classes. It is not at all contrary to human dignity to compare animal breeding and human breeding in this respect. The task is not easy, as I well know from my previous experience in animal breeding. The correct classification of offspring with regard to their breeding value is also one of the most difficult tasks in animal breeding. But difficulties are there to be overcome, and besides, I see no other way than this class division to really help our best women find suitable marriages. After all, the decision here is not how these difficulties are to be overcome, but merely whether we want to overcome them. In any case, the future of our people will more or less depend on this decision, and a very quick response is needed.

The whole four-tier proposal has the following advantages for our *hegehöfe*:

Class I: From this class, the young *hegehof* candidate can choose his future wife without requiring any sort of confirmation from the Noble Cooperative. This is a very simple means of preventing the Noble Cooperative from developing any caste-like blood separation, and also to make our best women accessible to the *hegehöfe*—all this without having to exert any direct coercion on the *hegehof* heirs.

Class II: In general, the *hegehof* candidate will also be able to make his choice from this class as he sees fit (if necessary, you can release a Class IIa in the same way you do a Class I), but in this case (or in the case of IIb) a confirmation by the Noble Cooperative (Herald's Office) will be necessary. Consider that in this class (or in IIb) there will be a lot of women whose marriage cannot be objected to, but who for special reasons (e.g., genetics) we would object to having on the *hegehöfe*.

Class III and IV: Women in these classes are not eligible for *hegehof* marriage.

If we consider that the people is a closed block in terms of blood value, then we see that this four-class division of women acts as a kind of filter which only allows the best German blood to be married into a *hegehof*, and if not a *hegehof*, then at least directs them towards German marriages. At the same time, this is a very simple device for keeping undesirable women away from the possibility of marriage on a *hegehof*. For we must gradually build the better up into the best by eliminating the below average—this is the only way to create perfection over time!

We summarize the tasks of noblewomen:

The noblewoman should exemplify true noble morality to all around her, for her spirit, as we explained in Chapter VII, Section 3, fills the house and thus also the souls of the growing children. If the German people provide a family with a *hegehof*, they also have a right to demand that the *hegehof* be exemplary.

The noblewoman is to provide the *hegehof* family with valuable genetic material in order to at least maintain the leadership qualities of the family—to be a mother is her most important function.

On the Question of the Breeding Objective

The following is a brief discussion of some special questions which play a role in today's debate about the application of expertise from the field of racial science, as well as the theory of heredity in general, to the living conditions of the German people—a task which must be considered if our goal of creating a new nobility can come to fruition.

The expertise of animal breeding can also be used as an example here, perhaps not least because the close connection between animal breeding and economic concerns has always given it a healthy balance with purely academic opinions. Animal stock is typically so economically valuable that only in exceptional cases can the owner allow himself to follow some emerging academic opinion in his breeding decisions or measures, regardless of the increased economic efficiency it may promise. Because of this, animal breeding scientists are forced to constantly deal with economic considerations, simply because the peasants' wallets represented a kind of healthy rapid arbitration between competing theories. This resulted in an interaction between reality and science which was extraordinarily fruitful for both sides, strongly promoting the development of both, and was not a small reason for why the young science of animal husbandry is already having a stimulating effect in many areas (recall the struggles of nutritional science), including the related science of the study of humanity.

Let us begin with the concept of constitution (physical condition). In the circles of human heredity and racial studies, there are currents today which want to explain what we call races as variations of a few constitutional forms. Although corresponding currents also exist in animal breeding and can still be found today among breeders who are inclined towards Lamarckism, animal breeding on the whole is today fundamentally moving away from such views. This is due in no small part to the fact that the classification of phenomena in the field of animal breeding was carried out much earlier than in the field of human science; it quickly became obvious that the concepts of "constitution" and "race" can coincide, but do not necessarily have to. For example, the Arabian thoroughbred horses and the English thoroughbred horses are constitutionally not different (even blood related), but in their performance they are still fundamentally different, because they were bred for different breeding goals—there is, therefore, a difference in terms of race. This is even clearer in the case of the noble so-called "trotters," which are neither constitutionally different from the English thoroughbred horses nor do they appear different to a layman. Nevertheless, all the scientific statements about the constitutional equality of these three horse breeds are of little use to the breeder, for he has to decide whether he wants to breed English thoroughbreds or Arabian thoroughbreds or racing trotters. All attempts to link or equate the concept of constitution with that of race must therefore be rejected.

Mendelism. Today, in so-called large animal breeding (breeding of horses and cattle), we have had to recognize that Mendelism (see Chapter VII, Section 2), while it has played a refining and illuminating role, has not yet played a role that was directly beneficial. Nor has it been possible in large animal breeding to obtain clarity about all the hereditary traits that exist in the animals. This is simply due to the fact that the developmental period of the individual animal until sexual maturity is quite long, the gestation period lasts almost a year, and the animals' number of offspring is quite small. Without a large number of offspring, additionally, it is not possible to make reliable estimations about the genetic make-up of a sire or dam. Although it is possible to obtain several hundred offspring from a sire, these are nevertheless infinitesimally small numbers when we consider that even if we only observe twenty hereditary traits—given all of their possible combinations during the hereditary process—we would require a trillion animals in order to even have the prospect of obtaining a single animal which possessed all twenty hereditary traits in a pure form and could pass them on accordingly. As we can see, the difficulties of doing anything tangible with Mendelism in the field of large animal breeding are considerable. Even if the birth of a trillion animals is not necessary in order to gain clarity on the existence of certain hereditary traits, this nevertheless shows that a truly flawless scientific investigation of all hereditary traits in reality will encounter enormous difficulties, and that we must anticipate from the outset that long periods of time will be necessary in order to achieve any appreciable success. In humans, things are even more complicated. Firstly, instead of a maturation period of three to four years (as, for example, in the horse), sixteen to twenty years must be calculated for the human child. Secondly, the possibility of obtaining an extraordinary number of offspring from one father is excluded for reasons of propriety. Thirdly, the possibility does not exist for the deliberate mating of certain traits (i.e. calculating a pairing in advance based on the possibility of combining hereditary traits), a means that has been useful in gaining clarity about certain hereditary processes in large animal breeding. And fourthly, whereas in large animal breeding only a relatively small number of traits have actual significance, the number of essential hereditary traits increases enormously in humans. In short, things are as unfavorable as they can be for genetic-based breeding in humans and the actual application of discoveries. For the time being, genetics and racial researchers will have no options other than the collection of documents and the pure observation and logging of hereditary processes. For the time being, Mendelism will only be of indirect use to them.

In general, it can be said that it was precisely the simplicity of the results of the early Mendelian research that nurtured unjustified hopes—

even initially in animal breeding—and that the successes of plant breeding had a confusing effect. It was not taken into consideration that plant breeding has tools at its disposal that animal breeding has to do without. These include, first and foremost, the production of offspring from a parent or a pair of parents numbering in the hundreds or even thousands. All hereditary characteristics can be regrouped, recombined, and exchanged on the basis of crossbreeding experiments, merely according to the laws of probability. Applied, however, this is not quite so. It has been shown that some heritable traits, especially in large animal breeding, are not as freely interchangeable as we would think, correlating with each other in specific groups; such a dependent relationship of hereditary traits is called coupling, and these couplings have already thwarted the efforts of many breeders by bringing into his animals not only the good traits of the foreign breeds he has attempted to cross with his domestic stock, but also the inferior, which the breeder could then no longer get rid of. Despite all recognition of the value of plant-breeding research for the geneticist, all those who want to apply genetics to humanity should never take plant breeding as a model—only animal breeding. And even within animal breeding, we should exclusively follow the expertise of large animal breeders, not those of small animal breeding, which has much easier conditions for these questions. Yes, actually only horse breeding offers clues for human breeding. The horse, with its slow maturation, still corresponds most closely to the slow development of man. Furthermore, the animals are so valuable that the breeder must consider every individual, a circumstance which is very similar to the conditions in man. And finally, horse breeding is the only example that not only has to take into account several physical hereditary characteristics, but also has to consider a lot of mental characteristics (courage, will to win, obedience, deviousness, fear, and so on).[160]

Health: Even within purebred herds, the health of the individual is of the utmost importance. Health can never replace breed. But since every chain is only as strong as its weakest link, the overall hereditary value of each individual member of a breed should be assessed from its weakest points and not from its strongest. Unhealthiness is under all circumstances the most dangerous enemy of any upward breeding

[160] For an introduction to horse breeding, we recommend Schwarznecker's work on horse breeding, newly published by Professor Dr. Fröhlich-Halle in Parey-Berlin.

development. This applies to purebred stock as well as to mixed-breed stock.

Performance: Each breed brings with it the abilities and strengths to perform certain tasks, i.e. for certain achievements. But it is wrong to assume that the breed guarantees performance, in this amateurs often find themselves making a fatal error. Nowhere does nature work according to a template or build neat little rows. Not even a factory does that. And just like, for example, a motor car factory is not able to deliver one motor car exactly like another—despite accuracies down to a fraction of a millimeter—so is it that a breed is not able to imprint the stamp of unconditional equality on all of its individual beings. For this reason, even the performance of the most pure-bred stock can only be maintained by continuous and relentless performance testing that meticulously identifies and weeds out all imperfections. There is no breed in this world more thoroughly bred than that of the English thoroughbred horse. But the two hundred years of experience in this field speak for themselves. Therefore, it is advisable to adhere to the following principle: a purebred pedigree is proof of performance parameters, but it is not proof of actual performance.[161]

According to which basic general rules does animal breeding work in terms of actual breeding?

Even if Mendelism has hardly brought any direct advantages to animal breeding (at least not in the realm of its conscious application), it has nevertheless had an indirectly beneficial effect by proving the hereditability of traits and clarifying many issues in the battle of opinions on heredity issues. Mendelism, however, did not shake the basic rules of ancient animal breeding experience, even though it did purge them of many superstitions and alleged mysteries. These rules of experience are roughly as follows, with the individual points roughly placed in priority order.

1. A selection model is set up in order to first determine the ultimate objective and to give each individual breeder a kind of inner compass, so to speak, as to in what direction he should strive. This selection model is intended to train the eye for defects and to give clues as to which animal

[161] In any case, it should be mentioned here what animal breeding has only clarified with time, and only after a few misguided steps: whoever utilizes performance testing to evaluate members of a breed must firstly be clear about what performance can be demanded from the breed in question, and secondly, must above all be clear about whether his testing means could be flawed in some way.

offspring should be selected. It is important to note here that even today, such selection models do not claim to be based on scientifically infallible documentation or to be actually achievable breeding objectives. The value of these selection models is as useful or as useless for animal breeding reality as, for example, the ideal image Plato created of the perfect ruler—we do not actually expect that there will ever be a ruler who could really perfectly correspond to the Platonic model, but it is nevertheless an excellent standard of value for judging real rulers and for maintaining an absolute set of requirements for them. It is much the same with the selection model in animal breeding. The selection model comes about in many different ways. It can be developed (this is extremely rare) on the basis of scientific knowledge and then artificially put together.[162] It can also be developed on the basis of visual traditions by identifying older breed features and striving to develop this breed type anew, a method that played a role in the history of the Holstein horses. In most cases, however, the selection model comes about through the memory of talented breeders, who know exactly what forms are and aren't necessary for a certain level of performance—this method has played a decisive role in the history of the development of the English thoroughbred horse.[163]

2. The best are paired with the best. Here, however, we have thoroughly retreated from an exaggerated worship of performance alone and value performance only in the context of a perfectly healthy body. The breeding of horses, for example, has shown that animals with the ability to perform at the very highest levels tend to have problems with their fertility.

3. Selection according to pedigree.

4. Every animal considered for breeding is subjected to a performance test, but rather than testing for a level of maximum possible performance—as determined by extraordinary individual members of its breed—it is tested for a minimum level of performance and it is this minimum level which is used as a point of reference for the assessment.

5. The performance of the offspring should be closely examined, because this, in a sense, is a test of the correctness of the first four

[162] This method, for example, has played a major role in the field of skeletal evaluation and biomechanical theory within horse breeding.

[163] A similar example for the use of memory in the evaluation and identification of performance is the way talented sports coaches assess the physique of a prospective athlete to locate their future "cannons." Here, they also tend to rely exclusively on their instinct and memory.

measures.

These are the basic rules. The animal is evaluated for breeding in detail by means of a very finely worked out evaluation procedure. The animal is given marks for certain things that the evaluator believes to be important, for example: health, pedigree, breed affiliation, breed appearance (type fidelity), performance and so on. Each of these areas is judged according to a certain scoring procedure with marks expressed in numbers—the sum of the numbers is determinant. If the total sum of the scores reaches a certain fixed minimum threshold, the animal is considered to be a breeding animal, if it does not reach this minimum threshold, it is strictly excluded from any further breeding. The advantage of this scoring system is that the assessment sub-areas can complement one another, so that, for example, lack of fidelity in the breed appearance is compensated by a good pedigree. Inferior overall performance, however, depresses the total sum of points in such a way that even the most perfect type fidelity or a brilliant pedigree cannot bring about the necessary compensation and the minimum number of points is not reached, thus excluding the animal from breeding.

9

Let us return to the human being! At the beginning, we said that breeding is a procedure that deliberately seeks to produce offspring whose value is at a minimum not below that of its producers—ideally increasing in genetic value over the course of time. The key word here is "deliberately." This means that we must be clear about the goal towards which we actually want to breed. We must therefore have a breeding objective. Breeding without an objective would be a contradiction in terms, simply because breeding is always the evaluation of produced genetic material in the context of a future goal.

This fact, which is actually self-evident, is the subject of the strangest uncertainties today. From the point of view of a person trained in animal husbandry, perhaps the most perplexing one is the opinion that the German people today are a mixed people, and that because of this, we must affirm them as a mixed people and must not promote any efforts whatsoever towards purity or any other breeding objectives. Such views are based on multiple errors, assuming that the underlying basis isn't simply the inability of un-Germanic people to creatively shape the current state of things according to their own will, and whose will is merely sufficient to resign themselves to the facts and adapt to them.

To some extent, such opinions are based on the idea that racial mixture is something similar to coffee with milk or raspberry lemonade—i.e. a mixture in the physical sense—which can be graded according to the proportion of the individual quantities of liquids poured together, but which can never again lose its characteristic as a mixture. Such a conception is a thorough misjudgment of the question of mixture in racial doctrine. Hereditary factors do not "mix" in the sense just explained, they only re-assemble in every newborn. Even if the following example is somewhat weak, it is nevertheless clarifying: think of a weaving mill where the individual threads on a loom can be put together in very different patterns without having to change themselves in any fundamental way—the type and color of the threads do not change, nevertheless no pattern needs to look like another. The appearance of the woven fabric is altered as new threads are woven into it, but it remains possible to unmix these new threads at any time by leaving them out, so to speak. Originally, the mixing misconception also played a role in animal breeding. People spoke of whole blood and half blood, of three-quarter blood and fifteen-sixteenth blood, and so on, until the science of heredity eradicated the terms from animal breeding terminology (perhaps not exactly eradicated, but rather explained the meaninglessness of the idea).[164]

Another wrong attitude towards the question of mixing is the opinion

---

[164] The word thoroughbred has acquired a special meaning today. Thoroughbred is understood as a certain stock of animals, of which the lineage of individual animals are meticulously recorded and, furthermore, are kept away from any foreign blood while being continuously subject to selection in very specific respects (breeding objectives). Since the scientific theory of classification (systematics) takes the bone structure of the breeds as the standard for their classification, the concepts of purebred and thoroughbred do not have to coincide at all, even though the thoroughbred can be very uniformly bred in the area of life processes (physiology), especially in the area of performance, and can give the impression of a separate breed. Under certain circumstances, one could consider the actual core of Jewry to be thoroughbred, even though the Jews are not an actual race in the sense of racial science, see Günther, *Rassenkunde des Jüdischen Volkes (Racial Studies of the Jewish People).* The term half-breed still has a meaning in heredity when two pure-bred representatives of different races produce offspring, because these first offspring of a cross-breed carry the hereditary traits in exactly equal parts. The terms three-quarter blood and fifteen-sixteenth blood and so on are pure nonsense and should be eradicated from linguistic usage as soon as possible.

that one should not set up any breeding objectives for our people because it may result in the unequal evaluation of individual members of our people. This objection is actually already invalid because in every sensible state system, the members of the people must be valued differently; we have already spoken about the value of gradient with regard to professions in Chapter VII, Section 5. Here the case seems to be rooted in the fact that valuation according to an individual's genetic material is, for the time being, still something unfamiliar. Moreover, the individual value and the genetic value (in other words, racial value) of a person do not necessarily coincide, i.e. an individual can be very capable yet still have undesirable genetic material. Additionally, from the point of view of the people as a whole, the case is as follows: first of all, every capable citizen in the nation (the precondition for obtaining German citizenship set forth in Chapter VII, Section 8 is a prerequisite here) is desirable—this is primarily a question of the value of each individual's personality, which is not necessarily dependent on his genetic material. In the case of the woman whom this man marries, however, it is above all the genetic value that is important, rather than the individual value, which of course is also of vital significance in a morally superior people. An evaluation of women with regard to their suitability for marriage has always taken place, whether they are married according to their father's purse, the beauty of their voice, the shapeliness of their body, or according to some other parameters, for all of history women have always been subject to evaluation with regard to sexual selection by a man. In this case, the evaluation according to genetics would not be the worst—wallflowers can never be avoided when it comes to marriage! Without this guidance or its application by growing young Germans in their choice of future spouses, no selection can be made. Evaluation according to genetic makeup, however, entails a breeding objective.

Here something else must be added: whoever affirms the doctrine of heredity and holds the position that germ cells are not influenced by their environment will also not be able to avoid admitting that the Germans which accomplished many of the great achievements of German history do not necessarily represent the same genetic material as that of some present-day Germans. It is not enough to only address the "Eastern Jewish question," since the Polish enclaves in the industrial areas of Westphalia are just as foreign to us. The correspondence of the genetic material of the historical Germans with present-day German families would be the minimum requirement for a view that could regard every single present-day healthy German woman as a valuable building block in the future construction of the German Reich. For the man, the case is always somewhat different (as already noted in Chapter VII, Section 8), since here an outstandingly capable personality proves his usefulness to the nation precisely through his performance, allowing the question of his genetic value to be treated as if of secondary importance, as long there are no serious misgivings. If today, however, we wanted to consider every healthy "German" to be valuable for the future of the German people simply because they happened to be a healthy German citizen and regardless of where their genetic material actually came from, one would be essentially be advocating for the most blatant Lamarckism, just as if one claimed that a healthy donkey or mule born in Trakehnen became a fully-fledged Trakehner merely because he or his ancestors were born at the Trakehnen stud farm.

Our eugenics or racial hygiene (i.e. the doctrine of genetic health and the racial improvement of our people) community is not entirely blameless in the view that today's mixed condition of our people must be affirmed and that there is no need for special objectives, so long as only healthy people marry each other. Hildebrandt says quite correctly in *Norm und Entartung des Menschen* (*Norms and Degeneration of the Human Being*):

> One-sidedly, the idea of a master race leads to racial chauvinism of a most doubtful basis, while the idea of eugenics leads to normless utilitarianism. The racial hygienist can, in his mind, certainly eliminate harmful and lowly lineages, leaving only the capable ones to then perhaps form a useful working community. But can a mixture of races bred according to such a principle condense into a race in the noble sense?

Racial chauvinism—Treitschke objected to the use of the word chauvinism in this context—is obviously understood to mean arrogance. This is a misjudgment of what is actually the essential point of the matter, but we will come back to this in more detail. Hildebrandt, on the other hand, is not so wrong in his accusation against the eugenics teachers and researchers. Von Verschuer once called racial hygiene the application of the sciences of race and man and saw its task as cultivating the people's good hereditary dispositions and thus serving to maintain its genetic health—there is not really any kind of objective expressed in this. The most basic objective in any cultivation is the weeding out of the undesirable. One tends to a forest by methodically pruning it; we must create an environment where the desirable have air and light to flourish, which is done primarily by ruthlessly weeding out the undesirable, see Chapter VII, Section 1. All weeding, however, requires clear decisions about what is to be cultivated and what is to be weeded. Therefore, the will to achieve a certain breeding objective is the primary deciding factor in any weeding. This will to decide, however, is largely lacking in our racial scientists. They either approach the topic in very general terms or they only talk about caring for what is valuable, avoiding clear decisions on what is actually valuable and what is not. This gives the aimless utilitarian impression, which Hildebrandt explains above, where only that which happens to be useful today is kept alive, while the rest is allowed to disappear. Furthermore, the impression is also created—undoubtedly unintentionally—that only the most useful workhorse possible, the healthy working ox, should be made available or preserved for today's age—a mentality caught up in purely economic thinking. In some respects, today's eugenics seems like a political and bourgeois Liberalism that has moved into the field of genetic health. There is no doubt that this is the cause of the often lamented phenomenon of our German-conscious youth having a thoroughly indifferent attitude towards the whole doctrine of genetic health. Although the young people know that there is something useful there, and therefore do not fight the movement, they do miss the rousing central objective—the belief that a state of perfection can be achieved by our people. The fact of the matter is that the mere identification and neat separation of good and bad components is not enough when it comes to the art of building. With good stones, one can erect both imperishable spiritual monuments as well as purely utilitarian buildings, yes, even banalities such as the Dessau Bauhaus style!

More serious is the objection that is often raised by the genetic health movement: the as of yet unclear range of heritable traits and the difficulty of researching the hereditary dispositions of the German people make it impossible for eugenicists, who have a sense of responsibility towards science, to set goals at this early stage. The only reply to this is that these difficulties will not be alleviated for a few more centuries, and it is doubtful if the German people will still be around then. Above, in Chapter VII, Section 8, the immense difficulties that are in the way of a flawless recording of the hereditary dispositions of human beings (or even of a people) was already admitted. But it makes no sense to let our people perish merely to follow proper scientific procedures.

It should also be noted in passing that even if science finally determined which selection model it should choose, it goes without saying that all thought experiments about the possibility of consciously employing the scientific findings of heredity to breed superhumans or utility-humans that are specially adapted to particular purposes belong more or less in the realm of delusion, at least with regard to our people's circumstances.[165] For the prerequisite of any conscious breeding on this scale is the full knowledge of hereditary characteristics as well as perfect control over the hereditary process. We have seen above what difficulties are associated with these requirements. I did not even mention that, for example, means to facilitate research into hereditary traits are available in large animal breeding that are absolutely impossible to use among humans—among these is linebreeding, i.e. the maximization of an individual's hereditary contribution through consistent incest and inbreeding. And even if we knew much, much more about the hereditary characteristics of man than is the case today, conscious breeding will always fail because of the following: the conscious creation of human beings on the basis of calculated hereditary trait mating requires the ability to carry out mating independent of the will of the people concerned, solely according to the determination of a person carrying out calculations in a laboratory. Apart from the fact that if this practice was employed it would effectively destroy the right of self-determination as well as all respect for the individual worth of the human being, along with our entire morality—simply thinking through the matter would allow the reader to realize that it would require a curious alienation from reality to even seriously entertain such thoughts or even to express them.

---

[165] About half a century ago, an entrepreneur in South America was faced with a difficulty: his White employees could not withstand the murderous weather conditions of the swamp area where his workplace was located, while the indigenous people were well adapted to life there but did not possess the mental abilities to work without Whites. Based on his observations, he eventually decided to employ Whites only on the condition that they produced children with indigenous women on the side during their short deployment to the worksite. This measure proved to be useful: it was possible to raise a well-adapted half-breed who had inherited health from his mother and sufficient intellect from his father to be a kind of foreman or master craftsman. Such a thing may be possible in special cases in hot latitudes and among savages, but it is not relevant to German conditions.

Rather, a more justified course of action is one that seeks to determine the genetic value (or lack thereof) of an individual through systematic research into family history and the compilation of genealogical tables. This is certain—without such a biological inventory of our national body, we will not make any progress in this regard anyway. Nevertheless, the pedigree will remain purely an aid, never replacing the breeding objective. For even the best pedigree can only tell us what hereditary qualities may be present in an individual, not what is actually present in his genetic material. Even if we use the pedigree methods common in Nordic countries and work out pedigrees which not only take into account the ancestors of the person in question, but also all of their siblings, we will always only learn what is possible, not what is. Only the descendants provide information about this. This is why the entrance to a well-known Prussian stud farm bears the words: "You shall know them by their fruits!"

It is an aspect of the independent nature of hereditary traits that we cannot easily say which of a person's four grandparents contributed to the inheritance of this or that trait. The situation is further complicated by the fact that genetic value and performance do not necessarily coincide; indeed, some performance is actually based on undesirable hereditary traits that happen to favorably couple to the performance type being considered. Therefore, the known performance levels of a person's ancestors are nothing more than clues. Those who have but a little experience in animal breeding know how difficult it is to use ancestors' performance in a useful way in the evaluation of the genetic value of a breeding animal (and to carry out breeding measures on this basis); they also know that the evaluation of a pedigree is among the most difficult tasks to master in the field of animal breeding, as absolutely necessary and indispensable as the well-elaborated pedigree itself.

Finally, it should be pointed out that we have many families in Germany who will never be able to produce a good genealogical table—be it that the church books have been burned or, as in some rural areas, no clear church book entries were ever created. Therefore, pedigrees can never replace the breeding objective.

We need a breeding objective, a selection model! It is not true that the breeding objective has to wait until science is clear about the genetic make-up of the German people (the German people would have to wait a very long time), the breeding objective should be set first—it would then be the task of science to expand or restrict this breeding objective according to the results it produces. For the living reality of the German people must always be judged with the aid of science, just as German science must always be judged through the lens of the reality of our people.

Let us say this once again: breeding without a breeding objective is a contradiction in terms, because breeding is the evaluation of given realities with a view to the future. The pure determination of racial and genetic facts belongs primarily to the field of systematics and has nothing to do with actual breeding questions until the breeding objective can be constantly checked against it. Therefore, the rapid establishment of a breeding goal (selection model) useful for the German people is one of the most important tasks of German racial and genetic health research.

10

How should we go about making the breeding objective (the selection model) for the German people, and what aspects must be taken into account when setting it up?

There are only three possible ways for accomplishing this:

1. Experience and knowledge of a purely scientific character (ideally from natural science) forms the basis of a selection model that is both scientifically-developed and from a scientific perspective. Apart from the fact that purely scientific mindsets frequently have something very anemic about them, thus generally being of very little appeal to the national spirit, I reject the possibility of a purely scientific basis for this endeavor based on the objections presented in Chapter VII, Section 8. This in no way denies that science will be and must retain a decisive advisory role in the matter.

2. Research into the German past establishes what the human beings who were the actual bearers of German civilization and German history looked like. This is probably the most fruitful way to reach the goal.

3. Memory, in connection with appropriate study, identifies certain human traits to be valuable outside the framework of purely pragmatic analysis, and accordingly as worthy of preservation in the nation. This option is not sufficient for a popular selection model and can only ever be implemented within a subset of the population, but there is no reason to underestimate its importance.

In general, none of the above three points can solely claim to be able to determine the selection model; point two should be considered first and foremost, while the other two points can be added to supplement or clarify.

Today, natural science has explained with complete clarity exactly which person has been the bearer of Germanism in history. So much work has been done on this subject, including some of a strictly scientific nature, that we need have no doubts or uncertainties whatsoever in this area. It has been shown that everything we call German was created exclusively and solely by the Germanic man (whom we now call the man of the Nordic race), whose Germanism was the basic building block of German culture and history. But beyond this, it has been shown—and this realization is even more significant—that the whole of Indo-European culture and civilization, especially the non-Germanic European cultures and civilizations since the Migration Period, have always had the same man—the same race—as its foundation, and that all of these civilizations consistently collapsed when this race disappeared from them.[166] A uniform scientific theory had to be established to account for the racial commonalities in all of these cultures and state creations, which were quite separated in time and space. Since it can be proven that the origin of this race is north-western Europe, it was agreed that this race of man should be given the scientific name of Nordic race and accordingly spoken of as Nordic man.[167] Herma Schemmel states:

> Many a true German inwardly rebels against suddenly using the term Nordic to describe what he had hitherto been content describing as Germanic or genuinely German. But it was precisely for the sake of conceptual clarity that a special word had to be coined for this newly-grown idea. We cannot possibly speak of a Germanic race, for then we would come to the incorrect conclusion that the cultures of the Romans, Greeks, Persians, and so on were created by Germanic peoples; on the other hand, we also need a term to express the race common to all of these peoples. The term

---

[166] Günther provides an overview of the work that has been undertaken on this in the introduction to *Der Nordische Gedanke unter den Deutschen (The Nordic Idea among the Germans).*

[167] The common spelling as "nordic" instead of "Nordic" race is wrong, because a "nordic" race is ultimately any human race in northern Europe. The East Prussian horse can be born outside of eastern Prussia, but it is also true that any horse born in eastern Prussian is an east Prussian horse without being an East Prussian horse.

> Indo-European used here has a purely linguistic meaning and would therefore have a confusing effect because peoples whose Nordic blood has long since dissipated may very well still speak an Indo-European language. So the only option remaining was to introduce a new term—the now long-established Nordic race. Ultimately, the Nordic idea means the deepening of being German beyond the Germanic into its prototypical roots—and it is precisely this inexhaustible source of strength that enables us to finally create for the German people a state of its own kind and thus to make possible a new and greater future.

While the English Jew and statesman Disraeli, Earl of Beaconsfield, had already asserted in the 1840s that the question of race was the key to understanding history (a viewpoint which, incidentally, the German Jew and statesman Walther Rathenau also expressly subscribes to in his *Reflections*), the conclusions drawn from this realization—which was really only reached towards the end of the nineteenth century by other thinkers—was actually far more important. If civilization is based on a certain race and collapses with the disappearance of the race in question, then it must be possible to keep this race-dependent civilization alive by preserving the race in question. In this way, the theorized laws put forward in recent times by Spengler describing the inevitable course of all cultures from their youth to their peak and down to decay in old age were evidently incorrect. In domestic questions, this present possibilities for setting objectives.

Hans F. K. Günther can be credited with bringing the results of racial science to the German people in a generally comprehensible way, but it is of even greater merit that he went one step further and consciously gave the German people the Nordic man as a target image—as the German selection model. Among those who recognize racial science and the importance of Nordic man to civilization, even the most uncompromising opponent of Günther, such as Prinz zur Lippe, could not avoid agreeing with him regarding the application of this science to German state policy. He states, "A change in the nature of our people means a change in the organization of its state. The people must therefore 'choose' which race they will participate in. Here, racial evaluation gains significance and justification."

Today, it is irresponsible nonsense to conceal from the German people the fact that the extinction of the Nordic blood in history has in every case also entailed the extinction of the corresponding civilization. It is even more irresponsible to try to lull the public's incipient attention to this question by saying, for example, that it is only the spirit that matters and not the body. Where in all of history do we have any proof that the spirit is capable of shaping history independently of the physicality of the race?

For us Germans, there can really only be one goal in this respect: to strive with all possible means to preserve and increase the creative blood in our national body—the blood of the people of the Nordic race—because the preservation and further development of our Germanness depends on it.

On the other hand, we must again warn against the opinion that all future German domestic problems will be solved if only as many Nordic children are born as possible. We explained in Chapter VII, Section 2 that we cannot breed a race against an environment that does not suit it. The race in and of itself does not determine the state's form—it can do so if certain conditions apply, such as among the Icelandic peasants—but it is not the case that this condition always applies. For example, the entire structure and nature of the political system of the Roman Empire since Gaius Julius Caesar was thoroughly un-Nordic. In fact, it was so un-Nordic that even today's Germans still suffer from the contradictions between the Germanic and the late Roman political systems, which has neither been fully carried out nor been examined through to the last detail. Since the time of Caesar, Germanism had been penetrating the Roman Empire in ever-greater numbers and had attained increasingly higher ranks and honors, meaning that it would have been in a position to exert influence on the state. In fact, one of the very first governors of Gaul—a prisoner of war of Caesar and his house slave—was a Germanic, to whose influence, for example, the conquest of Germania under Tiberius can be attributed. Constantine once raised 40,000 Goths for military service in a single campaign. According to a conservative estimate by Kauffmann in *Altertumskunde (Ancient History),* half of all senior officers in the Roman army were Germanic under Julian. This alone, therefore, should have been enough Nordic blood to steer the development of the Roman state—which since Caesar had visibly taken an un-Nordic course—back into a Nordic direction. The fact that this indeed did not happen, that the high percentage of Germanic peoples in the Roman state were not enough to stop the disintegration and decay of the declining Roman civilization (or even to renew it) proves quite clearly that the physical presence of the race alone is in no way sufficient to actually shape the state corresponding to it. In this respect, things have deeper roots! In addition to the physical presence of the race, an understanding of its own kind of state and a desire for it must also exist in order for this state to come into being—in order to, as it were, prepare the seedbed upon which it can first develop.

The situation is somewhat different when the Nordic race is forced to adopt an alien form of government and is later allowed to administer this form of government independent of foreign influences. In this scenario, one can observe that the Nordic race tries to shape, or at least to administer, the alien form of government in a way that it suitable to its nature. The end result is a state that may not, strictly speaking, be called Nordic, but rather can be classified as "Nordic-modified." Undoubtedly, a classic example of this remains Frederick the Great—he is an absolute monarch and is thus also the state. Such absolutism is as un-Nordic and thoroughly late Roman as can be, see Chapter II, Section 1. Significantly, however, Frederick the Great managed his absolutist state with a Nordic sense of stewardship—he placed the state above himself and felt, as it were, only charged with running the state responsibly. Thus the non-Nordic concept of absolutism was changed, if not in form, then at least in meaning, to the Germanic-Nordic political system of a responsible (i.e. commissioned) leadership of the people (see Chapter II, Section 1). One could demonstrate the same of the political systems of many rulers of the German Middle Ages, just as the behavior of the Ostrogoths as lords of Italy is particularly instructive in this respect. Nordic man can clearly shape or at least administer a non-Nordic state, the prerequisite for this being that he is free of non-Nordic control. If he does not have this independence, the result will be nil, as is demonstrated by the Goths in their capacity as administrators and officers of the Roman Empire before their conquest of Italy. Or alternatively—as German history shows—it results in a struggle that has lasted for millennia: German history is, for the most part, nothing more than an attempt to force a non-Nordic political system onto Nordic man in order to control him by assimilating him into a non-Nordic condition—and, on the other hand, the continual rebellion of Nordic man against this.

But these facts must not mislead us into believing that the political system is so much more significant than the concept of race that race can be disregarded altogether—that it is therefore enough to simply create a Nordic state and everything else will follow. This is the mistake that certain "nationalists" are making today! Certainly, a German state shaped in the Nordic sense and based on Germanic concepts would indirectly and, so to speak, automatically promote Nordic blood in the nation—but a prerequisite for this is that Nordic blood still exists in the first place for this purpose. If this is no longer the case, then even the most beautiful state structure is of no help. It is therefore necessary to combat both the narrow-mindedness of a purely "nationalistic" point of view (i.e. one that only pays attention to the political system) and that of a purely racial point of view, which expects that all salvation will come from the physical existence of the race alone. Instead, we must promote the idea that only from the interaction of both views can something which is beneficial and profitable for our people arise.

For example, one cannot seriously imagine that merely the study of the old German spirit and the spirit of antiquity would have sufficed to rekindle the light of spiritual freedom and development lost following the German people's plunge into spiritual darkness during the Thirty Years' War. Here spoke what no oppression of the spirit has ever been able to destroy—blood. It was the blood of ancient people, who felt the same impassioned resonance within themselves and from their blood mustered the courage to stand against the misguided spirit of their contemporaries. If, however, artists are permitted today to exhibit works in the German capital that reveal with astounding openness the low state of their morality to every clear-sighted German, then their blood also plays a decisive role in this regrettable fact; this shows to what depths a person can sink when their Nordic blood has disappeared or when perhaps never they possessed it, compare Paul Schultze-Naumburg in *Kunst und Rasse (Art and Race*; Munich 1928). For today every ambitious person has sufficient education at his disposal—no one can complain of too little in this regard—so civilizational decay cannot be explained by those origins.

Recently, another objection has been raised against the Nordic idea, which strives to set the Nordic human being as the model of selection for the German people. It is pointed out that within the German nation there exist races other than the Nordic race, and that they should also be taken into account. In my opinion, however, this objection is only justified if it can be proven that certain valuable phenomena in German history and in the history of German civilization and customs can only be traced back to this or that non-Nordic race, rather than to the Nordic race. However, there is no proof of this thus far, nor do I know how one would want to prove it, for to my knowledge, German moral and civilizational history does not offer the slightest evidence for such an assumption.[168] The presence of non-Nordic traits in important people only proves that a certain admixture of non-Nordic blood need not be an obstacle to the emergence and development of a distinguished personality, or that a certain admixture of non-Nordic blood creates a certain versatility in the creative human being—whose creative power would perhaps be limited to certain areas peculiar to the Nordic race if he had purely Nordic traits. This evidence certainly does not justify the demand to preserve non-Nordic races in Germany or even to recommend them to the German people as a breeding objective, and so clearly does not justify recommendations of hybridism, such as those made by E. G. Gründel in *Menschheit der Zukunft (Humanity of the Future).*[169] The latter would be about as logical as claiming that because a glass of champagne has a stimulating effect, drunkenness must be encouraged. If, on the one hand, it is certain that a particularly versatile individual (who, by the way, is only valuable to his people through proven performance, not merely because he is versatile) has only acquired his versatility through the addition of non-Nordic blood to his fundamentally Nordic being, and if, on the other hand, it is also certain that the elimination of Nordic blood extinguishes the creative element in the nation, then only one conclusion can be drawn from this: that non-Nordic blood is stimulating only up to a certain point, not necessarily harmful up to a further point, and beyond that point is pernicious. To recommend hybridization would therefore only make sense if it was within our power to regulate the degree of mixture consciously and artificially, that is, we are able to prevent the mixture from going beyond a certain degree. But we do not have this possibility and never will have it (excluding special cases where this could be possible). If, therefore, we observe today a heavy mixture of our people, this alone is no reason to continue down this path[170]—on the contrary, this is an occasion to put a stop (at least indirectly) to the mixture, precisely by clearly developing a selection model as a breeding

---

[168] Compare Kurt Gerlach, *Begabung und Stammesherkunft im Deutschen Volke: Feststellungen Über die Herkunft der Deutschen Kulturschöpfer in Kartenbildern (Talent and Tribal Origin of the German People: Findings on the Origins of German Civilization-Builders in Maps)* (Munich: J. F. Lehmanns, 1930).

[169] Gründel's point of view can be explained by his conception of racial relations in German history. But Gründel's conceptions cannot claim to be based on real evidence.

[170] This would be as logical as living in a house that is in a state of disrepair simply because the state of disrepair is its natural state.

objective for our people. We have absorbed so much non-Nordic blood into our nation that even an immediate, unerring, and exclusive preference for marriage to women of Nordic, predominantly-Nordic, and somewhat-Nordic blood would still preserve non-Nordic blood within the body of our people for millennia to come, which could continue to richly stimulate the versatility of creative men. Regardless, any over-correction in breeding matters can later be very easily compensated for by carefully letting in desirable blood, even if non-German. Whereas it is difficult to purify a nation's genetic material after it has become uncreative through thoughtless mixture with foreign blood, it is borderline impossible once a certain degree of mixture has been achieved because one cannot control the human condition with the same thorough ruthlessness that one can employ in animal breeding.

German civilization blossomed on a foundation of Germanic blood. Today, this basic building block has absorbed a great deal of non-Nordic blood. One may regret this and also largely connect it to the undoubted decline of today's civilization.[171] But our present condition will become particularly dangerous when the German people no longer want to remember the basic Germanic core of their being. For in this question, wanting is now everything.

From a purely breeding point of view, the case is as follows — we have practically no German among us who is German by blood and who does not still have at least traces of Germanic blood in him. This reality becomes even more important when we combine it with the fact that no other race in Germany can claim the same. Consequently, purifying the German genetic material of non-Nordic blood is far more within the realm of breeding possibilities than, for example, answering the question of which non-Nordic races could be unhesitatingly recommended to the German people as a selection model.[172]

From the more recent scientific findings about the Nordic man as the historical bearer of German civilization we can draw the simple

---

[171] Wherever we observe a pronounced cultural or civilizational decline in Germany today, every single time there is evidence of non-German blood of non-European origin in the person or persons concerned. But these people are not ours regardless, so what they do has a limited bearing on the above question.

[172] On the other hand, in the case of the Westphalian and Dinaric races, one can certainly consider preserving these two racial components within our national body; this circumstance is not sufficient to recommend either race as the definitive selection model, however.

conclusion that Nordic blood must be preserved in Germany, along with sufficient justification for presenting the Nordic man as the selection model for the German people.

If we may now again draw from animal breeding experience, it follows that the German people must first be educated to recognize the Nordic man, and in particular to recognize its identifiers in a crossbreed, because this is ultimately the decisive factor.

When reading racial literature today, one often has the feeling that the prevailing opinion is that anyone is able to easily judge the breed or racial composition of a human being. Animal breeding experience, however, teaches just the opposite—it has been proven that the gift of identifying a breed without special guidance is something innate and that this gift is relatively rare. Far more often it is the case that, in spite of good and correct instruction, the ability to identify a breed cannot be obtained. In such cases, the person concerned must refrain from becoming an animal breeder—he may then become a plant breeder, where things are much easier, or he may request the guidance of an animal breeding consultant.

But just as it is not acceptable in the field of agriculture to refrain from training a peasant merely because he is not innately gifted in animal breeding, so is it not acceptable for the German people, because of existing difficulties, to refrain from training themselves to identify racial differences. It is perhaps worthwhile to show here how animal breeding skills are trained in agricultural studies.

The teacher or the school in question first presents a purely template image of the breed to be explained that is based on experience or average calculations or other indicators. Once the pupil comprehends this "ideal image" of the breed and is able to correctly recite from memory its characteristic features, as well as gained the ability to explain the characteristic differences between the breeds on the basis of pictures of other breeds, the pupil's gaze is shifted from the ideal image to reality using photographs or, if possible, live animals. For there are no perfect animals in any breed that actually reach the ideal image. The student must first learn to recognize, for example, the faults and common deviations from the ideal (without taking foreign crossbreeding into account). The art of breeding does not consist in identifying faults, deviations, crossbreeding, and so on (i.e. becoming a more or less amusing "fault checker," the plague of all animal lovers!), but in learning to appreciate what breeding value the animal still possesses in spite of its faults or foreign crossbreeding and assessing what is objectionable in relation to the whole and in view of what is being striven for. Complete beginners in animal breeding are therefore usually first cured of their "purity obsession," because most seriously believe that one may or can only work with pure breeds. This leads them to demand things from reality that reality cannot fulfill, and that is where they fail. In actual reality, the case is always that even in the most well-bred herds, one never finds animals that correspond perfectly to the established purebred template. In addition, it is often required to lead mixed-breed herds towards purebred status, i.e. to carry out so-called purification or grafting or designer crossbreeding.

Undoubtedly, applied human racial science will not be able to avoid using essentially the same techniques in training the German people on racial questions. Since we do not have the ability to teach race by means of living human beings at the moment, it will perhaps be expedient to produce textbooks which present a scientifically-established racial template alongside photographs to train the reader's or pupil's eye in identifying the features and traits of our people.

So far, only a few have dared to take this obviously useful method from animal breeding and apply it to human racial science. Strangely enough, some anthropologists accuse such proposals of being unscientific. From an animal breeder's perspective, one could say that we could patiently wait to see what kind of "more scientific" approach these experts actually come up with. Animal breeding did not develop its training know-how just yesterday, either. Just as how in the army the guidelines for general officers are somewhat different and more finely worked out than those for frontline officers, the same is probably true for the training of the anthropologist in technical racial science and the training of the German in applied racial science. Firm and clear guidelines taught in a way that make them second nature, even if they are not "strictly scientific," would still be better for our people than paying too much attention to academic concerns, which in the end only paralyzes the decisive "get to work" approach. A nation lives from the will of its citizens, not from their concerns.

One way or another, something must be done now in our disintegrating nation. The usual indifference to the fate of our precious heritage is akin to the robbery of our heritage—this state of affairs cannot last much longer. It is common knowledge today that a non-Nordic-looking German may very well have predominantly Nordic hereditary traits, so that an un-Nordic appearance is no reason (for instance out of injured pride) to oppose the Nordic idea; Günther once said, "A person's appearance may be an indication of his racial affiliation, but it is not incontrovertible evidence." That a German who marries a predominantly Nordic-looking woman is more likely to have children who at least match his level of talent than if he married a palpably un-Nordic woman is, after all, also common knowledge and is not exactly very difficult to understand if one has even a cursory understanding of racial science. This leads to the very simple conclusion that in matters of breeding, our people should evaluate their men primarily according to their achievements while also recommending that they follow the Nordic selection model as far as possible when choosing their wives. In this way, both the idea of performance and the idea of racial breeding can be integrated into our national consciousness in a very simple and undoubtedly realizable form, thus bringing it to life.

Certainly, one should not judge a woman only by her racial value. We have no use for blondes without heart or health; how this can be recognized has been indicated in Chapter VII, Section 8. But do not underestimate the importance of appearance in the selection of a wife. Breeding for appearance has the advantage that mixing (i.e. with very apparent foreign blood), with its completely unpredictable effects on the blood heritage of the offspring and the people, can be largely prevented. In animal breeding we have a thoroughly convincing example of this in the breeding of horses—during a time when competing theories clashed fiercely with one another, breeding for breed and appearance was the one point of agreement that preserved the quality and consistency of the genetic material and thus also performance. Without the surprisingly strong sense of mutual equality in our old peasant families, the German people would have never preserved the genetic material from which an abundance of important minds arose in the eighteenth and nineteenth centuries, earning our nation its world reputation as the nation of thinkers and poets.

In this sense, Hildebrandt once spoke of the importance of becoming inwardly clear about these things and the direction-giving power of a physical target image:

> Design is the meaning of life, and therefore love of form is the meaning of experience. In it, opaque desires receive a clear image, the dull impulses ignite in anticipation of their own design, and

> the seen form becomes the direction of all action, the standard of all beauty.

The question of whether such a breeding objective will be successful for our people cannot be answered with certainty in the affirmative, simply because there is a lack of experience—but it should by no means be answered in the negative. The lessons learned from animal breeding speak with such clear language about the value of a breeding objective (a selection model) that there can be doubt. It remains more difficult to predict whether this animal breeding fact can be applied to human conditions without adjustment. But here, too, we have a clue that does not necessarily prove the possibility of success, but makes it very probable.

By Holbein the Elder we have a lot of portraits of sixteenth century English society and the English nobility. It is striking that these portraits almost never depict people with the distinctly Nordic appearances that we recognize in the eighteenth century English and today consider characteristically English: those narrow, long, blonde heads with consummately Nordic facial features. The portraits of the English nobility in the sixteenth century do not appear as uniformly Nordic as those of the English lords of the eighteenth and early nineteenth centuries—it seems as if the English nobility had become more "Nordic" over the course of the past three centuries. The reasons for this strange fact, which has drawn the attention of art historians for some time, cannot be easily explained. The cause cannot be attributed solely to the painter Holbein, or to a certain style of the time, since he also painted some excellent Nordic leaders, and thus undoubtedly mastered the art of depicting the Nordic man. If the English nobility had the tendency to segregate themselves in a caste-like manner as a German ruling class, then one might be tempted to assume that the phenomenon can be traced back to a certain over-refinement caused by a culture of separation—animal breeding proves that it is at least as easy to over-refine a race as it is to coarsen it. But this can by no means be true of the English nobility, see Chapter VII, Section 5. Moreover, the English leaders of the eighteenth and nineteenth centuries have a perfect refinement in their appearance—anything but an over-refinement.

Thus only one explanation remains, to which Charles Darwin once referred, namely that in England the possibility of marrying a woman purely according to her own worth, irrespective of dowry or class (at first unconsciously and then more and more consciously) led to a preference for high-quality representatives of the female sex—the epitome of beauty and femininity—complementary to the model of the "gentleman" that was becoming ever more cemented within the world of men. This occurred in such a way that direct interaction with this social model subjected both men and women to a selection process that was to find its culmination in the familiar noble figures of today's English society. Additionally, England benefited from the fact that many of its territories had a predominantly Nordic (Lower Saxon) peasant class, which was an excellent pool from which the upper class could continually, if indirectly, supplement itself. Since the situation remains similar in our country—and our peasantry in particular still has an excellent blood heritage—there is no reason to doubt the possibility of a re-Nordicization of our people through a clear selection model such as the one laid out in Günther's *Nordischen Gedanken (Nordic Ideas).*

VIII

Some General Guidelines for the Education of the Young Nobility and for Their Position in the German Nation

"What is culture but a higher conceptualization of political and military concepts? What matters to nations is the art of proper conduct in the world and taking action when required."

Wolfgang von Goethe

1

Nobility only makes sense if it is made up of leaders and is therefore able to provide the people with leadership. Nobility that does not want to do this or can no longer do this is superfluous. This means that our *hegehof* nobility must not only educate its children in becoming conscious German citizens, it must also strive to shape its growing youth into a civic-minded generation that is truly capable of leadership.

In the previous section we stated that physical racial conformity alone is not sufficient to fill a state with the spirit of the physically predominant race when the state in question is dominated by a spirit alien to it. The German state—the Third Reich we are striving for—cannot be realized by breeding for a certain physicality alone! Therefore, it is our duty to imbue the spirit of the growing German youth with genuine German political concepts. These concepts must be particularly alive in the young nobility of the *hegehöfe*, so that they can truly fulfill their task of being an exceptional example of Germanness to the German people.

Only in this way will it be possible, over time, to carry the true spirit of the state into the entire German people and, without coercion or heavy-handedness, induce every German to strive for the same ideal noble civilization. It is conceivable then that the German people will one day be able to exemplify to the world a political system and citizenry akin to that which Plato saw in the noble spirit, but which history itself has not yet experienced.

The leadership of a people by its nobility is basically only possible in two ways: either the nobility compels the people to follow its leadership by virtue of some kind of force, or the nobility is the leadership expression of the people's will as a genuine nobility of the people and thus, to a certain extent, acts as the most perfect embodiment of the people's spirit. If the latter is currently out of reach for our people, it can still be realized if our people grow together to form a nation and are also made aware of the fact that their good leadership blood can lead them in this way. Without an understanding on the part of the German people of what should and must actually happen, even the most perfect people's nobility will not be able to lead. We must be quite clear about these relationships and correlations! This makes it abundantly clear that the leadership education of the young nobility can never be a matter for the nobility alone, but must represent a special function within the framework of the civic education of all German youth. For the young nobility, the special education necessary to train them to be conscientious and responsible leaders will essentially be a matter for the *hegehof* families, i.e. the noble community; it is unnecessary to discuss it in detail here, because it will follow naturally from the spirit of the whole system. However, we cannot deal with the civic education of the young nobility without taking a brief look at the education of German youth as a whole.

The bearer of all civilization, whether indirectly or directly, is always the state—a truth that Fichte clearly recognized. As Dahlmann said:

> For the state is not just something that men have in common, not merely something independent, it is also something that has grown together—a personality united both physically and spiritually. The family, thought of independently, is people and state and completely permeates both concepts.

But Savigny also clearly states that state power can neither enforce morality nor prevent immorality.

This clearly explains that the state, as the bearer of civilization, must have a say in the education of growing youth, but it is also clear about the limits of its educational responsibilities.

"Education is the process of integrating the offspring into the community and national order. Education continues the work of procreation."[173] If we combine this with what Fichte and Savigny have said above, we can conclude that education must begin in the family, continue in community education, and end in the civic maturity of the pupil. The question is when and how the transition from family education to vocational and then to civic education should take place.

In the preface to his work on England, Dibelius says:

> The Prussian schoolmaster had won the war of 1866, for he had given the Prussian people all the human qualities that enabled them to achieve hegemony in Germany. But the Prussian schoolmaster, namely at the grammar school and university level, lost the World War, because since 1870 he had not been able to implant in his race the political qualities necessary to become a world power.

If only it were only a question of the lost World War of 1914–18! But it is an unfortunately undeniable fact that since 1918, every year has brought us more and more proof that our entire German education system not only lacks an education for civic-mindedness, but must also be fundamentally wrong in some other way. Almost every day we can convince ourselves anew that the transmission of knowledge and the careful training of the powers of reason are obviously in no way sufficient to prevent, for example, brutal cruelty, lasciviousness, state irresponsibility, and so on; every day the newspapers report on things that no one would have thought our people capable of doing in such abundance at the turn of the century. The years after 1918 seem almost like a scornful footnote in world history about the complacency of the average German regarding the state of his school system.[174]

There is no doubt that although we created an excellent school system to develop intellectual abilities, we forgot that the human being should be whole and that his attitude towards his self and his nation is worth at least as much, if not more, than all the knowledge he was transmitted and internalized. In short, the state forgot to educate its growing youth in

---

[173] Krieck, *Das Naturrecht der Körperschaften auf Erziehung und Bildung* (*The Natural Right of Authorities in Upbringing and Education*) (Berlin, 1930).

[174] See R. Richard, "Der Nordische Gedanke und die Schule" ("The Nordic Idea and the School"), *Die Sonne* (*The Sun*), November 1928.

becoming citizens. The task of our time is to integrate the citizen-education of the young German into our present-day youth education. In this regard, we can use some aspects of English youth education as a model. Wildhagen states:

> School and home go hand in hand and work together for the education of the citizen. In England, the educational ideal has changed little in its essential features since the fourteenth century, just as the core character of the people has changed very little in that time. Then, as now, the primary aim was to educate people in becoming healthy, practical, real human beings by training their bodies and developing their individual natural aptitudes and abilities. The secondary aim was to educate them in becoming citizens by nurturing their social instincts and sentiments and by strengthening their will and character; instilling the will to self-reliance, self-discipline, and self-government based on the principle of "government by the governed," in accordance with the constitutional form of the state. The tertiary aim was then educating them as gentlemen and as members of society by awakening their sense of honor and decency and acclimatizing them to social forms.[175]

Dibelius (volume II, pages 97 and 129) explores England's policy of deliberately utilizing its youth's passion for sport by exploiting it in education in order to develop a man who is determined to act, but who always feels himself to be part of a whole. Wildhagen writes:

> Sport, which in England is thoroughly bound to the outdoors, to nature, embraces the whole man—body and soul—and these again in two very different directions, which are causally connected with the nature of the Englishman. It places the individual in a difficult but lively struggle against his fellow man, a struggle that daily life cannot offer more strongly. This develops and strengthens all the natural qualities which are constantly demanded in the political and economic struggles of the individual, the corporation, class, party, or even the nation itself

---

[175] Wildhagen, *Die Treibenden Kräfte im Englischen Bildungswesen (The Driving Forces in English Education)* (Langensalza, 1923).

> against its competitors. At the same time, it places him in a community and teaches him to use his strength and honor in its defense and to subordinate his own interests to the higher and more important ones of his community.

Apart from sport, another major feature of education in England is the cohabitation of young people. The boys are placed in a community, thus accustoming them with fitting into a whole and, by means of extensive self-governance, ensuring that their leadership talents become evident and assert themselves. Dibelius writes, "The English schools educate every Englishman in being a citizen, not by merely teaching civics, but by accustoming every boy to self-government at an early age. All this must be a model for us." The success of these measures is quite obvious—indeed, this type of education is recognized as one of the domestic pillars that England can absolutely rely on in times of foreign distress, and which has played a major role in enabling England to hold out steadfastly in times of domestic distress. The disadvantage of this method of education is, however, that the free development of the self is inhibited to a certain extent. By comparison, we take care of the spiritual and moral development of the individual (a training to which we owe a great number of our important intellectual figures) but we forget, as already mentioned above, the education of the character and, in addition, that of the German citizen.

What we need, therefore, is to combine German educational principles[176] with English ones (i.e. retaining the good principles of our German education system and taking from the English educational system what is valuable with regard to the civic education of the youth) in order to educate not only the individual's intellect as before, but also the German human being and citizen, so that every future German has a combination of all.

How could the positive aspects of German and English education be

[176] German in this sense is, for example, German physical education, with its training in individual performance. In German physical education, the community's only purpose is the promotion and bringing together of people who want to compete against each other, so to speak, through individual performance. In English sport, on the other hand, the individual performance serves to subordinate an individual to the community and to fight with one's community against another community. There is therefore a fundamental difference between German physical education and the English concept of sport.

united in such a way that they become a vibrant German entity?

Eduard von Stackelberg said:

> The essential thing in political life is not academic impressions, programs, and theses, but the indisputable: the mindset, the innermost attitude, the passionate will, the sacrifice of everything for the preservation of one's own kind.

In other words, everything that we understand as "character." Action is born out of character—we can see that wherever energetic action is vital, the qualities of character are always in the foreground. Von Seeckt once expressed this very clearly:

> The essential thing is the deed. It has three parts: the decision born of the thought, the preparation for the execution or the command, and the execution itself. In all three stages of the deed, the will leads! The will arises from character, and is more decisive for the person than the spirit. Spirit without will is worthless, will without spirit is dangerous.[177]

Seeckt's words here hold clues for the possibility of uniting German and English education.

It is a fact that no sensible person doubts that in our pre-war army and in the general conscription we had institutions that were able to replace, to a certain limit, the English citizen education system. Two circumstances prove that this assertion is not just a baseless assumption, but that our army education really did function as a civic education school to some extent. Firstly, that the frontline soldiers were the only class of people in Germany willing to save the German state from ruin in certain critical periods of time in the years after 1918. They displayed a civic will even following their general disbandment and completely without orders or instructions—exclusively on their own initiative and often inhibited by German state authorities. And secondly, that even in left-wing circles, the value of the soldierly period of service is recognized and even sought out. The value of the civic education of the pre-war German army is thus already historically substantiated. If Treitschke

---

[177] Von Seeckt, *Gedanken eines Soldaten (Thoughts of a Soldier)* (Berlin, 1929) and *Schlußkapitel: Das Wesentliche (The Final Chapter: The Essentials)*.

believes that the German state of 1870 can ultimately be traced back to the creator and realizer of the idea of universal compulsory service—to Scharnhorst—then we can calmly extend Treitschke's word to the effect that the salvation of the German state from the hands of murderers and plunderers in the years after 1918 is also due to the spirit of Scharnhorst and his disciples, above all Moltke and Schlieffen.

It is therefore important to provide citizen education to young Germans through a general period of service, for here is the place where German education and the English experience of citizen education can be very easily coupled. We will see in a moment that this also offers the possibility of eliminating from the very outset any caste mentality that might possibly take root in the growing *hegehof* nobility, as well as keeping them always conscious of their national nobility.

In view of the extraordinary diversity of the German school system, the diversity of the German tribes, and the individuality of the German people in general, there can be no consideration of any kind of standardization of German youth education for the time being—this would not even be desirable. In general, Germans are not easily persuaded to let their children grow up and be educated outside the parental home, as is customary in England. I would even like to take the view that German family education must be preserved to a large extent because it can be a wonderful source of spiritual development, provided, of course, that the parents live in a truly German marriage and that they live in a real residence, i.e. that the parents are able to offer the children a home.

If, on the one hand, German family education is retained to a large extent, but, on the other hand, the tried and true character training of our old army is added with the stipulation that the period of service this entails is subordinated to the idea of a conscious education of the youth in service and citizenship (along with the employment of certain principles of self-governance), then the possibility would exist for the adoption of the good aspects of the English education system without abruptly disturbing the uniqueness of the existing German education system. Through a properly implemented compulsory service, a space could be created where the state could methodically educate the next generation of Germans in becoming strong German citizens. This institution would also be an excellent counterweight to the increasing number of special schools which, through increasing self-governance in all areas (the advantages of which for vocational and general education need not be doubted), may harbor the danger of developing idiosyncrasies that could result in Germans no longer developing sufficient camaraderie; as a result—as so often in German history—Germans may end up placing their own benefit above the benefit of their people due to a lack of community solidarity. A general compulsory service, however, affects every German and gives him the opportunity during this time to develop a genuine comradely connection with his fellow Germans and simultaneously subjects him to genuine tasks of self-governance; this experience is likely to be as decisive for his life as it is advantageous for the state, particularly with regard to the fostering of comradeship and solidarity in the nation.

I believe that the era of standing armies, as it was in the pre-war period, is nearing its end, if not already over. The giant standing armies of the nineteenth century were a historical curiosity and actually only find a historical counterpart in the armies of Xerxes. One must bear this fact in mind in order to properly judge this question. There is no doubt that we are approaching a second European war. But it is questionable whether the huge national army that is customary today will, after this war, still retain any meaning. As urgently as we require general conscription today, given our unprotected central position in Europe, it makes little sense to believe that this necessity will exist for eternity.

Among proponents of compulsory military service here in Germany, two things are generally not discussed individually: on the one hand, the meaning of compulsory military service and, on the other, its organization in peacetime. The concept of compulsory military service only means that every citizen is obliged to defend the homeland, whereby, strictly speaking, it is up to the citizen to decide how he wants to teach himself the skills of soldiering. The standing army, on the other hand, is essentially a professional soldiery, based on a state salary. Our compulsory service of the pre-war period was a peculiar fusion of the two, born of the standing mercenary armies of absolutist kings and the Prussian popular uprising of 1813. The conscript of the pre-war period became a professional soldier for a period of time, so to speak, and learned the skills of soldiering during this time, whereas previously he would have had to teach himself. Our peacetime imperial army therefore suffered from a certain internal contradiction which it had not overcome by 1918 and which even its excellence in other matters could not compensate for.

In order to get right to the heart of the matter, it is advantageous to answer the question of conscription not so much from the perspective of compulsory military service, but more from that of a right to military service—considering the question of military service from the latter is inherently Germanic. For all healthy rational people, it is a matter of course that the homeland in distress is defended with arms when necessary. Strictly speaking, the question of who has the privilege of being called a citizen is of vital importance, as the duty to defend the homeland derives from this privilege. From this point of view, it is understandable that among the Germanic peoples, acceptance into the national community coincided with making the person in question liable for military service, and that arms became the outwardly visible expression of honorable membership in the national whole. Since the Germanic derived his entire attitude towards the nation from honor, it was logical that arms should also be an expression of the undisputed honorableness of their owner as well as of his belonging to the people. Arms symbolized—and were the defender of—said honor and people.

We too must return to this basic Germanic idea that fuses honor, arms, and citizenship into a unity, and we must do this by creating a general compulsory service that provides the citizen education called for above. This could be arranged in such a way that becoming a citizen and acquiring civil rights is only possible upon the honorable completion of compulsory service. The outward sign of these well-acquired civil rights would be the right of the German to bear arms and, on occasion, to carry them in public. Arms would thus once again be an expression of full German citizenship. How the training of the German citizens in weapons usage should be carried out is a question of secondary importance: foundational skills can incorporated into youth education, while the professional soldiery—intended more as a framework to provide leaders with the most complete training possible—provides military training to those who fulfill their official duty to compulsory military service. This could perhaps be described as follows: we are expanding the pre-war compulsory military service into a school of education in German citizenship.

Accordingly, lack of moral worth naturally excludes a person from the right to serve, and thus also excludes them from attaining full civil rights. Admission to service is thus the first and coarsest screen through which the state can filter its youth in order to determine which future citizens are useful and which ones are inferior and should be kept away. The honorable discharge from service—on which the granting of citizenship depends—then represents a second, somewhat finer filter. The final authority in breeding is then the professions, which, by granting the right to marry, methodically identify the Germans willing to work or are otherwise useful. This final filter, of course, only concerns the young men, not our women, for reasons which are explained in Chapter VII, Section 10.

With regard to the establishment of such a period of service, it must be said that it will have to be allotted a sufficient period of time and should be obligatory for both sexes—because the spirit imbued into the mothers of our people, which is in turn consciously and unconsciously imparted onto their children, is just as important for the welfare of the state as the education of the growing male youth. The training is, of course, segregated by gender. The aim of the training is to bring the individual as close as possible to moral, physical, and spiritual perfection, since this perfection is needed for their own good and for the good of the state as a whole. With this provision, it is already implied that physical unfitness would not exclude a person from compulsory service. Those who are physically unfit may perhaps be grouped together into special cohorts that conduct their training under the care of physicians so that they can re-enter life and their profession in the best possible health. The granting of citizenship rights cannot be made solely dependent on whether someone is fully physically fit or not—the only decisive factor here is whether he has been honorably discharged from his service. In times of need, a soldier can be recruited from the ranks of the less physically fit to serve as a type of rear guard in the homeland. A man who is able to work a profession in times of peace is never so unfit that he would be incapable of helping somewhere in the defense of his nation in times of need. It is a different question, however, whether a physically unfit person should be allowed to marry and have children—this is a question of genetic health, not of citizenship.

The training during this compulsory service will essentially be centered around the development of gender-related virtues, with the *tugend* (virtue) to be understood in the old German sense of *tauglichkeit* (fitness). With this, the guiding principle of male and female training is clearly highlighted, as well as their fundamental differences in certain areas. In order to avoid misunderstandings, the emphasis on the feminine education of our women is not to be understood as a call for the future expulsion of German women and girls from all places in public life, as they have fought for these positions in fair competition with men. In my opinion, this is and will remain the affair of the people in question on a case by case basis and can therefore not be appropriately incorporated into a period of service established by the state for the education of future nation-conscious female citizens. In a healthy nation, the responsibilities of women and men will always be different, even if it is often not possible to clearly delineate between professions, and even if some things can be done jointly by both sexes. The future German state, which will strive to place the family at the center of civic life, will, depending on the situation, have to prioritize the development of the means necessary for the formation and preservation of the family idea in young women. Training courses commonly found in the so-called women's agricultural schools offer pointers as to how such compulsory service for women could be handled.

As far as the male youth are concerned, it will not be possible to recommend "barracking" during the period of service; instead, something similar in nature to the rural women's schools is recommended. The youth must be prevented from cohabitating in the form of barracks because these are typically administered by an autocratic authority under conditions where self-governance tasks are not possible, lest they merely result in the mirroring of their superiors. Obedience and rank structures—where they belong and must be demanded—should be ruthlessly insisted upon! But if we want the form of their cohabitation to impart something civically valuable on the youth during their time in compulsory military service, then we must implement the forms of self-governance shown above; in this we must somehow adopt elements of the English model. This is where the pre-war period of service must undergo its further development. In this respect, the *Kolonialhochschule* (German Colonial School) in Witzenhausen-an-der-Werra could possibly point the way. There, the students live together in a university cooperative with extensive self-governance and are, contrastingly, given clearly directed education and academic ranking and are unambiguously subordinate to the teaching staff. This institution has proven itself for three decades, and valuable experiences for its field have been gained, after overcoming the usual growing pains. The method used in Witzenhausen's agricultural settler program, which combines scientific academic training with hands-on training, could also be used as a guideline for the different tasks of general compulsory service. A plausible model for this could be developed by substituting both the physical training and the weapons training of the conscript for the agricultural training customary at the colonial college, and by replacing the comprehensive and integrated scientific training of the students with the civic training of the conscripts (which instructs in Germanness as well as their duties and rights as German citizens).

However, one difficulty arises for our plan: during the compulsory service period, members of all aptitudes come together. This is even deliberately strived for in order to realize the idea of a national community and building camaraderie among the men—in this way, to a certain extent, the frontline experience of the World War (1914–18) is preserved for all time. Thus, young people with very different backgrounds come together during their time of service. If physical and mental training are one-size-fits-all (as was unfortunately often the case in the old army), the more advanced or gifted students only lose interest in the matter. In this respect, however, the following solution is recommended: the teaching of these young people—who come from such different environments and have such different educational backgrounds—should not be carried out according to an apathetic template or divided into classes based on some external point of view, rather, subjects concerning either the mental or physical training of the person should have multiple tiers, thus meeting the educational needs of the beginners, the advanced, the very advanced, and the particularly gifted in the individual areas. By employing multiple levels within individual subjects, the state also has a very simple means of identifying the particularly gifted among those in service and later either favoring them for the civil service or promoting their progress in some other way; upon discharge, even career advice could be given to the conscript on the basis of the these experiences. These multi-tiered lessons, however, do not affect the actual comradely life of the conscripts, who continue to eat, sleep, and otherwise live together, as we frontline soldiers of the World War experienced to our benefit. The institution of the "one-year volunteer," a concession to bourgeois resistance against the introduction of compulsory military service at the beginning of the last century (which was quite unappealing to the imperial army), naturally has no place in the compulsory service period being discussed here. The period of compulsory service is the same for all citizens.

In this way, an institution would be created that, despite far-reaching concessions to special vocational and general youth education, would unite the German youth in a general period of compulsory service which would develop in them an awareness of their nationality and educate them in their civic responsibilities to the German state, thus welding them together into a vital unity of the German people.

In this respect, the youth of the *hegehöfe* follow the same path as their peers. After the honorable discharge from the period of compulsory service and the subsequent granting of citizenship and civil rights by the state, the *hegehof* aspirant can be recognized and appointed by the Noble Cooperative as the heir of a *hegehof*. Restricting the nobility from confirming an heir to a *hegehof* until after the state has granted him citizenship is an excellent means for state leadership to prevent from the outset any simple-minded caste-like boorishness or arrogance on the part of the nobility—but also to show the young heir in a forceful manner the sovereign rights of his people.

Many things could be said about other forms of training for the budding nobleman. Here, at least, only this much: the nobleman administers and cultivates German soil—he must therefore understand the peasant's trade. But he should also be able to set an example for his fellow countrymen in this field. Therefore, a good scientific and technical education of an agricultural nature will be necessary for him. He may only take over the *hegehof* after passing an agricultural examination; today's agricultural state examination, administered by the Noble Cooperative, would probably be sufficient proof of training. In any case, the nobleman must be able to master the management of his *hegehof* from a business point of view. However, whether the nobleman (after his appointment to the *hegehof*) actually carries out the business management himself or whether he hands this task over to a civil servant (a lease of the *hegehof* is, of course, never an option, because this would contradict a central tenet of the *hegehof* idea) is a completely irrelevant question, provided that the nobleman has received a thorough agricultural education. After all, it is not important for a nobleman to farm the territory of his *hegehof* from morning to evening, but that he is able to oversee the business management and can judge the quality of his subordinates' work. The purpose of the requirement that professional agricultural training must precede the taking over of a *hegehof* is not the breeding of master peasants, but rather the prevention of agricultural mismanagement, which could endanger the values of the Noble Cooperative exemplified in the *hegehöfe*, and thus indirectly also those of the German people. What other special training the young *hegehof* candidate should receive in addition to his agricultural training is a question that will be answered in time by experience.

2

About the sons of a nobleman who do not inherit a *hegehof*.

The sons of noblemen who do not inherit a *hegehof* after they have completed their service and have been granted their civil rights have a special task to fulfill in the German nation, about which a few things must be said here. These sons of noblemen are to become the backbone of the leadership class of our people. They are to be role models and, as guardians of noble values, cultivate social tradition and thus impart noble spirit and noble attitudes on those called from other national circles to become leaders. Joseph von Eichendorff writes:

> For the nobility, according to its imperishable nature, is the ideal element of society; it has the task of chivalrously preserving everything great, noble, and beautiful, however and wherever it may appear among the people—of mediating the eternally changeable and new with the eternally existing, thus making it truly viable."

In general, it is lamented that we Germans are pretty much the only people in Europe with the dubious distinction of not having a national style, and that we even tend to cultivate a style of styles, so to speak. Some circles are eager to reinterpret this phenomenon, which can no longer be easily overlooked, as a special advantage of our nationality, i.e. to explain it away as an individualist tendency which is supposedly particularly German. Recently, racial science has also investigated this question, either trying to derive the phenomenon from the "degeneration" of our people or connecting it to our nation's high levels of mixed blood (which is essentially the same thing). All of these explanations, however, fail to recognize that in the countries surrounding us, things are more or less similar to ours in terms of blood purity, yet the peculiar attitude that often characterizes Germans is not to be found there, or at least not to the same extent as in our country.

In my opinion, the causes lie much deeper and affect us directly here, even if the attempts at explanations on the part of racial studies undoubtedly make good points. To a large extent, the historical disruption of our state life explains why neither an external state consciousness (as in France, for example) could develop and thus create an external national style shaped by the state, nor could a sense of belonging for the German to his people develop out of an inner national consciousness and thus establish an inner national style to regulate its outward appearance.[178] All this explains a lot! But the real cause lies in the fact that for centuries we have not had a uniform and exemplary upper class to imperceptibly influence and educate the lifestyle of the Germans. In England, the nobility succeeded in this educational task, but not in Germany, although some things were achieved in certain cases and in some quarters. What are the reasons for this?

In his *Deutschen Schriften (German Writings;* Munich 1924), Paul de Lagarde correctly recognized in his essay "Konservativ?" ("Conservative?") that our custom of passing on the noble name to all sons of a noble must and has led to very disastrous consequences. This custom dates back to the age of chivalry, when all sons of a noble were considered noble—not just the eldest who inherited the fief. From this, over the centuries, a divide developed which resulted in the worthy bourgeois never becoming equal to the nobles, inhibiting the upper classes from coalescing into one. Whereas in England the nobility, surprisingly wise in this respect, knew how to absorb worthy members of the non-noble classes and how to weed out the incompetent from their own ranks by means of self-acting processes, the German nobility had been erecting artificial partitions since the Middle Ages, nesting within themselves and sealing themselves off from the outside world. In the end, the most incompetent nobleman, solely by virtue of his birth, was socially superior to the highest-ranking commoner, because even the ennobled commoner was still considered an upstart, along with his family (original nobility, letter nobility,[179] personal nobility, and so on). Thus a thoroughly unhealthy state of affairs was reached.[180] Dibelius states:

---

[178] Since the Migration Period, we have been the oldest historical people in Europe. The Frankish Empire of the Carolingians was built on German blood and continued in the Ottonian Empire, so there is no reason to cede the honor of being the oldest European people to the French, as is often done today. At a time when Emperor Otto the Great, born of Lower Saxon blood, ruled over a world empire and the Germans were indeed the masters of the Occident, the French king was a thoroughly insignificant affair in France, the Germanic north was still pagan, Italy was sinking into internal rot, and a half-Asian barbarism was still raging in the lands east of the Elbe.

[179] Editor's note: Known as *briefadel,* these were nobles who had been ennobled by means of letters patent, a practice that began in the fourteenth century. This compares with the *uradel* (original nobility), whose nobility preceded this practice.

[180] The worst aberration in this regard probably arose in recent history, when

> In contrast to continental development, only the eldest son of the nobleman inherited the title of nobility with the undivided fief,[181] thus preventing the emergence in England of a nobility that was poor, haughty, and incapable of achievement, and fully merging it with the bourgeoisie.

The sons of a noble called to abandon the property because they did not inherit a title form the "gentry," a word which is very difficult to translate into German and can best be described as "the well-born." While all landed lords belong to the nobility[182] and are therefore all members of the English House of Lords, their brothers and sons—who are not endowed with landed property—remain bourgeois, insofar as they are perceived as noble and are noble by virtue of their origin, but never by outward appearance. Dibelius writes:

> Thus, the nobiliary particle "von" was never able to erect a barrier between the bourgeoisie and the nobility. The younger sons of the nobility formed a bourgeois middle class that actually stood between the bourgeoisie and the nobility.

The already very close inter-penetration of the nobility with the valuable leadership of the bourgeois camp is made even closer by the fact that particularly distinguished non-noble individuals, just like members of the gentry, were awarded the title of "Sir"; wives and daughters did not use the title of their husband or father, but remained bourgeois.

---

nothing better was done with men of merit than to make them *talmibureaukraten* (fake bureaucrats), that is, to confer on them official titles such as the title of councilor of commerce, title of privy councilor, etc.

[181] In England, property is—not legally but in practice—firmly bound like a *fideicommiss*: the son is appointed heir by the father only on the condition that he passes on the property undivided to his own son. Compensation for the departing heirs only takes place from the stock of movable monetary assets (insofar as the estate is not burdened by this) or indirectly by arranging for an accelerated track in the civil service instead of payment. Until the twentieth century, therefore, the position of the English nobility had been unassailably firm. Since 1918, tax legislation has made a breach in this firm foundation.

[182] On the gradations of the English nobility, see Dibelius, *England*, volume II, notes page 284. This also contains information regarding the gentry-related positions of Knights (personal nobility) and Baronets (hereditary), which roughly correspond to our lower *von* lords; the bearer of these titles being called, for example, Sir William Smith or Sir William Smith, Bt—abbreviated in England always as Sir William (in German newspaper always incorrectly written as "Sir Smith").

Wildhagen explains in *Der Englische Volkscharakter* (*The English National Character*; page 87):

> And much like during Anglo-Saxon times, since then and until today, the English nobility has never formed a closed and privileged class like in many continental countries. Whereas elsewhere the titles and rights of the father generally pass to the children, in England the rights connected with the title of nobility are by law only passed on to the bearer of the title, the "peer;" his wife and children are only bourgeois ("commoners") and, in the case of the latter, could freely marry non-nobles without any concerns. Only the eldest son inherits from his father, and only after his father's death. Even in the king's family, apart from the king, only the queen, the eldest son,[183] the eldest daughter, and the wife of the eldest son are endowed with privileges—all the other children are not legally distinct from commoners and are therefore treated as such by the justice system.

The peers, the members of the gentry, the bourgeois bearers of the title Sir, and the other members of the bourgeoisie who are in some way leaders together form London society, where the landed lords have a natural and decisive influence on the state of affairs.[184] This society is

[183] England does not use our whole "prince" system either. The "Prince of Wales," the official title of the English heir to the throne, does not mean "prince" in the German sense, but rather *fürst.* Editor's note: While both translate as "prince" in English, the German noble titles of *prinz* (prince) and *fürst* (from the Old High German *furisto,* meaning first) are different. *Prinz* merely referred to male members of a royal family, while *fürst* referred to the head of a *fürstentum,* meaning principality.

[184] The influence of these lords in England is generally underestimated by the Germans, as can be seen from the fact that we like to describe English foreign policy as "shopkeeper politics." Until 1832, only the landed lords determined English foreign policy. It was not until that year that a non-noble influence began to assert itself, essentially starting with Benjamin Disraeli, later Lord Beaconsfield. But the influence of the lords remained more or less decisive up until the World War (1914–18), despite the fact that by that point the lords had half of the influence they once possessed in 1830. But the extent to which the landed lords still determine society (London society) today is demonstrated by the timing of the famous London social season. The grouse and deer hunts begin on August 12th and the fox hunt on November 1st, with the overall hunting season not ending until April. Because of this, big social events can only begin in May and then can only last until the end of July. In other words, because the landed lords must have

essentially a model for English social life in general and is a very effective educational tool for the entire English upper class of this vast world empire. This society is actually the means by which the huge English empire is held together inconspicuously and firmly. However casually and loosely the English world empire is structured in its individual parts, there is no danger of it falling apart as long as English society in the old sense remains present. Its influence is imperceptible, but more pervasive than any treaty or legal bond could ever be. Incidentally, the supreme and absolutely recognized leader of English society is the English monarch. Related to this fact is that while the English royal house does not legally have a great deal of influence on English politics, its indirect influence through the society is, in fact, extraordinarily strong.

England, through her continuous, genuine, and imperceptible absorption of all emerging leaders from the lower classes, and through her custom of attaching the title of nobility to ownership of the soil, succeeded in keeping her nobility a healthy and vigorous leadership class. But beyond that, it achieved even more—it prevented any discontent on the part of the lower classes under noble authority from being organized and weaponized by a born leader of these classes, since the prospect of possibly belonging to the nobility himself one day extinguished any incentive to initiate a struggle against it. On the other hand, the upper classes demonstrated their qualifications through their actions, so that doubts about the necessity of the nobility did not arise at all. The advantages of such views for the English nobility are obvious and explain the fact that even today among the English people, the respect for the nobility and the belief in their special talents for leadership stand unshaken—and stand so unshaken that the average German is incapable, without an understanding of the context, of reconciling this fact with the otherwise liberal manner of the Englishman.

In our country, the situation is generally the other way around. The result is that basically every valuable German of non-noble origin is somehow imbued with a heartfelt hostility to the nobility. This is clear proof of a healthy Germanic feeling in the people, because the Germanic hates any privilege that is not based on merit or that derives its claims only from birth. Considering how this affects the current state of affairs, however, it is nevertheless worrying for our people and must therefore

---

their hunting pleasure, the London social season takes place during the time of greatest summer heat.

disappear.

There can be no doubt that the gulf between the nobility and the bourgeoisie, which has enlarged since the age of chivalry due to unhealthy developments within the German nobility, is essentially the reason why no exemplary, unified German upper class emerged to give the German people a model to emulate – it is also the reason why we have found ourselves in a state of continuous upheaval since the Middle Ages. For it is not true that the disturbances in Germany during the nineteenth and twentieth centuries are rooted in the French Revolution of 1789, even if that year may have been the strongest impetus for bringing the upheavals to public attention, as they had been more or less obscure until then. The real causes of our national upheavals are rooted in our history – in the centuries since the Middle Ages!

This is where the *hegehöfe* have their very special task for our people's future. The non-inheriting sons of the *hegehöfe* must become the backbone of the German leadership in all estates. Just like the branched structure of the body's nervous system interconnects its individual parts to form a unity, the noble spirit of the *hegehöfe* must penetrate the other professional estates through its non-inheriting sons and daughters – not by virtue of external class designations, but merely by virtue of their innate nature and noble education. This may only have an indirect effect, but it is nevertheless a vital task for the children who leave the *hegehöfe*.

In this way, we create with the noblemen's non-inheriting children something similar to what the English gentry has been for England. Without titles of nobility and other privileges, this young nobility will be influential on its non-noble surroundings merely by virtue of its nature, imperceptibly filling the whole leadership of the German people with a uniform noble spirit. Outwardly purely bourgeois and thus in a position to devote themselves to any profession without – as is the case today – having their lives complicated by a noble name; they would then only be left with the choice of either living in an exemplary manner through performance and a noble attitude (thus having an educational effect on the broader population) or disappearing into obscurity – this means they either live in an exemplary manner or at the very least do not stand in the way of non-noble exemplary leadership.

Günther described the enormous educational significance of such an institution on the people's spiritual and, just as importantly, physical breeding development in *Adel und Rasse (Nobility and Race)*, saying this about the importance of the gentry for England:

> Thus England possessed a class that approached the genuine Nordic model of the "gentleman" and the "lady" in lifestyle and choice of spouse, and is broader and better preserved in our time than any other elite class in Europe. It was in this class that England preserved its best blood. The gentry was the class in which, according to a genuinely Nordic trait, an individual's possessions and education could not win them recognition if they lacked poise, demeanor, restraint, or self-control—if he lacked the characteristics which the sagas regarded as noble and which the Nordic Hebbel, the mason's son, possessed. Because it was essentially the Nordic in body and soul that constituted a gentleman, selection for these traits had to take place in the English upper class, which today still provides so many exemplary Nordic people and so many leading men to the British Empire, all of this without the concept of equal birth having created barriers.

In this way we enable the circulation of blood: the proven leadership of the German people is continuously absorbed into the Noble Cooperative and there, purified of hereditary inferiorities over generations through clear breeding laws;[185] valuable leadership blood then flows continuously from the *hegehöfe*, as the source of renewal, back into all classes and strata of the nation, either actually leading it or, in the case of only mediocre talent, seeping away unnoticed back into the people.

But we must also create something similar to the English society, so that a certain uniform spiritual style can be imparted on Germans throughout the world and, as a result, an outward attitude can finally develop. Germanness must finally be brought out of the swinging dichotomy of arrogance and spinelessness and educated to a noble attitude which gives others what is due to them but does not cede what it is due. However, I do not want the word "society" to be understood here in the sense of our pre-war "society," which was to a very large

---

[185] With the *hegehöfe* we will have fulfilled another of Günther's wishes. He says in *Der Nordische Gedanke unter den Deutschen (The Nordic Idea among the Germans), second* edition: "What must be achieved is that as many predominantly Nordic families as possible return to the land. A Nordic upbringing will present as its target image the 'landed rural gentleman' who has been at the core of England's racial strength and whose representatives have given England's state leadership the valuable Nordic trait of steadfastness, while was well-preserved in this race."

extent only the preferred playground of bourgeois and aristocratic pomposity.

We must create a truly exemplary upper class composed of the worthy among the non-nobles and the worthy descendants of the *hegehöfe*. In this upper class, merit must always play a decisive role, regardless of the class from which the meritorious person originated; additionally, the non-inheriting sons and daughters of noblemen must ensure that a noble attitude is not lacking. Like in England, where members of the gentry and the bourgeoisie are honored and knighted with the titles of Sir and Knight in cases of extraordinary achievement, so too should our country have such a title—bestowed only for achievement—to outwardly characterize the leading upper class of society and thus effectively unite them; in other words, a nobility of merit (i.e. not inheritable) of the German people is necessary. This nobility of merit, whose influence would reverberate through the broader stratum of society to all classes and estates of our people, would, by virtue of its existence and despite the diversity of the German people, slowly evolve and converge into a society of uniform style. This is the new German society.

It is difficult to say which title should be chosen for the meritorious person. The bestowal of the word *von* as has been customary up until now should be rejected because this can easily lead to linguistic confusion, namely if the word *von* does not refer to any place designation. Additionally, this is not even an option for a non-hereditary nobility of merit. Perhaps the word *Edler* or *Edle* should be considered as a simple addition to the name, displayed as an "E" after the name like the English addition of "Bt" for baronet. Such a title should only be a distinction, not a designation.

Within the nobility of merit, however, a special title of *Ritter* (Knight) should be created, which would only be acquired in the face of the enemy: for saving lives at one's own risk, for warding off attacks against the lives and safety of the German people, for faithful fulfillment of service under life-threatening circumstances, and so on, and which—in addition to the nobility of merit based on manual or intellectual achievement—rewards and thus cultivates and promotes the spiritual values of our people. Here, too, a simple "R" after the name would sufficiently identify the Knights. For special distinction on the battlefield, such as the *Pour Le Mérite* order of merit, the title of duke could be used as an extraordinary honor, as an addition to the name similar to *Edler* and

Ritter. The very future of our people is absolutely dependent on the special cultivation of soldierly virtues.

This nobility of merit, along with the nobility of the *hegehöfe* and other leading individuals of our people, will form our society, which we suggest naming with the old German term *die Gebildeten* (the cultured), from *bildung* – meaning culture. In the older usage of the word, as is still the case in natural science, culture actually meant a thing's physical form, shape, likeness or structure – a defect of culture meant deviation from the usual bodily form. Only since J. Möser has the word also been used in a figurative sense for a person's level of education and intellectual state.

At the moment, there is a complete lack of clarity as to what a "cultured person" actually is. People generally believe that being "cultured" and "intellectually cultured" is not necessarily the same thing. Indeed, the people are far more likely to consider somebody "cultured" if they behave appropriately in public life than if they simply know a great deal, and they are likely to consider someone "uncultured" if they behave unseemly out of a lack of self-control.

Attempts to grasp the concept of culture exclusively in terms of intellect fail completely. It is instructive to observe that even a clear thinker like Paul de Lagarde is unable to make any headway with a purely intellectual explanation of the word *bildung* – in his *Deutschen Schriften (German Writings)*, for example, he says: "Culture is the form in which civilization is possessed by the individual," (page 147). Later in the text, he defines a cultured person as someone who handles life properly (page 209). Another time, "culture is the ability to distinguish the essential from the unessential, and to take this distinction seriously," (page 364). If one takes a closer look, one realizes that Lagarde repeatedly refers to a person's innate dispositions – rather than their education – in order to explain the word "culture," a realization that is particularly significant when one realizes that *kultur* (civilization) in literal translation is nothing more than "refinement of innate disposition."

The *Gebildeten* would primarily have the task of becoming the guardians and bearers of the genuinely German character, a task that goes well beyond that of the English society. The English society was ultimately a means by which the English nobility, so clear-sighted and wise in their treatment of people (according to Dibelius, they owed these qualities to an inheritance from the Norman period), ruled England and later the British Empire indirectly and therefore imperceptibly but nevertheless securely. Our *Gebildeten* need not conform to English society in this sense, but must become an expression of perfect Germanness—thus exemplary in this sense, but nevertheless responsible to the people.

Among these *Gebildeten* would primarily be where the "Nordic idea" of Hans F. K. Günther would have to be cultivated—they would have to become the primary bearers of a "Nordic movement." In *Der Nordische Gedanke unter den Deutschen (The Nordic Idea among the Germans; second edition),* Günther says of the Nordic movement:

> The Nordic movement wants the "great health" (Nietzsche) of body and soul, and the struggle for it serves as a selection model, acting as a physical and spiritual target image. The Nordic movement sets before its adherents the example of the healthy, creative, preeminent Nordic man. There must be something to strive for in order for aspiration to arise. Tension between the present reality and the timeless archetype cannot help but ignite a vibrant life. It is precisely the Nordic movement (which recognizes the Hellenic pleasure of the hero with the joyful heart, a pleasure that is also of the Nordic soul) that bears witness to the spirit that is expressed in exercise and care for the body. It points to a physical and spiritual model of selection for the German people, to which its attainment is worth every effort. The genetically healthy Nordic man could be called the selection model that the Nordic idea has proposed for the Germans.

If the Nordic idea thus guides every individual member of the *Gebildeten,* it is the task of all of them to integrate this Nordic idea into the German national idea and thus to convey it to our people.

Unfortunately, we do not yet have an actually German political system. It can only be developed out of the Prussian political system, for reasons that cannot be discussed in detail here. Unfortunately, this is quite easy for non-Prussians to misunderstand. For the Prussian political system has very often been discredited in Germany by those who were the actual bearers of its greatness, namely the Prussian civil servants.

The Prussian political system is itself a thoroughly moral concept—placing the whole above the individual and evaluating the morality of the individual with regard to his service to the state according to the requirements of the whole. One could call the Prussian political system the Germanic political system and national idea that have been adapted to modern conditions.

Therefore, the morality of the Prussian political system does not lie merely in obedience commanded from above, but rather in the voluntary integration of the individual into the whole and the naturally resulting limitation of individualism. Understanding the idea of Prussianism requires both study and experience—indeed, a certain moral aptitude and maturity on the part of the individual is required in order for it to be properly grasped. Therein lies its greatness, but therein also lies the reason why it is easily misunderstood by outsiders.

States, just like houses, cannot be built on spirit alone, see Chapter VII, Section 1. Here, too, the spiritual and the material must first be brought into harmony before a whole can be created. Without the Prussian civil service, the framework of the Prussian state would never have come into being, and the Prussian spirit could never have been realized in its people and history. Ultimately, however, the viability of the entire system depended on the sincerity and honesty of the Prussian civil service, and it is no coincidence that King Frederick William I began the creation of his Prussian state with the education of his civil service.

But the Prussian civil service was only the framework of the Prussian state, and as much as it breathed the Prussian spirit, it was not, in its essence, a truly Prussian civil service—at least not Prussian in the sense that it was able to act independently out of an innate sense of responsibility. For the nature of a good civil service is to be obedient and not self-serving, it is not optimized for acting on its own initiative. Responsible, independent action—the hallmark of every true leader—does not coincide with and is in fact the exact opposite of civil service, in the best sense of the term. The Prussian civil servant was the responsible guardian of the gears of the Prussian state, who saw to it that no cog in the Prussian state's great machinery came to harm—but he was not a leader, let alone capable of setting the gears of the Prussian state into motion on his own accord. Thus it is no wonder that Prussia produced outstanding civil servants of consummate honesty, but hardly any leaders—leading Prussians were almost always Prussians-by-choice, i.e. born as non-Prussians, then voluntarily becoming Prussians. Around 1809, the Prussian Minister of the Interior at the time, Count Alexander Dohna, noted with surprise:

> In no other country in Europe are all the qualities necessary for a capable representative as unheard of as in Prussia; on the other

> hand, in no other country can you find so many excellent people for the details of business.

On the same occasion, Freiherr vom Stein wrote about the Prussian civil service (and thus, incidentally, uttered prophet-like words that were to prove surprisingly true in the years after 1918):

> Our misfortune is that we are governed by bureaucrats who are salaried, academic, disinterested, and landless. This list goes on and on. These four words: salaried, academic, disinterested, landless—embody the spirit of our mindless government machine. Whether it rains or shines, whether taxes rise or fall, whether old traditional rights are destroyed or left in place, whether all peasants are considered merely day laborers, and whether bondage to Jews and usurers is substituted for bondage to the lord of the manor—all this is of no concern to them. They raise their salaries from the state treasury and write, write, write in their quiet, well-locked offices, raising their children to be equally useful writing machines.

This Prussian civil service has been the mediator and representative of Prussianism among non-Prussians and has therefore induced completely erroneous ideas about Prussia.

Before 1914, the introduction of non-Prussians to the morality of the Prussian political system was a matter that few people took into consideration. What the non-Prussian experienced as Prussianism was essentially just the Prussian civil service. These civil servants inspired respect and admiration, but not exactly enthusiasm. This was expressed very nicely in the thoughtful Baltic R. V. Engelhardt's *Skizzen* (*Sketches*; Berlin, 1905):

> The precision, the almost machinelike regularity with which the great apparatus of the German state functions creates an atmosphere of order and so-called welfare that can almost replace education in freedom and morality, and therefore possesses a certain compulsory method of ennobling man.

We have seen that, properly understood, Prussianism is voluntary service—in thought and deed—to the national whole out of moral conviction. Now contrast this with Engelhardt's words above about "forced ennoblement." It is immediately apparent that the old Prussian civil service, in itself an excellent institution, has unfortunately given rise to completely incorrect ideas regarding the Prussian spirit and the Prussian political system.

But to grasp the deep moral core of the Prussian political system and elevate and expand it into the German political system is a task well worth the efforts of the noblest of our people. To understand and experience this in oneself and to fulfill it in the German state should be the moral duty of all *Gebildeten* (in the sense described above). In harmony with Günther's Nordic idea, a German political system could arise and a German humanity could be formed, which, out of the spiritual and physical perfection drawn from its service to the German state, would give rise to the style of the future German man. Perhaps then we will see the realization of the old prophecy that the world will once again be healed by German nature.

But only when the German has, in a sense, learned to be himself—and only if there exists a fully developed Germanness—can the German one day fulfill his mission for humanity! Otherwise, a gravestone will one day be set with the inscription that Georg Stammler warningly wrote:

"Here the German people have slain themselves
In gruesome strife, not one remained."
Why? One will ask, shaken.
On the stone it is written: "For human happiness."

Appendix A

Recommended Works

Editor's note: This section, included in the original text, presents a collection of works either recommended by the author or promoted by the original publisher. While many of these are not available in English at this time, many readers will find the literature's subjects and themes, hopes and dreams, fears and anxieties extremely relevant to our modern world. This list of books gives us a rare glimpse not just into the intellectual zeitgeist of National Socialist Germany, but also the daily lives and concerns of the average person.

The fundamental work of
Reichsbauernführer (Reich Peasant Leader) and Reich Minister of Food and Agriculture R. W. Darré

Das Bauerntum als Lebensquell der Nordischen Rasse (The Peasantry as the Source of Life for the Nordic Race). 1933 Edition. 480 pages.

Darré's book on the peasantry was first published in 1928 in Wehnachten. At the time, the author was still an unknown researcher, so publishing the extensive book was a significant risk. Since then, Darré has proven that he is far more than a scholar—he has realized the conclusions of his research and carried out the unification of the German peasantry under his leadership. He now gives the newly unified peasant class the laws which (based on his knowledge of history) he believes are necessary for the salvation of not only the peasantry, but also of the Nordic German people. His inheritance law was the first step on this path, others will follow.

The basis for this legislation, so necessary for the German

peasantry, is contained in this book. In it, he shows that the Indo-Europeans were not a wandering, nomadic, pastoral people, but that they lived as farmers and drew their national strength from the soil. As an animal breeder, Darré is well-versed in the history of our animals and from this basis has drawn valuable conclusions about the origins of our ancestors. The book places particular emphasis on the things that ought to be of particular importance to Germans of today—the basic principle that only efficient, land-based farming can serve as an inexhaustible source of life for the people. We must take the measures that our ancestors employed to secure and protect our peasantry and transform them into new forms for the present day—in this way, we can stop the downfall wrought by urbanization, proletarianization, and disorganization altogether, we can escape the fate of Sparta and Rome. The book received recognition in the political and scientific press alike, in a time when it was still dangerous and offensive to profess a Nordic peasantry.

More writings from R. W. Darré

Das Schwein als Kriterium für Nordische Volker und Semiten (The Pig as a Criterion for Nordic Peoples and Semites).

Stellung und Aufgaben des Landstandes in einem nach Lebensgesetzlichen Gesichtspunkten Aufgebauten Deutschen Staate (Functions and Tasks of Government in a German State Built on Principles of Life-Law).

Walther Rathenau und die Bedeutung der Rasse in der Weltgeschichte; Rathenau und das Problem des Nordischen Menschen (Walther Rathenau and the Importance of Race in World History; Rathenau and the Problem of the Nordic Man).

Zur Wiedergeburt des Bauerntums: Aufgaben des Landstandes (For the Rebirth of the Peasantry: Tasks of the State).

Das Zuchtziel des Deutschen Volkes (The Breeding Objective of the German People).

Two wonderful books on race by Dr. Ludwig Clauß

Die Nordische Seele: Eine Einführung in die Rassenseelenkunde (The Nordic Soul: An Introduction to Racial Souls).

"Clauß examines the style of the Nordic soul in all areas of her passion: in the chaste shyness of shame, in the confession of love, in the duel of swords, in the absence of speech, in jokes and wit. The differences and limits of our spiritual understanding of racial souls, their connection to the Germanic type (which is evenly mixed between Nordic and Dalic races), and their separation from the Mediterranean and Eastern types can be read in this book filled with examples and the lively perspectives, written by an interpreter and visionary who sought out the Nordic figure—be it in the Black Forest or on the North Sea coast or among Frisian fishermen." *Deutsche Zeitung (German Newspaper).*

Rasse und Seele: Eine Einführung in die Sinn der Leiblichen Gestalt (Race and Soul: An Introduction to the Meaning of Physical Form).

The reworking of an out of print book: *Von Seele und Antlitz der Rassen und Völker (On the Soul and Face of Races and Peoples)* as well as the earlier, immensely popular book also titled *Rasse und Seele (Race and Soul).*

"In contrast to scientific anthropology, which is based on measurements of physical characteristics, here Clauß examines the distinguishing characteristics of the souls of different peoples and races. As part of the methodology of his research, Dr. Clauß lived for many years with the peoples he was examining. Living with those whom we want to explore with understand—this is the only source from which expressive research draws. The captivating presentation will be a pleasure for everyone, as Clauß opens our eyes to a deeper understanding of foreign peoples." *Lokal-Anzeiger (Local Gazette),* Berlin.

Works of Professor Dr. Hans F. K. Günther

Deutsche Köpfe Nordischer Rasse (German Headshots of the Nordic Race), with Professor E. Fischer (Berlin).

The result of a competition organized by the Werkbund (German Association of Craftsmen) in the interests of research into the German race and people.

"These headshots are indeed a selection of gorgeous, genuinely Germanic looking German men and women." *Deutsche Zeitung (German Newspaper),* Berlin.

Der Nordische Gedanke unter den Deutschen (The Nordic Idea among the Germans).

"The Nordic movement is not directed against other races, nor does it deny the value of other races. It only knows one positive goal: to counteract the frightening anti-selection of the Nordic people, i.e. the gradual decline of this physically and mentally superior race among the German people." *Deutsche Zeitung (German Newspaper).*

Rasse und Stil: Gedanken Über ihre Beziehungen im Leben und in der Geistesgeschichte der Europäischen Völker, Insbesondere des Deutschen Volkes (Race and Style: Thoughts on Their Relationships in the Life and Intellectual History of the European Peoples, Especially the German People).

"You don't know what is more admirable about the new work: the creativity of the racial thought therein, or the often unheard-of novelty of the questions and solutions." *Deutsche Zeitung (German Newspaper).*

Rassenkunde des Deutschen Volkes (Racial Studies of the German People).

"The elegant, factual, and carefully considered presentation, combined with a brilliant style, makes studying this excellent book a pleasure." *Blätter für Deutsche Vorgeschichte (Journal of German Prehistory).*

"The best and richest easy-to-understand explanation of our people's racial problem that we know." *Zeitschrift für Deutschkunde (Journal for German Studies).*

Kleine Rassenkunde des Deutschen Volkes (Pocket Edition of Racial Studies of the German People).

"Rightly called the 'People's Günther.' It outlines the essentials regarding racial issues and sets forth the latest research in historical, linguistic, and prehistorical studies. Despite this, it is written in such a way that everyone can read and understand it." *Die Heimat (The Homeland).*

Rassenkunde Europas (Racial Studies of Europe).

"Günther's findings and the conclusions drawn from them are based on an incontrovertible scientific basis." *Deutsche Akademikerzeitung (German Academic Newspaper).*

"By critically evaluating all new observations and findings and wisely eliminating everything that is remains disputed or unexplained, Günther's new edition of Racial Studies of Europe has considerably progressed; in its present form it is an excellent treasure trove of knowledge about racial matters." *Niedersachsen (Lower Saxony).*

Rassenkunde des Jüdischen Volkes (Racial Studies of the Jewish People).

"Without any fear or false shyness and in no way one-sided or unjust, let alone motivated by hatefulness. Both the content and format are exemplary – in-depth, knowledgeable, flawless, and irrefutable." *Die Kommenden (The Coming).*

Ritter, Tod und Teufel: Der Heldische Gedanke (Knight, Death, and the Devil: The Heroic Idea).

"A worthy German companion to Carlyle's work, all the more valuable to us as it portrays German heroes." *Deutsche Zeitung (German Newspaper).*

Works of Professor Dr. Ludwig Schemann-Freiburg

Studien zur Geschichte des Rassengedankens (Studies on the History of the Idea of Race). Volume I: *Die Rasse in den Geisteswissenschaften (Race in the Humanities).*

"With an extraordinary mastery of the vast subject and with extraordinary conscientiousness, a very broad topic has been brought together here and presented with liveliness and enthusiasm. The strong arguments set forth in support of the author's personal convictions will convince not only the educated layperson but also the expert." Professor Dr. von Eggeling in *"Anatomischen Anzeiger" (Anatomical Gazette).*

Studien zur Geschichte des Rassengedankens (Studies on the History of the Idea of Race). Volume II: *Hauptepochen und Hauptvölker der Geschichte in ihrer Stellung zur Rasse (Major Epochs and Major Peoples of History and their Concepts of Race).*

"The book is written with the most refined objectivity, an admirable mastery of the subject, and the impartiality and sense of responsibility that distinguish our best historians. An excellent, extremely interesting work." Professor Dr. A. Drews in *Karlsruher Tagblatt (Karlsruher Daily).*

Studien zur Geschichte des Rassengedankens (Studies on the History of the Idea of Race). Volume III: *Die Rassenfragen im Schrifttum der Neuzeit (The Racial Question in Modern Literature).*

Some of the 280 individuals thinkers discussed by Schemann:

Spinoza / Rousseau / Voltaire / Leibniz / Kant / Goethe / Fichte / Hegel / Schopenhauer / Feuerbach / Nietzsche / Luther / Grotius / Jhering / Stahl / Konstantin Frantz / Schäffle / Schmoller / Napoleon / Lavater / Virchow / Ratzel / Kossinna / Burckhardt / Breysig / Chateaubriand / Thiers / Renan / Taine / Johannes von

Müller / Wilamowitz / Mommsen / Macaulay / Carlyle / Lagarde / Bopp / Jakob Grimm.

This volume, Schemann's third, concludes the great racial work: *Studien zur Geschichte des Rassengedankens (Studies on the History of the Idea of Race)*. The evolution of the concept of race in literature and science has been traced from the Reformation to the most recent times.

Works on Genetics

Graf, J. *Die Bildungs- und Erziehungswerte der Erblehre, Erbpflege und Rassenkunde (The Educational and Nurturing Values of Genetics, Inheritance, and Racial Studies)*. Lecture.

Graf, J. *Vererbungslehre und Erbgesundheitspflege: Einführung nach Methodischen Grundsätzen (Heredity and Genetic Healthcare: An Introduction According to Methodological Principles)*.

"Graf offers an excellent introduction to heredity and genetic healthcare (racial hygiene). This book is aimed at the educated of all classes and is written especially for teachers and educators." *Deutsche Erziehung (German Upbringing)*.

Lenz, Fritz. *Menschliche Auslese und Rassenhygiene/Eugenik (Human Selection and Racial Hygiene/Eugenics)*.

"The book presents profound thoughts on every important issue facing our people today. Genetic predisposition and social structure are seen as factors of biological selection, along with illnesses. We learn things of the greatest seriousness regarding the relationship between the decline in the birth rate and women's professions—about migration selection and the fate of whole races and peoples.

The whole book is an intense and mortal struggle for fate of the German people, presented in a language understandable to everyone. For all of those who do not want to, and cannot quietly watch, the death of our people, it is an incentive to start the renewal from within—to start with themselves." *Der Türmer (The Tower Keeper)*.

Schultz, Bruno K. Head of the Department of Racial Studies at the Race and Settlement Office of the *Schutzstaffel* (SS). *Erbkunde, Rassenkunde und Rassenpflege: Ein Leitfaden zum Selbststudium und für den Unterricht (Genetics, Racial Studies, and Racial Care: A Guide for Self-Study and Teaching)*.

The new, popular, and comprehensive presentation of all three subjects for teaching in schools of all kinds.

Siemens, H. W. *Vererbungslehre, Rassenhygiene und Bevölkerungspolitik (Heredity, Racial Hygiene, and Population Policy).*

"A first-class guide! The low price makes it accessible to those who cannot buy more extensive publications in the field. I really want to see Siemens' work in the hands of every true German." *Alldeutsche Blätter (Pan-German Newspaper).*

Works on German Racial History

Bang, Paul, Heinrich Claß, Generalmajor Graf von der Goltz, Professor Dr. Hans F. K. Günther, Professor Hartmann, Councilor von Hertzberg, General of the Infantry A. Krauß, Councilor Dr. H. Stellrecht, and Professor Mar Wundt. Edited by W. von Müffling. *Deutschlands Erneuerung (Germany's Renewal).*

Monthly magazine for the German people. For more than sixteen years, with the help of outstanding men, *Deutschlands Erneuerung* (Germany's Renewal) has been fighting to restore and consolidate the political, economic, and cultural foundations that our people need in order to regain their place among the nations.

Baur, Erwin. *Der Untergang der Kulturvölker im Lichte der Biologie (The Decline of Civilized Peoples from the Perspective of Biology).*

Hart, Franz Theodor. *Alfred Rosenberg.*

The long-time editor of the "*Völkischer Beobachter*" (Volkish Observer) is one of the intellectual leaders of the National Socialist movement. His main work "The Myth of the 20th Century" is about as popular as a book can be. Anyone who wants to learn about the intellectual foundations of National Socialism will happily welcome Hart's new writing, which introduces us to people close to Rosenberg and at the same time provides insight into the thought processes and arguments behind his main work.

Kern, Fritz. *Stammbaum und Artbild der Deutschen und ihrer Verwandten: Ein Kultur- und Rassengeschichtlicher Versuch (Family Tree and Breed Pictures of the Germans and their Kin: An Attempt at Cultural and Racial History).*

"I consider Kern's book to be the most ingenious that has been written since Gobineau's essay on the importance of race in history—it is far more significant than that. The contributions from the fields of anthropology, ethnology, prehistory, and history have made it possible to build a no less magnificent building on their very stable foundations. Kern has a very unusual understanding of biology for a historian, with a keen eye for body shapes and a fine ear for the expressions of the soul." Professor Dr. Fritz Lenz.

Krog, Fritz. *Lagarde und der Deutsche Staat (Lagarde and the German State).*

Kuhn, P. and Dr. H. W. Kranz. *Von Deutschen Ahnen für Deutsche Enkel: Allgemein Verständliche Darstellung der Erblichkeitslehre, der Rassenkunde und der Rassenhygiene (From German Ancestors to German Grandchildren: A Presentation of Heredity, Race, and Racial Hygiene for General Audiences).*

A book for everyone. Even the simplest German comrade should be able to understand it (this is why the author avoids foreign words as much as possible or only uses those that are officially introduced). It seeks to get every German to share responsibility for the future of their people and to awaken in them a love and pride for their race.

de Lagarde, Paul. Volume 1: *Deutsche Schriften (German Writings).*

Complete with an index of persons and subject matter and a portrait of Lagarde.

de Lagarde, Paul. Volume 2: Ausgewählte *Schriften (Selected Writings).*

Edited by Paul Fischer. Complete with an index of persons and subject matter.

Helmut, Otto. *Volk in Gefahr: Der Geburtenrückgang und Seine Folgen für Deutschlands Zukunft (A People in Danger: The Birth Rate Decline and its Consequences for Germany's Future).*

The text gives a clear and convincing explanation of the danger we are facing and points out the need for an appropriate racial hygiene and population policy.

Ploetz, A., editor, in cooperation with Dr. Agnes Bluhm, Professor Dr. F. Lenz, et al. *Archiv für Rassen- und Gesellschaftsbiologie, Einschließlich Rassen- und Gesellschaftshygiene (Archives of Racial and Social Biology, including Racial and Social Hygiene).*

Official journal of the Reich Public Health Service Committee and the German Society for Racial Hygiene.

Schulz, Bruno R., editor. *Volk und Rasse (People and Race).*

Monthly illustrated magazine for the German people about racial studies and racial care.

Contributions by: Professor Michel (Riel) / Präsident Astel (Weimar) / Professor Baur (Müncheberg) / Minister R. W. Darré

(Berlin) / Professor Fehrle (Heidelberg) / Professor Günther (Jena) / Councilor Gütt (Berlin) / State Minister Hartnacke (Dresden) / SS-Reichsführer Himmler (München) / Professor Mielke (Berlin) / Professor Mollison (München) / Professor Much (Wien) / Professor Reche (Leipzig) / Dr. Ruttke (Berlin) / and more.

The magazine publishes research on the racial composition of the German people. Not only the physical, but also the mental and emotional properties are taken into account. Related research into the relationship between race and language and culture, as well as the cultural differences within the German people, are also published.

Professor Dr. Staemmler, M. *Rassenpflege im Völkischen Staat (Racial Care in the Volkisch State).*

Contents: Why do we need racial ideas? / What everyone should know about race and heredity. / The law of fertility. / In 1900, Germany had a population of 52 million with two million births per year—today it has 65 million with only one million births. / The abnormal age structure of our people. / The best should be expected to reproduce. / How can one work towards racial hygiene? / Racial care or "eugenics"? / Keeping the race clean. / The struggle between blacks and whites in America. / The Jewish system. / Our goal is: separation of races. / Penalties for those who desecrate our race. / Immigration of foreign races. / What the parents' house means for their children. / The transformation of "family morality." / Love without inhibition. / 40,000 divorces in 1930 in Germany. / Protect the youth from degenerate sexual literature. / Purge theater and film. / We need the four-child marriage. / Against biological pacifism. / Should contraceptives be freely sold? / Against Marcuse and Hirschfeld. / Protecting large families. / The different genetic groups. / Who can marry whom? / The health passport. / And the illegitimate children? / Women and jobs. / Population policy is living space policy. / Balancing family burdens. / Child benefits and child support. / School and the number of children. / Protecting the farmer. / Create new living space. / Who should settle? / Some data on offspring of inferior quality. / How do you prevent inferior people from reproducing? / Racial care and criminal law. / Castration of sex criminals. / Is abortion permissible? / How a volkisch school should look like. / The task of the race offices. / Health surveillance until a person's twentieth year. / Determining genetic value. / *Volksgemeinschaft.*

Works on History and Government

Bang, Paul. *Geld und Währung: Eine Gemeinverständliche Darstellung (Money and Currency: A Guide for Non-Experts).*

State Secretary Dr. Bang is not only a legitimate expert, but he also knows how to present information to others in a clear and enjoyable way. First, he explains the often misused terms of inflation and deflation, then he clarifies what is money and what is not, identifying what makes a usable currency. Imaginative proposals for a capital-based currency are correctly discredited for their worthlessness. Money can only be based on the creation of goods—not on land, mortgages, or other similar things. Connected to this, the serious disadvantages of a gold-based currency are shown."

Böhmer, Rudolf. *Das Erbe der Enterbten (The Inheritance of the Disinherited).*

Böhmer details the social bondage of the landless disinherited. The surplus children of the rural country and the small towns—compelled to leave their homes to earn a living—greatly enlarge the masses of the dispossessed and the disinherited. Your legacy should be returned to you. Among other possibilities, this can be done by transplanting industry to the countryside and developing smaller new cities. These cities, which would house every worker, would bring the worker's home and workplace closer together. This frees him from the depressing reality of having to remain a wage slave just to keep his land. He becomes down to earth and thus more satisfied, eventually finding his way back to his "fatherland." The realization of Böhmer's ideas can only be comparable to Stein's reforms (which made Prussia's rise possible). Böhmer conclusively said this: national freedom is based on social freedom alone!

"Probably none of the previously published essays on the plight of the German people investigates the root causes as deeply as Rudolf Böhmer's book, the title of which sounds like that of a novel, and whose economic discussions are rare in their deepness, thoroughness, and uniqueness." *Ubersee- und Kolonialzeitung (Overseas and Colonial Newspaper).*

Danielcik, Hans Peter, et al. *Deutschlands Selbstversorgung (Self-Sufficient Germany).*

"This work can be better described as the "primer of autarky." In any case, there is no book that is better suited to spreading and underpinning the idea of self-sufficiency. It is not surprising that these insightful proposals for a new economic structure come very close to our National Socialist ideas – sometimes matching them exactly – and that the ideological basis of this book is ultimately National Socialism." Oberpräsident Wilhelm Kube in *Der Märkische Adler (The Märkische Eagle).*

Contents: The path to self-sufficiency. / The labor service. / Fundraising. / Economic and trade policy. / Grain farming and bread supply. / Potato growing. / The German tobacco industry. / Fruit cultivation. / Beekeeping. / The sugar supply. / German sheep farming. / Meat supply. / Margarine supply. / Dairy industry. / Livestock feed. / Fishing industry. / Poultry farming. / Coffee-tea-cocoa. / Industrial raw materials and the finished goods industries. / Metal industry. / Chemical industry. / Textile industry. / Lumber industry. / Mining. / Fuel supply. / The quarry industry. / Glass industry. / Leather industry. / Shoe industry. / Rubber industry. / Motion picture and cinema industry.

von Dickhuth-Harrach, Gustaf. Compiled. *Im Felde Unbesiegt: Erlebnisse im Weltkrieg, Erzählt von Mitkämpfern (Undefeated in the Field: Experiences in the World War, Told by Fellow Combatants).*

Table of Contents:

Major General Hugo Kerchnawe. *Im Felde Unbesiegt: Band Österreich* (Undefeated in the Field: Austrian Edition).

Vice Admiral Eberhard von Mantey. *Auf See Unbesiegt* (Undefeated at Sea).

Air Force Major George Paul Neumann. *In der Luft Unbesiegt* (Undefeated in the Skies).

von Dickhuth-Harrach, Gustaf, Compiled. *Wie Wir uns Zur Fahne Durchschlugen: Erlebnisse von Auslandsdeutschen und Seeleuten im Weltkriege (How We Won Our Flag: The Experiences of Germans Abroad and Sailors in the World War).*

Eckehard, Kurt and Dr. Battenberg. *Fieberkurve oder Zeitenwende? (Fever Curve or Turning Point?)*

An excellent propaganda pamphlet that is particularly aimed at the bourgeoisie.

"Anyone hesitating as to whether they should take part in the Party will find an explanation of everything that was previously unclear to them. Hardly any text has brought so many thousands of Germans their 'day in Damascus' as this by Eckehard." *Völkischer*

Beobachter (Volkish Observer).

Contents: Is the NSDAP a "bourgeois" or a "proletarian" party? / The nature of the bourgeois parties. / Reactionary? / Imitation of fascism? / Beyond "bourgeoisie" and "proletarians." / The idea of a blood community. / The idea professional estates. / What about socialism? / Revolutionary? / Legal or illegal? / Stumbling blocks. / The rough-bodied clay. / The "Nazi" press. / Brawls and "provocations" / Why uniforms? / The "right to the streets." / Is anti-Semitism necessary? / What is the stance of National Socialism towards the Christian churches? / Aim of revanchist war? / Rethink the big one.

Contents of the afterword: The shots of Potempa. / Traffic strike. / Gregor Straßer. / Schleicher. / Harzburg Front.

Engel, J., member of the Prussian diet, and Franz Eisenberg. *Millionen Klagen An! Altenmäßige Aufdeckung Marxistischer Mißwirtschaft in der Sozialversicherung (Millions Accuse! Marxist Mismanagement of Social Insurance).*

This manifesto explains the shocking manner in which local health insurance funds—intended as helpers and friends of the working class—had become the strongest bulwark of social democratic nepotistic crony capitalism, abusing the funds of more than 22 million insured persons over decades. The authors bring forth a wealth of facts, often proven by publicly available court judgments, from which it can be clearly seen that these are not individual cases of abuse, but a system. The local health insurance scandal screams this reality to the heavens. The book should be read by all insured persons, as well as doctors and health insurance officers.

Freiwald, Ludwig. *Die Verratene Flotte: Aus den Letzten Tagen der Deutschen Kriegsmarine (The Betrayed Fleet: The Last Days of the German Navy).*

"Freiwald describes in gripping form the penetration of revolutionary ideology into small circles of sailors, the failure of the administrative offices, and the resulting indecision of some of the officers. We read about the deaths of officers loyal to their flag and the final journey to Scapa Flow." *Kieler Zeitung (Kiel Newspaper).*

Hartz, Gustav. *Die National-Soziale Revolution (The National Socialist Revolution).*

Gustav Hartz's new book, both captivating and clearly written, will convince everyone of the need for a fundamental change in the state and in the economic principles that still prevail among the majority of our people today. Only a radical rethinking and relearning will free us from the curse of the individualist economic ethos of the past decades, whose unrestrained capitalism made individual advantage the sole driving force behind all economic action.

It is extremely interesting what the author has to say about the restructuring of our economic system, about new forms of organization for the workforce, about the state of wages, about private and joint ventures, about a new form of social insurance, about public health care, about the social retirement fund (which gives the retired worker as large a share as possible of his paid contributions) that is completely absent today, as well as other contemporary emergency issues. In general, the sections that offer practical suggestions are the best parts of the entire book.

Helmut Stellrecht. *Trotz Allem! Ein Buch der Front (In Spite of Everything! A Book from the Front).*

"I consider the book to be very meritorious and I wish it widespread circulation, its spirit is brave and pious, qualities found in and inherent to war." Hanns Johst.

Hitler, Adolf. *Warum mußte ein 8. November kommen? (Why did November 8th have to come?).* Pamphlet from *Deutschlands Erneuerung (Germany's Renewal).*

The Führer's program: in powerful sentences he shows how Marxism caused Germany to collapse. He also outlines the path to a cure: "The salvation of the Fatherland is complete the instant that the last Marxist is converted or destroyed.

Hoffman, W. *Mein Weg zum Glück: Erlebnisse Eines Deutschen Kriegsblinden (My Way to Happiness: The Experiences of a German Man Blinded in War).*

"Grenade shrapnel tore the optic nerve of the barely thirty-year-old soldier. In the following years, he blindly walks the long road to independence, learning all over again these things that are so self-evident and yet are now so difficult: walking, eating, reading. This is a book of valor. Every National Socialist should campaign for the distribution of this book." Baldur von Schirach in *Völkischer Beobachter (Volkish Observer).*

Lehmann, Fritz. *Wir von der Infanterie: Tagebuchblätter aus Fünf Jahren Front- und Lazarettzeit (We, The Infantry: A Diary of Five Years on the Front and in the Hospital).*

"Here we are shown the experience of the war in its entirety, with its infinite versatility, insightfully describing its deep, revolutionary effect on the soul of the frontline soldier. Above all, this book includes keen, relentless introspection and a complete and unrelenting openness. It is the war book of the German man." *Völkischer Beobachter (Volkish Observer).*

Ludwig Freiwald. *U-Bootsmaschinist Fritz Kasten (Submarine Machinist Fritz Kasten).*

Fritz Kasten really lived. In his trips on many of our dashing submarines, the tremendous experience of our intrepid and doomed men is reflected on in an impressive way. Submarine machinist Kasten is a symbol for all members of our submarine fleet, whose deeds still shake and inspire us today. The book is written with passion and inexorable truth, leading us from event to event in gripping, hard-hitting language—it is the anthem of the submarine fleet.

von Müffling, Wilhelm Freihern. Compiled. *Wegbereiter und Vorkämpfer für das Neue Deutschland (Precursor and Pioneer for the New Germany).*

"A splendid collection of works by all those who contributed to the reacquisition of Germany's freedom and sovereignty. The national revolution can only be sustained by an intellectual and political ruling class that stands out in all essential fields from the stressed and complacent satiety and arrogance of the elites of November Germany. A valuable little book that deserves to be seen and handed down to future generations." Der S.A.-Führer (The S.A. Leader), Karlsruher.

Paul, Walther. *Als Kanonier in Ost und West: Fronterlebnisse eines Deutschen (As a Gunner in the East and West: Frontline Experiences of a German).*

Not a diary from an officer's point of view, it is—for better or worse—the war memories of a poor rural Stormtrooper who was drafted in the middle of the war at almost forty years of age. His unique experience allows the reader to view the events of the front not just from the perspective of a common soldier, but also that of a mature man.

Reventlow, Graf Ernst. *Kriegsschuldlüge und Kriegsschuldlügner (War Guilt Lie and War Guilt Liars).*

Contents: You are guilty—because you are alive. / The enemy begins to march. / The Balkans become a base for attack. / The Balkan Wars. / German fleet construction to blame for the world war? / Organization and preparation. / Belgium. / The German guilt. / The guilty lie before the war... / ...and during the war. / Germany's "attack." / "Not solely to blame," the guilt "confession." / "Fulfillment."

"The author explains the Belgian question and highlights those actually guilty for the war in a compelling way. As a relentless investigator of the past and the cowardly and mendacious present, Reventlow delivers with a book that both enlightens and admonishes taboos." *Sächsischer Beobachter (Saxon Observer).*

Rosenberg, Alfred. *Das Verbrechen der Freimaurerei: Judentum-Jesuitismus-Deutsches Christentum (The Crimes of Freemasonry: Judaism – Jesuitism – German Christianity).*

"Thanks to the work of in-depth researchers, the realization that international Freemasonry was the driving force behind the unleashing of the world war continues to grow. This book deals with the spirit of Freemasonry (i.e. Judaism) and contrasts these two with the seemingly opposed—but in reality aligned—Jesuitism, showing that all three have one striking commonality: striving for world domination. All in all, an excellent book that is enlightening in every respect." *Der Michel (The Michel)*, Graz.

Schöpke, Karl. *Deutsches Arbeitsdienstjahr Statt Arbeitslosenwirrwarr (A German Year of Service Instead of the Clutter of the Unemployed).*

"One of the most daunting tasks facing Germany, the year of service and the solution to the unemployment question is presented here in such a way that one truly believes that these proposals are possible and can greatly improve our people body and soul. With complete mastery of his subject in both theoretical concepts and practical applications and with a fanatical enthusiasm for the promotion of the people's mental welfare, the author unfolds his ideas regarding the implementation of a service year and answers all objections and concerns in advance of the reader." *Deutsche Zeitung (German Newspaper).*

"This extremely valuable book explains one way to eradicate the clutter of unemployed people: the idea of the service year. The author is a real leader, a man of action who knows exactly what is possible and what is necessary." *Deutsche Akademikerzeitung (German Academic Newspaper).*

Sorokin, Pitirim. Translated and edited by Dr. H. Raßpohl. *Die Soziologie der Revolution (The Sociology of Revolution).*

"Reading Sorokin's book is not recommendable enough. A rare source of information about the natural genesis, artificial operation, and general course of revolutions; those who know understand revolutions also have a means of defending against them." *Deutsche Allgemeine Zeitung (German General Newspaper).*

Spieß, Theodor. *Minenwerfer im Großkampf (Mortarman in a Great Battle).*
His personal war diary with supporting information from his war comrades.

"With its dramatic descriptions of the major battles in the west and east and on the Isonzo Front from 1914 to 1918, the book gives a vivid picture of the development of the short-range mortar during the four years of the war." General of the Infantry Ewald von Lochow.

von Volkmannleander, B. *Soldaten oder Militärs? (Soldiers or Military?)*
"This book speaks to my soul." General of the Infantry Karl Litzmann.

Weinreich, Eckart. *Die Nation als Lebensgemeinschaft (The Nation as a Life Community).*
"The self-evident facts of political contemplations regarding God and divinity—of the highest goals and eternal tasks—are now finally being considered. This book pulls the curtain aside with the power of true belief and true morality, demanding a world that is guided by more than organizational, economic, and political concepts alone. It calls out to all those who are preparing to lead us into the much-awaited future 'In this sign you will conquer!'"

Wichtl, Friedrich. Edited by Ernst Berg. *Weltfreimaurerei—Weltrevolution—Weltrepublik: Eine Untersuchung über Ursprung und Endziele des Weltkrieges (World Freemasonry—World Revolution—World Republic: An Investigation into the Origins and Ultimate Goals of the World War).*

Contents: Introduction and overview. / Introduction to the Masonic order. / Masonic institutions, customs, and symbols. / St. John's Freemasonry—St. Andrew's Freemasonry. / Masonic clothing, badges, etc. / Freemasonry and Christianity. / Freemasonry and Judaism. / The role of Jews in Freemasonry. / Freemasonry: Charity and Politics. / World revolution as a means for a Masonic world republic. / Freemasonry and the world war. / Conventions of Freemasonry's war. / Freemasonry, Zionism, etc.

Zarnow, Gottfried. *Gefesselte Justiz (Shackled Justice).*
Volume I Contents: The New German Iliad (Sklarz-Rutisker). / The overthrow of the Barmat public prosecutors. / In the shadow of the dead tribunes. / The tragedy of justice in Magdeburg. / The secret of Dr. Nicola Moufang. / Rogues, speculators, and councilors: the Boeß-

Sklarek case. / Judge Pontius (Feme Trials). / The Leipzig Reichswehr high treason trial.

"Examine each of the works in this text and see whether such a situation does not demand a duty higher than silence." Adolf Hitler.

Volume II Contents: The treatment of Nordic farmers compared to that of the rebellious winegrowers on the central Moselle (Klaus Heim). / Public Interest—the decree granting special protections to Jews. / Red hate speech. / The bombing case. / Judge Beinert: Justice and reciprocity. / State Secretary Weismann's oath. / Barmat and the Prussian government. / Barmat-Heilmann. / The oath of the *Reichskanzler* A. D. Bauer.

"This is a reference work of the highest usefulness for future historians—it is a moral act to arouse conscience." *Der Weltkampf (The World Struggle).*

Works on Nature

Bertsch, Karl and Franz Bertsch. Compiled. *Flora von Württemberg und Hohenzollern: Zum Gebrauche auf Wanderungen, in Schulen und Beim Selbstunterricht (Flora of Württemberg and Hohenzollern: For Use on Hikes, in Schools, and for Self-teaching).*

Demoll, Reinhard. *Instinkt und Entwicklung (Instinct and Development).*
The book is not only of special importance to the expert (because of the new theory of instinct, which was first proposed here), but also to the non-scientifically trained reader and nature lover. In a stimulating way, it offers an insight into an aspect of nature and compels us to admire.

Hegi, Gustav. Alpen*flora: Die Verbreitetsten Alpenpflanzen von Deutschland, Österreich und der Schweiz (Alpine Flora: The Most Common Alpine Plants in Germany, Austria, and Switzerland).*

Hegi, Gustav. *Illustrierte Flora von Mitteleuropa (Illustrated Flora of Central Europe).*
"The most magnificent and most important work of botany in Central Europe." Professor E. Ulbrich, Berlin.

Lehmann, Ernst. *Biologie im Leben der Gegenwart (Biology in Everyday Life).*
A great era has dawned for biology—it has been placed at the center of the National Socialist worldview and has thus become the focus of the interests of our entire people. It is important to enlighten all types and classes of people with regard to biological issues and to make it

clear to them what biology means to the life of an individual in the German present and future. This is what Professor Lehmann's book does! It should be widely distributed to educate all types of people about life science issues.

Lehmann, Karl Bernhard. *Frohe Lebensarbeit: Erinnerungen und Bekenntnisse eines Hygienikers und Naturforschers (A Happy Life's Work: Memories and Confessions of a Hygienist and Naturalist).*

The book of the multi-faceted and well-educated university professor is captivating on every page. The description of his teaching days are not only quite charming, it can also teach today's teachers a lot about education. The book is a grateful retelling of a rich and varied life.

Ruckuck, P. *Der Strandwanderer: Die Wichtigsten Strandpflanzen, Meeresalgen, Seetiere, Strand- und Seevögel der Nord- und Ostsee (The Beach Walker: The Most Important Beach Plants, Sea Algae, Sea Animals, Beach Birds, and Sea Birds of the North and Baltic Seas).*

The textbook for all leadership courses.

University of Politics of the NSDAP

A textbook. Published with the collaboration of lecturers from the politics department of the NSDAP School of Politics in Bochum by Gauleiter Dr. Joseph Wagner and the scientific director Dr. F. Alfred Beck, Councilor in Prussia. Sponsored by Ministry of Culture.

The work has been tried and tested in leadership courses! The basics of political knowledge and action are given in an easily understandable format.

Table of contents:

Introduction:	J. Wagner: The task of a National Socialist university of politics. / Dr. F. A. Beck: The idea of a National Socialist university of politics.
J. Wagner:	General and current politics: 1. Concepts and ideas of National Socialist politics. 2. The German concept of leadership. 3. The German way of life as a political problem. 4. Current political problems.
Dr. F. Jeß:	Racial studies of the German people.
Dr. H. Schultz:	Heredity.

Judge Dr. Reimer: The law under National Socialism.

Judge Dr. Roebling: State and people.

Colonel Kirchheim: The German armies from the German p eople's armies to the *Reichsheer*.

Dr. A. Schlitter: The economic system and its problems.

Businessman H. Heiner: Breaking bondage.

E. Stürz: Organization as a realization of an idea: 1. Classical forms of organization in history and the present. 2. Modern forms of organization, particularly the National Socialist movement.

A. Meister: Foundations and applications of psychology in advertising.

Dr. E. Schwarzschulz: From Germanic to German: a brief look at great Germanic early history.

Appendix B

Glossary of Cited Figures

Aereboe, Friedrich: Born July 23rd, 1865 in Horn, Hamburg; died August 2nd, 1942 in Berlin. He was an agricultural economist, advocating for the integration of business principles into agriculture. He pioneered a method of phosphate fertilization that lessened Germany's reliance on phosphate imports.

von Amira, Karl Konrad Ferdinand Maria: Born March 8th, 1848 in Aschaffenburg, Bavaria; died June 22nd, 1930 in Munich, State of Bavaria. He was a legal historian, dealing primarily with German and medieval law.

Ammon, Otto Georg: Born December 7th, 1842 in Karlruhe, Baden-Württemberg; died January 14th, 1916 in Karlruhe, Baden-Württemberg. He was an anthropologist and archaeologist. His claims on Nordic ancestry within ancient European aristocracies set the groundwork for many future works of Nordicist theory and scientific racialism.

Arnold, Wilhelm Christoph Friedrich: Born October 28th, 1826 in Borken, North Rhine-Westphalia; died July 2nd, 1883 in Marburg, Hessen. He was a politician, legal scholar, and legal, economic, and cultural historian.

Bauer, Karl Heinrich: Born September 26th, 1890 in Schwärzdorf, Bavaria; died July 7th, 1978 in Heidelberg, Baden-Württemberg. He was a surgeon and university lecturer in Breslau and Heidelberg. Among other things, he was co-editor of human genetics publications, director of the Surgical University Clinic in Heidelberg, and founder of a cancer research institute in Heidelberg in 1964.

Baur, Erwin: Born April 16th, 1875 in Ichenheim, Baden-Württemberg; died December 2nd, 1933 in Berlin. He was a botanist, geneticist, and eugencist. His application of eugenics to racial advancement with Fischer and Lenz proved highly influential to National Socialism.

Bebel, Ferdinand August: Born February 22nd, 1840 in Deutz, North Rhine-Westphalia; died August 13th, 1913 in Passugg, Switzerland. He was a socialist politician and publicist. He was one of the founders of German social democracy and is still regarded as one of its preeminent historical figures.

Caesar, Gaius Julius: Born 12 July, 100 BC in Rome, Italy; died 14 March, 44 BC in Rome, Italy. He was a Roman military tactician and politician whose conquests, reforms, ambitions, and eventual assassination would eternally echo (for better or worse) in the politics, philosophy, and culture of Western civilization.

Clauß, Ludwig Ferdinand: Born February 8th, 1892 in Offenburg, Baden-Württemberg; died January 13th, 1974 in Huppert-Taunus, Hessen. He was a German psychologist and influential racial theorist from the 1920's through to the National Socialist era.

Dibelius, Wilhelm: Born in 1876; died in 1931. He was a Professor of English at the University of Berlin and a member of the Society for German Abroad, a German cultural association that promoted closer relations between Germans in Germany and Germans in the diaspora.

Disraeli, Benjamin: Born December 21st, 1804 in London; died April 19th, 1881 in London. He was a British statesman, one of the founders of that country's Conservative Party, and a staunch supporter of British imperialism. Disraeli and his family were Sephardic Jews of Italian origin.

von Dungern, Otto Karl Ludwig Freiherr: Born October 14th, 1875 in Neuwied, Rhineland-Palatinate; died October 4th, 1967 in Graz, Austria. He was a German-Austrian legal scholar and historian.

von Eichendorff, Joseph Karl Benedikt Freiherr: Born March 10th, 1788 at Lubowitz Castle near Ratibor, Silesian; died November 26th 1857 in Neisse, Silesian. He was an important lyricist and writer of the German Romantic period.

Ferrero, Guglielmo: Born July 21st, 1871 in Portici, Italy; died August 3rd, 1942 in Mont-Pélerin, Switzerland. He was an Italian historian, sociologist, journalist, and novelist. Ferrero was committed to Liberalism in his writings.

Fichte, Johann Gottlieb: Born May 19th, 1762 in Rammenau, Saxony; died January 29th, 1814 in Berlin. He was a philosopher and the founder of German idealism, which further developed many of the ideas of

Immanuel Kant. He was an ardent German nationalist.

Fischer, Eugen: Born June 5th, 1874 in Karlsruhe, Baden-Württemberg; died July 9th, 1967 in Freiburg im Breisgau, Baden-Württemberg. He was an anthropologist, racial theorist, and eugenicist. His application of eugenics to racial advancement with Baur and Lenz proved highly influential to National Socialism.

Fuchs, Carl Johannes: Born August 7th, 1865 in Nuremberg, Bavaria; died December 4th, 1934 in Tübingen. He was an economist, with an emphasis on the role of economics in historical class relations.

George, Henry: Born September 2nd, 1839 in Philadelphia, Pennsylvania; died October 29th, 1897 in New York City, New York. He was an economist and political progressive. His economic ideas would form the basis of Georgism, which advocated that all value derived from land should be equally owned by all members of society.

Giesebrecht, Friedrich Wilhelm Benjamin: Born March 5th, 1814 in Berlin; died December 18th, 1889 in Munich, Bavaria. Known as "von Giesebrecht" from 1865 onward. He was a historian, professor, and writer. Giesebrecht was one of the first to apply the scientific method to historical research.

von Goethe, Johann Wolfgang: Born August 28th, 1749 in Frankfurt; died March 22nd, 1832 in Weimar, Thuringia. He was a German renaissance man—making major contributions to the fields of literature, science, poetry, theater, philosophy, and politics. Von Goethe is best known for his play "Faust," considered by many to be one of the greatest works of German literature.

Goetz, Bruno: Born November 6th, 1885 in Riga, Latvia; died March 19th, 1954 in Zurich, Switzerland. He was a Baltic German poet, writer, and translator. His novels frequently included elements of surrealism.

Günther, Hans Friedrich Karl: Born February 16th, 1891 in Freiburg im Breisgau, Baden-Württemberg; died in Freiburg im Breisgau, Baden-Württemberg. He was a pioneer of racial science and an advocate of Nordicism and eugenics. He greatly influenced National Socialist philosophy, joining the NSDAP in 1932. He was affectionately referred to as the *Rassenpapst* (Race Pope).

von Hardenberg, Karl August: Born May 31st, 1750 in Essenrode, Lower Saxony; died November 26th, 1822 in Genoa, Italy. From 1814 onward, known as Prince von Hardenberg. He was a German statesman and reformer. Hardenberg entered the Prussian civil service in 1792. After publishing the Riga Memorandum for a Modern

State, Hardenberg was appointed Chancellor of State by King Frederick William III in 1810 and continued the Prussian reforms begun under his predecessor Karl Freiherr vom Stein.

Hasse, Traugott Ernst Friedrich: Born February 14th, 1846 in Leulitz, Saxony; died January 12th, 1908 in Leipzig, Saxony. He was a university teacher of statistics and colonial politics and a politician of the National Liberal Party.

Hebbel, Christian Friedrich: Born March 18th, 1813 in Wesselburen, Schleswig-Holstein; died December 13th, 1863 in Vienna, Austria. He was a German playwright and lyricist.

Hentschel, Willibald: Born November 7th, 1858 in Łódź, Poland; died February 2nd, 1947 in Leoni am Starnberger See, Bavaria. He was a natural scientist, writer, and propagandist of the Völkisch movement in Germany. Hentschel was an early proponent of racial breeding plans.

Holbein the Elder, Hans: Born in 1460 in Augsburg, Bavaria; died in 1524 in Issenheim, France. He was a painter, pioneering the transition of German art from Gothic style to Renaissance style.

Holfelder, Hans: Born in 1900 in Vienna, Austria; died in a motorcycle accident on January 30th, 1929. He was an Artaman youth leader and a member of NSDAP. Holfelder was honored after his death by both Heinrich Himmler and R. Walther Darré.

Horthy, Miklós: Born June 18th, 1868 in Kenderes, Hungary; died February 9th, 1957 in Estoril, Portugal. He was an Austro-Hungarian admiral, Hungarian politician and, as imperial administrator, long-time de facto head of state of the Kingdom of Hungary (1920-1944).

Jung, Edgar Julius: Born March 6th, 1894 in Ludwigshafen am Rhein, Rheinland-Palatinate; died July 1st, 1934 in Berlin. Sometimes known by his pen name Tyll. He was a conservative politician and journalist. Despite having racialist views and being generally supportive of revolutionary violence, he was opposed to National Socialism. Jung was arrested and executed during the Night of the Long Knives.

Jünger, Ernst: Born March 29th, 1895 in Heidelberg, Baden-Württemberg; died February 17th, 1998 in Riedlingen, Baden-Württemberg. He was a writer whose personality and work were shaped by his participation in the First World War. He is best known for his war experience books such as *In Stahlgewittern* (Storm of Steel), fictional novels and stories, and various essays. In his elitist, anti-bourgeois, and nationalist early work, which is attributed to the so-called Conservative Revolution,

Jünger resolutely opposed the Weimar Republic.

Kant, Immanuel: Born April 22nd, 1724 in Königsberg, Prussia; died February 12th, 1804 in Königsberg, Prussia. He is one of the most well-known figures in German (and Western) philosophy. One of major figures in Enlightenment philosophy, he developed doctrines such as transcendental idealism.

Klages, Friedrich Konrad Eduard Wilhelm Ludwig: Born December 10th, 1872 in Hanover, Lower Saxony; died July 29th, 1956 in Kilchberg, Switzerland. He was a natural philosopher and psychologist as well as the founder of expressive scientific graphology. He was a representative of a special science studying character and biological metaphysics.

Krauß, Alfred: Born April 26th, 1862 in Zadar, Croatia; died September 29th, 1938 in Bad Goisern, Austria. He was an Austro-Hungarian officer, Privy Councillor, and last General of the Infantry of the Austro-Hungarian Army. Krauß was leader of the National Association of German Officers in Vienna from 1920. In the last year of his life, he became a member of the Reichstag for the NSDAP and was appointed SA brigade leader.

Kretschmer, Ernst: Born October 8th, 1888 in Wüstenrot, Baden-Württemberg; died February 8th, 1964 in Tübingen, Baden-Württemberg. He was a psychiatrist and researched the human constitution, establishing a theory of classification.

Kummer, Bernhard: Born January 21st, 1897 in Leipzig, Saxony; died December 1st, 1962 in Klingberg, Saxony. He was a Germanist and a specialist in Old Norse languages that was fondly known as "Germanenbernhard."

Lagarde, Paul Anton de: Born November 2nd, 1827 in Berlin; died December 22nd, 1891 in Göttingen, Lower Saxony. Born Paul Anton Bötticher, he was a theologian, cultural philosopher, orientalist, and one of the most influential German anti-Semites of the nineteenth century.

Lauffer, Otto: Born February 20th, 1874 in Weende, Lower Saxony; died August 8th, 1949 in Hamburg. He was a folklorist and cultural historian.

Lenz, Fritz Gottlieb Karl: Born March 9th, 1887 in Pflugrade, West Pomeranian; died July 6th, 1976 in Göttingen, Lower Saxony. He was highly influential in the field of eugenics and racial care. An avowed Nordicist, his application of eugenics to racial advancement with Baur and Fischer proved highly influential to National Socialism.

Mack, Eugen: Born in 1882; died in 1947. Vicar in Rottenburg in 1907, municipal archivist in Rottweil in 1912, appointed as archival councilor to the princes of Waldburg-Wolfegg in 1923.

Mann, Ernst: Born November 7th, 1886 in Pillau, Prussia; died July 18th 1945 in Hagenow, Meclenburg-Vorpommern. He was a lawyer and financial administrator.

Marx, Karl Heinrich: Born May 5th 1818 in Trier, Rheinland-Palatinate; died March 14th, 1883 in London, England. He was a philosopher and political theorist whose ideas would result in the development of Marxism and communism, resulting in nearly two hundred years of revolutionary activity and violence. His family were Jewish secularists.

Mayer, Ernst: Born January 22nd, 1862 in Algertshausen, Bavaria; died August 16th, 1932 in Würzburg, Bavaria. He was a legal historian and a professor of German legal history in Würzburg.

Merk, Walther: Born October 12th, 1883 in Meersburg, Baden-Wuerttemberg; died February 6th, 1937 in Freiburg im Breisgau, Baden-Wuerttemberg. He was Profesor of Law and supporter of the NSDAP. His legal writings would heavily influence racial law in the Third Reich.

Meyer, Eduard: Born January 25th, 1855 in Hamburg; died August 31st, 1930 in Berlin. He was a historian and researcher of classic civilizations. Meyer was one of the founders of the nationalist and *volkisch* German Fatherland Party.

von Moltke, Helmuth Karl Bernhard Graf: Born October 26th 1800 in Parchim, Mecklenburg-Vorpommern; died April 24th 1891 in Berlin. He was the first Chief of the German General Staff and pioneered the use of railways to deploy military forces.

von Münchhausen, Börries Albrecht Conon August Heinrich Freiherr: Born March 20th, 1874 in Hildesheim, Lower Saxony; died March 16th, 1945 in Windischleuba, Thuringia. He was a German writer and lyricist of the neo-Romantic period. Von Münchhausen was an anti-Semite and was close to the *Völkisch* movement. In the late Weimar Republic, he founded the elite German Poets' Academy.

Mussolini, Benito Amilcare Andrea: Born July 29th, 1883 in Predappio, Italy; died April 28th, 1945 in Giulino di Mezzegra, Italy. He was an Italian frontline soldier, political theorist,t and Prime Minister of the Kingdom of Italy (1922-1943). His fascist ideology, while influenced in part by previous revolutionary nationalist ideologies, would itself greatly influence the political landscape of early twentieth century Europe.

Nietzsche, Friedrich Wilhelm: Born October 15th, 1844 in Röcken, Saxony-Anhalt; died August 25th, 1900 in Weimar, Thuringia. He was a philosopher, poet, and critic who is a major figure in the modern Western philosophical canon. Aspects of his philosophies have been influential on leaders and theorists from across the political spectrum.

Plenge, Johann: Born June 7th, 1874 in Bremen; died September 11th, 1963 in Münster, North Rhine-Westphalia. He was a sociologist, economist, and propagandist. Plenge developed the term "volksgemeinschaft" (national community), which would go on to being a major tenet of National Socialism.

Pliny the Elder: Born in 23 AD in Como, Italy; died in 79 AD in Pompeii, Italy. Also known by his full name, Gaius Plinius Secundus, he was a Roman author, philosopher, traditionalist, and military commander. He would be killed leading a rescue expedition to the city Pompeii, which had been destroyed by an eruption of Mount Vesuvius.

Rathenau, Walther: Born September 29th, 1867 in Berlin; died June 24th, 1922 in Berlin. He was a German industrialist, writer, and liberal politician (German Democratic Party). During the First World War, he assisted in the organization of the war economy and campaigned for a "victorious peace." After the war, he joined the left-liberal German Democratic Party and became Foreign Minister of the Weimar Republic in February 1922. Numerous journalistic attacks against him accused him of take advantage of the "politics of fulfillment," i.e. collaboration with the victorious Entente powers. Rathenau was assassinated by ultranationalists while in the back seat of his vehicle.

Reibmayr, Albert: Born in 1848 in Meran, Italy; died October 6th, 1918 in Sarnthein, Italy. He was an Austrian physician. As a researcher, he was concerned with medical massage, curative issues, human biology, social hygiene, and anthropology, as well as cultural and racial theory from the 1890's onwards.

Ricardo, David: Born April 18th, 1772 in London, England; died 11 September 1823 in Gatcombe Park, England. He was a British economist and a leading exponent of classical liberal economics. Ricardo and his family were Sephardic Jews of Portuguese origin.

von Scharnhorst, Gerhard Johann David: Born November 12th, 1755 in

Bordenau, Lower Saxony; died June 28th, 1813 in Prague, Czechia. He was the first Chief of the Prussian General Staff and was responsible for numerous reforms to the Prussian military, including the establishment of a strategic military reserve and abolishing non-meritocratic promotions.

Schauwecker, Franz: Born March 26th, 1890 in Hamburg; died May 31st, 1964 in Günzburg, Bavaria. He was a writer and political publicist. His writings had prominent supporters in the Third Reich, including Minister for Propaganda Joseph Goebbels.

Schleich, Carl Ludwig: Born July 19th, 1859 in Stettin, Poland; died March 7th 1922 in Bad Saarow-Pieskow, Brandenburg. He was a surgeon and writer.

von Schlieffen, Alfred Graf: Born February 28, 1833 in Berlin; died January 4th, 1913 in Berlin. He was the Chief of the German General General Staff from 1891 until 1906. Schlieffen pioneered aggressive maneuver and encirclement tactics and was an advocate of universal military conscription.

Schultze-Naumburg, Paul: Born June 10th, 1869 in Almrich (now within the city of Naumburg), Saxony-Anhalt; died May 19th, 1949 in Jena, Thuringia. Also known as Paul Eduard Schultze. He was an architect, art theorist, painter, publicist, and politician (NSDAP).

von Schwerin, Claudius Wilhelm Engelbert Franz Johann Maria Freiherr: Born September 2nd, 1880 in Passau, Bavaria; died June 13th, 1944 in Munich, Bavaria. He was a German legal historian.

von Seeckt, Johannes Friedrich Leopold: Born April 22nd, 1866 in Schleswig, Schleswig-Holstein; died December 27th, 1936 in Berlin). He was a German general and chief of the army command of the *Reichswehr* from 1920 to 1926.

Sokolowski, Paul Ernst Emil: Born July 6th, 1860 in Ronneburg, Latvia; died November 16th, 1934 in Kaunas, Lithuania. He was a Professor of Law and Roman Studies, teaching at Friedrich Wilhelm University in Berlin from 1906 to 1908.

Spengler, Oswald Arnold Gottfried: Born May 29th, 1880 in Blankenburg am Harz, Saxony-Anhalt; died May 8th, 1936 in Munich, Bavaria. He was a philosopher and secondary school teacher. Spengler was active as a scholar and writer in the fields of historical philosophy, cultural history, and cultural philosophy. As an anti-democratic political author, he is considered an intellectual forerunner of National Socialism.

von Stackelberg, Eduard Otto Emil Karl Adam Freiherr: Born November 6th, 1867 in Sillamäggi, Estonia; died April 7th, 1943 in Munich, Bavaria. He was an Estonian chemist and politician. The Stackelberg family estates were confiscated by the Bolsheviks during the Russian Civil War; he would fiercely advocate for anti-Russian positions until his death.

Stammler, Georg: Born February 28th, 1872 in Stammheim, Baden-Württemberg; died May 16th, 1948 in Gießen, Hessen. Also known by his real name, Ernst Emanuel Krauß. He was a poet and a writer active in the nationalist youth movement, joining the NSDAP in 1942.

Stein, Heinrich Friedrich Karl Reichsfreiherr vom und zum: Born October 25th, 1757 in the Duchy of Nassau; died June 29th, 1831 in Cappenberg, North Rhine-Westphalia. He was a statesman and reformer. Stein entered the Prussian civil service in 1780. After publishing the Nassau Memorandum for a Modern Administration, he was appointed Chancellor of State by King Frederick William III in 1807 and initiated the Prussian reforms.

Stieve, Hermann Philipp Rudolf: Born May 22nd, 1886 in Munich, Bavaria; died September 5th, 1952 in Berlin. He was a physician and anatomist with a particular interest in human reproduction. He was closely aligned with the NSDAP, studying the effects of stress on imprisoned women.

Stoddard, Theodore Lothrop: Born June 29th, 1883 in Brookline, Massachusetts; died May 1st, 1950 in Washington, D.C. He was an American historian, Nordicist, and journalist. Stoddard is considered one of the founders of modern racial science and was a prolific author in the field. His works were influential both at home and abroad. Stoddard's ideas greatly influenced the Second Klu Klux Klan as well as many National Socialist thinkers of the time.

von Sybel, Heinrich Ernst: Born March 28th, 1885 in Gummersbach, North Rhine-Westphalia; died 22 March 1969 in Schweinfurt, Bavaria. He was a German estate owner (Haus Isenburg near Cologne) and politician (Christian National Peasants' and Country People's Party, later NSDAP).

Teudt, Wilhelm: Born December 7th, 1860 in Bergkirchen, Bavaria; died January 5th, 1942 in Detmold. He was a Völkisch amateur researcher who found archaeological evidence of a Germanic advanced civilization.

von Treitschke, Heinrich Gotthard: Born September 15th, 1834 in

Dresden, Saxony; died April 28th 1896 in Berlin. He was a German historian, political theorist, and a member of the Reichstag from 1871 to 1884. Initially a deputy from the National Liberal Party, von Treitschke was without party affiliation from 1878. He was one of the best-known and most widely-read historians and political and political theorists in Germany at his time.

Vollgraff, Karl Friedrich: Born November 4th, 1794 in Schmalkalden, Thuringia; died March 5th, 1863 in Marburg, Hessen. Also known as Carl Friedrich Vollgraff. He was a German legal scholar and early social scientist.

Wildhagen, Karl: Born August 23rd, 1873 in Hanover, Lower Saxony; died August 7th, 1945 in Leipzig, Saxony. He was an anthropologist and linguist who specialized in English culture, history, and philosophy. His German-English dictionary remained popular in Germany well after his death.

CPSIA information can be obtained
at www.ICGtesting.com
Printed in the USA
LVHW041130290423
745665LV00006B/405